HAMISH BROWN'S
Scotland

HAMISH BROWN'S
Scotland
(A Chapbook of Explorations)

ABERDEEN UNIVERSITY PRESS

First published 1988
Aberdeen University Press
A member of the Pergamon Group
© Hamish Brown 1988

British Library Cataloguing in Publication Data

Brown, Hamish M
   Hamish Brown's Scotland: (a chapbook of explorations)
   1. Scotland—Description and travel—1931-
   I. Title
   914.11′04853   DA867.5

   ISBN 0 08 036391 1

PRINTED IN GREAT BRITAIN
THE UNIVERSITY PRESS
ABERDEEN

For Mary, who kept the home
fires burning

Glen Coe across Loch Leven

CONTENTS

Introduction   xiii

I: The Chatter Box   1

A Boy in the Ochils   3
Ochil Memories   10
Above the Devil's Elbow   11
The Snowdrop Miracle   17
Memory-haunted   19
Salute to Adventure, without Cars   21
A Day Of Glory Given   23
A Night out on Beinn a' Bhuird   26
Snow Sets On   31
Wade and Caulfeild, Road Builders   32
Game of the Name   35
Rounding up Round Towers   38
The Seasons   41
Clouty Wells   42
Birds of the Mountain   44
Fieldfares, November's Vikings   51
The Open Door (SYHA Jubilee)   52
Silent Stones   56
Peaceful Places, Caithness   60
Munro of the Munros   61
A Highland Lament   63
Extinction   66

II: Ranging Scotland   67

Cairnsmore, The Highest of the Three   69
Hermitage Castle   71
An Eastern Iona   74
Ben Lomond, Eventually   79
The Blackmount and Rannoch Moor   83
Glen Tilt and its Hills   88
Summit Search   96
Storm Joins the Munroists   97

The Glen of Rowans   102
Blizzard '78   105
Behind the Ranges   110
Jubilee Jaunt   115
Sourlies Bothy   123

III: Western Wanderings   125

Knoydart, Just Passing Through   127
Glenelg   131
Ben Attow   137
By The Crags   141
Bagging Benula   142
The Coulin Pass   146
The Anvil of the Forge   149
Familiarity Breeds Content   153
Peanmeanach   156

IV: Islands, Islands, Islands   157

On Jura's Empty Quarter   159
Arran is Magic   165
The Cocktail Islands: Eigg   169

The Cocktail Islands: Muck 173
The Cocktail Islands: Canna 177
The Cocktail Islands: Rhum 180
Skye High 184
Bonxies on the Shiants 191
A Day in the life of Handa 194
Hurryings 198
Orkney's Italian Connection 199
Shetland, a Summer Sojourn 202
St Kilda, a World of its Own 205
The Strange Case of Lord and Lady Grange 209
Hodden Solitude 213

V: Stories of Places

V: Stories of Places 215

The Ornithologists 217
Tait's Tomb 222
The Cross 226
The Fisherman's Release 233

LIST OF ILLUSTRATIONS

	Frontispiece: Glen Coe across Loch Leven.	vi
1	Castle Campbell in the Ochil Hills above Dollar.	1
2	'A Day of Glory Given'.	23
3	The granite 'tor' or 'barn' marking the summit of Ben Avon in the Cairngorms.	27
4	Wade's finest bridge. The showpiece of Aberfeldy.	34
5	One of the old iron milestones across Fife naming Pettycur, the old ferry to Edinburgh.	36
6	The old market cross and Round Tower at Abernethy.	39
7	Craig, Scotland's remotest youth hostel.	53
8	Ben Loyal seen across Loch Hakel.	56
9	Silent stones—a pictish symbol stone at Abernethy.	58
10	Hermitage Castle, one of the most dramatic castles in the Borders.	72
11	Inchcolm, in the Firth of Forth.	75
12	Loch Lomond. The *Maid of the Loch* at Inversnaid.	78
13	Ben Lomond seen from the top of Duncryne at the south end of the loch.	81
14	Looking down from the Blackmount hills to Loch Tulla and the hills of Bridge of Orchy.	83
15	Above Glen Tilt—on the great ski day described.	94
16	Storm beside the Cross Stone above Tarfside.	99
17	Geal Charn from Aonach Beag—the peaks of Storm's last Munro.	101
18	The Buachaille.	106
19	The head of Loch Nevis near Sourlies Bothy.	123
20	Hamish and his dog in the hills of Knoydart.	128
21	A quiet bay at Glenelg.	131
22	The Eas Mor Falls in Glen Beag near Glenelg.	134
23	Storm in his glory—looking to Ben Sgriol.	136
24	The view south from the summit of Ben Attow.	137
25	On the ridges of The Saddle, Kintail.	140

26 Ardessie Falls near Dundonnell, with Sail Mhor behind.   147
27 From the slopes of An Teallach looking over to Beinn Dearg Mor.   150
28 Cir Mhor, Arran—a poem in granite.   166
29 The Sgurr of Eigg.   169
30 Port Muck—the view from the tent door.   174
31 The Cuillin of Rhum from the Island of Eigg.   181
32 Skye. Looking to Blaven from the Marsco-Glamaig ridges.   185
33 The view from Blaven, looking towards Sgurr nan Gillean.   186
34 Skye. Bruach na Freithe, one of the easier Cuillin peaks.   188
35 The classic view of Sgurr nan Gillean across the Sligachan moors. 190
36 The sea cliffs on the island of Handa in Sutherland.   195
37 The Italian Chapel, Orkney.   200
38 The broch of Mousa, Shetland—the best preserved in Scotland.   203
39 St Kilda. Stac Lee, speckled with gannets with Stac an Armin
    (left) and Boreray (right) behind.   206
40 An abstract on the frozen surface of a loch.   216
41 The Meikelour Beech Hedge near Blairgowrie—planted
    after the Forty-five and the country's highest hedge
    (trimmed by the fire brigade).   221
42 Leuchars Kirk in Fife—a Romanesque treasure.   225
43 The summit of Scotland—Ben Nevis.   232

MAPS

 1 The Ochils   2
 2 East and West of the Devil's Elbow   13
 3 Cairnsmore of Carsphairn   68
 4 The Black Mount   84
 5 Glen Tilt Hills   89
 6 Bealach Dubh Hills   98
 7 Knoydart   126
 8 Glenelg—Glen Shiel   132
 9 Beinn Attow   138
10 Beinn Fhionnlaidh and Loch Mullardoch   143
11 An Teallach   151
12 The Islands   158
13 Jura   160
14 Arran   164

INTRODUCTION

Being unable to travel abroad has never struck me as a deprivation. A great deal of my life has been spent out of Scotland, enjoyably so, rewardingly and enrichingly so but the basis of a happy internationalism is a deep-rooted, tenacious, love of a home country. Scotland happens to be mine.

Were I to be left with Scotland only I would still be a happy man for it is a country of great variety, a long history and a rich heritage, which could fill a score of lifetimes of exploration, never mind the hundred years I've asked for! I have been lucky to have spent so much time wandering in Scotland, as a mountaineer, teacher, writer and photographer but I am equally happy at home with my alpine garden, the wildlife of the coast at the foot of the garden, Edinburgh's cultural opportunities across the water, and a house full of books, books and books—to which I have managed to add a few of my own. And here is another!

This book is a collection of purely 'Scottish' pieces which I hope will show our visitors something of the country's attractions, particularly in the wilder corners, and will also give fellow-enthusiasts new angles on familiar places and themes. A few short stories end the selection and they too are redolent of particular places, as are the poems scattered throughout. A country is the sum of its parts and these are parts of one man's Scotland.

The selection was difficult as so much had to be left out but I have tried to include pieces which at the time drew a special response from readers of the magazines and journals in which they appeared and I would like to thank all those publications (and the *Glasgow Herald* in particular) for welcoming their appearance here. A temptation to re-write has been resisted and only minimal comments have been made where an explanation is needed. This is a book to dip into while sitting in the garden, or reading in bed, or perhaps *en route* to some of the places mentioned. If it sets you dreaming I will be pleased. If you set feet to those dreams I will be delighted.

The pieces previously appeared in the following publications: *Alpine Journal, Chapman, Climber, Countryman, 'Eye to the Hills', The Field, Footloose, Glasgow Herald, Great Outdoors, High, Mountain Bothies Association Journal, New Writing Scotland, Other Poetry, Rod and Line, Scottish Field, Scottish Mountaineering Club Journal, Scots Magazine.*

Hamish M. Brown
Kinghorn, 1988

The Chatter Box

When friends joined me for odd days in the course of my big, solitary walks (such as All-the-Munros or The Groats End Walk) I apparently talked non-stop—a natural reaction to the rather monastic life of such lonely tramping and also, I am sure, an unconscious desire to share all the interesting sights and experiences along the way. This book is a quite conscious effort to share such experiences and the loquacity is no doubt still in evidence. My earliest Scottish ramblings, and my earliest Scottish writings, took place under the Ochils, so that is where I would choose to open my chatter box.

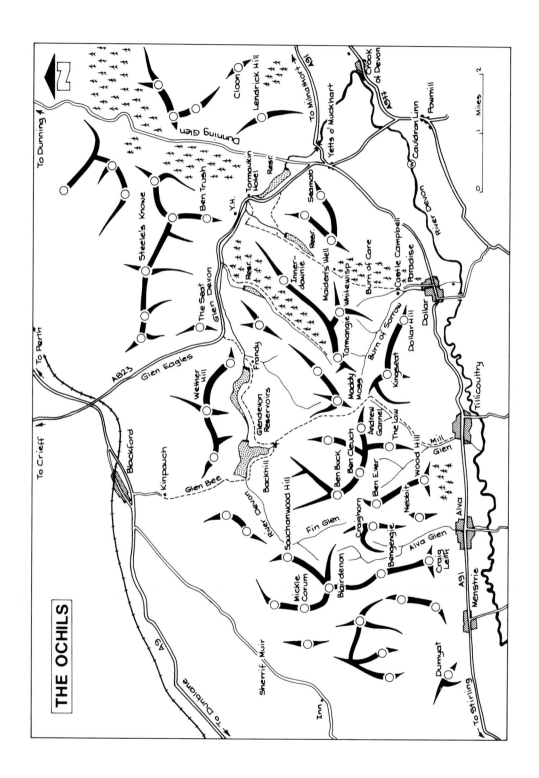

THE OCHILS

To Dunning

To Perth

To Crieff

AB23   Glen Eagles

Blackford

To Dunblane   A9

Sherrif Muir

Inn.

To Stirling

Cloan

Lendrick Hill

Dunning Glen

Steele's Knowe

Ben Trush

Y.H.

The Seat   Glen Devon

Wether Hill

Kinpauch

Glen Bee

Frandy

Glendevon Reservoirs

Backhill

River Devon

Souchanwood Hill

Fin Glen

Mickle Corum

Blairdenon

Bangengie

Craig Leith

Craighorn

Nebbit

Ben Ever

Ben Cleuch

Ben Buck

Andrew Gannel

The Law

Wood Hill

Mill Glen

Alva Glen

Alva

Menstrie

A91

Inner-downie

Maiden's Well

Whitewisp

Tarmangie

Maddy Moss

Kingseat

Burn of Sorrow

Dollar Hill

Burn of Care

Castle Campbell

Paradise

Dollar

Tillicoultry

Tormaukin Hotel

Resr.

Resr.

Resr.

Seamab

Yetts o' Muckhart

To Milnathort   A91

Crook of Devon

A977

Cauldron Linn

Powmill

River Devon

Dumyat

0   1   Miles   2

N

A Boy in the Ochils

When, a few years ago, I gained a new dog—Storm, a Shetland Collie the colour of autumn bracken—it just did not enter my head to take him anywhere else but the Ochils for his introduction to the hills. Alva was our chosen gateway.

Alva Glen, the Mill Glen above Tilly and Dollar Glen all have man-made paths to give convenient access to the steep grassy hinterland. Menstrie lacks such a glen, but is backed by its own private hill, Dumyat, which some people are sure is the original Spyglass Hill of *Treasure Island*. These towns, strung between the scarp steepness of the Ochils and the meanderings of the River Devon, are collectively known as the Hillfoots—or Hillfits if you belong to them, as I did through a Dollar childhood.

The Devon was always the boundary of 'our' Ochils. Its headwaters lie only two or three miles north of Alva but they do a great sweep east to the Glendevon–Gleneagles road, then at the Crook suddenly back-track in classic river-capture fashion so that, instead of joining Loch Leven, they flow west under the Ochils to enter the Forth at Cambus—a 25 mile progress for 7 miles as the crow flies. It is always tempting to head for the source.

Storm and I pushed up Alva Glen, a tree-shady gorge, following first the east bank and then zig-zagging up the west on to the sparser open grasslands which eventually cover the crumbly volcanic rocks. The path ends at the junction of the Alva Burn and the Glenwinnel Burn. The latter has a thin tail of waterfall, green-edged and sparkling, which is an irresistible lure onwards. It leads up between Craighorn and Ben Ever to Ben Buck, a spur of Ben Cleuch where we were glad to rest ourselves.

Kincardine and Grangemouth with their towers and lights set a pattern, day or night, that has changed utterly since childhood. The patchwork of Lowland lights was so familiar when I used to roam the hills at night with a Tilley lamp until the Police asked me to use a torch: my legs swinging made it look like a distress flash and we were twice 'rescued'.

Storm, after two years of showring life, found the freedom of the hills intoxicating. It was interesting to see him having to learn much that I thought he would have known automatically—such as the fact that steep, wet rocks are slippery. He learnt fast, however, and fell in a burn only once. He met his first sheep with curiosity. No problems there.

We shared a piece on Ben Cleuch, then hit one of the source streams of the Devon in the Fin Glen. We kept northwards round Sauchanwood Hill for the Danny Burn, Kinpauch and Blackford on the A9. I can't think of many areas with more attractive hill-names than the Ochils. Taste a few more: Seamab Hill, Cloon, Ben Trush, Simpleside, Mickle Corum, Bengengie, Andrew Gannel, The Nebit.

Growing up in Dollar, our usual routes to Ben Cleuch led up the Burn of Sorrow to Maddy Moss, or over King's Seat, then on by Andrew Gannel—a name which deserves to be the hero of a John Buchan yarn. From Maddy Moss a track from Tilly led on by Skythorn Hill and the Braich Burn to the lonely shieling of Backhill from which Blackford and the A9 was reached by Glen Bee. Backhill has since been inundated by one of the many Ochil reservoirs. Maddy Moss, remembered as a real floundery bog, seems to have dried out considerably over my lifetime, though the Ochils don't give the impression of being any drier.

Possibly the finest long route we evolved (rather than taking these old drovers' ways across the range) was to join up all the 2000-foot summits. The last time I did this was with three of my Fife pupils when we made a two-day traverse of the Ochils—heading west to east, 'with the weather'. We bivouacked above Menstrie on a chilly October night and climbed Dumyat by moonlight simply because it was a night of rare beauty.

The Second Inchna Burn helped us to gain the first 2000-foot top just west of Blairdenon. Ben Buck led to Ben Cleuch and the spur of Tilly Law. The map has The Law, but to us it was Tilly Law as Dollar also had its Law Hill (on which a stand of firs gave rise to all sorts of legends). Andrew Gannel led to King's Seat, then there was a sweep back and round to the other side of the Sorrow: Tarmangie Hill and Whitewisp before the interminable tramp out to Innerdownie completed the haul and led us wearily down to Glendevon—about 22 miles from the start. The Tormaukin Hotel gave us such an immense mixed grill (for 7s 6d) that we could stagger on only another mile before camping on a site now under the waters of the most recent dam.

The next day led through what is now Glen Devon Forest and is chiefly remembered for the destroying heat and my pupils learning the gentle art of guddling trout. We came down to Milnathort like redskins—our warpath leading straight to the chip shop where we did not need to pay the deposit on the lemonade bottles—we finished them on the spot.

It is amazing how much has changed over the years. One assumes hills don't change, but forestry plantings, reservoirs, radio/TV masts, new tracks, longer grass from less grazing, the more industrialised view of the Lowlands, the influx of walkers, all make the Ochils now quite different from the hills I knew as a boy.

The railway still existed in my youth. The loss of its viaduct over the Devon was regretted. Rackmill Bridge was not so handy to someone living on the Muckhart Road. Our neighbours were George Blake, the novelist, and family, but they did not seem to have deep roots so far from the Clyde. Less than a mile out of the town, I can recall being able to descend into old coal-mine workings. It scared me silent and now there is simply a field. Even the operational mine at Pitgober has gone. The former bleach-works by the Devon also provided subterranean passages which I could not find years later when the site was a sawmill providing pocket-money for student days. Now it is a camp and caravan park.

For one brief spell there were riding stables in Dollar and in return for working there, some of us enjoyed magnificent free rides—usually after delivering clients back to their homes. One I'll never forget was on a horse called Silver when we rode through from Glendevon. As this was the way home we were soon galloping along Glenquey Reservoir and through the pass by the Maiden's Well. I lost my stirrups but maintained my seat for an exciting few miles.

There used to be the gable-end of a former shepherd's house on the slopes of Whitewisp. Library Farm we called it and tradition says that, in the eighteenth century, a shepherd living there was something of a scholar and had a collection of four hundred books which were auctioned off at Dollar Bridge after his death. The farm may have served the castle anciently and the field system can still be traced despite the rampaging bracken. Now even the gable has gone.

Dollar Academy began as John McNabb's School, McNabb having been a poor boy who ran away to sea and made a fortune which he left to the parish. After plenty of legal wranglings the classical Playfair building was completed in 1821, using stone quarried on the Sheardale Braes. It soon became a famous institution and links with overseas developed quickly, and have continued. For many games, the school divides into 'Britishers' and 'Foreigners', the latter being those who were born abroad, have lived abroad or whose parents are abroad.

For one year my neighbour in Junior II was one Alexander Desta, a grandson of Haile Selassie. Some years ago, I travelled through Ethiopia and at once wanted to return to explore the remoter areas of the harsh 'roof of Africa'. Prince Iksander seemed a good contact as he was in charge of the Navy. I wrote a draft letter, but before I had time to type it out there was a coup and he and scores of others were killed.

In 1960 I was in Glencoe climbing when Ingrid Feeney, the youth hostel warden, rushed me through to her TV set to see the old Academy going up in flames. Fortunately the shell survived and within it a three-storey building replaced the original two. The Queen and Prince Philip visited the restored building in 1963. Her Silver Jubilee saw the cairn on top of Dollar Hill rebuilt in commemoration. As a boy we lugged stones up to it after the war to rebuild the then decayed cairn as a Victory memorial. It is a long way from John Christie, shepherd, born in 1721, who lived with his books in the cottage of Brewlands up under Whitewisp by the Glenquey road.

The path from Glenquey comes down by the Burn of Care to the house, now a Scout Adventure Centre. Our family nearly bought it after the war, but considered it too much for my grandmother—the south face of the Ochils is unrelentingly steep. It would have been interesting to live up there though, really on the hills instead of looking up to them, on nodding terms with Castle Campbell.

Castle Campbell is all one can imagine a castle should be: a keep and circling walls perched on a knoll, moated by nature and with a stunning view out over the rich lands of Fife, the silver slither of the Forth and the Pentlands behind Auld Reekie. It suffered neglect during the war as did the paths and bridges in the Glen—not that this stopped our youthful explorations. Funds were raised to restore the Glen, owned by the National Trust for Scotland. The Ministry of Works accepted guardianship of the Castle.

1 Castle Campbell in the Ochil Hills above Dollar.

Our family must have been among the most regular customers at Castle Campbell, eventually becoming honorary visitors. One skilled mason, with occasional help, laboured for a decade, restoring the worst of time's decay. We found this work as fascinating as I'm sure he found it satisfying. The tidying up of the Glen was rather regretted, we liked it wild and full of secret places. We knew all the pools for swimming, learnt to climb on its slimy walls and with an ordinary axe I cut steps up Kemp's Score—my first winter climb and probably its first winter ascent. Hamid, the long-suffering childhood dog, even shared that adventure. One of the biggest avalanches I have ever seen in Scotland stripped the northern slopes of Whitewisp.

The Gloom Hill Quarry gave me my initiation in rock climbing. Six-inch nails served as pitons and years later, when I was introducing school parties to climbing in the glen, I came on some rusted remains.

We should have broken our necks a dozen times considering the liberties we took with rock, snow, water and the slippery grass pelt of the bulging hills. Cricket boots with their studs were excellent for this last surface. Seldom, if ever, did we meet other people. I was astonished, years later, to discover Harry Bell, our Headmaster, had been a member of the Scottish Mountaineering Club. We learnt the best way of all—from our own volition.

One person we did meet regularly was W K Holmes and much of my own mountain philosophy came from this gentleman. He would watch us hammering away in the quarry without comment—or lead us away up the Burn of Sorrow to the old copper mines—or tell us stirring tales of John Knox and the Great Montrose and the Campbells who had left their mark on the Castle of Mary Queen of Scots who visited it for a wedding and on her flight from Loch Leven Castle—or of Ben Nevis and Skye and those peaks that rimmed the horizon when we stood on top of Ben Cleuch, at 2363 feet, the highest summit in the Ochils. Postcards in his spidery hand followed me to far places during my National Service or later expeditions and his gentle encouragement helped my first literary efforts. Autographed copies of his poems and his wee book, *Tramping Scottish Hills*, are amongst my most treasured possessions.

> Still a child in a world of wonder,
> Heir of the sky and the earth thereunder . . .

The Ochils have inspired a surprising amount of poetry over the last hundred years. Hugh Halyburton had one line, 'It's no aye raining on the misty Ochils' which became one of our catch phrases as we'd descend to Dollar in a deluge and Anon provided another (repeated with Hillfoot gutterals):

> What hills are like the Ochil hills?
>   There's nane sae green tho' grander.
> What rills are like the Ochil rills?
>   Nane, nane on earth that wander.

There is great comfort even in lowly hills.

> *Paradise re-visited*
>
> I find my peace in
> the Pole Star
> standing above Whitewisp
> for there it stood
> throughout my youth
> a safe constancy
> there it may stand in
> years to come
> when the kind Ochils and I
> have ended—however
> the world ends.

I am glad to see Paradise survives. Up above Scott's Farm and the demolished Hillfoot House, on land now all planted over by conifers, were a series of pools (an abandoned curling pond, a water supply and just a pool) to which we gave the names First, Second and Third Paradise. Second Paradise became a firm favourite, a camp site used over a score of years, so that the numbers were eventually dropped. The name Paradise stuck and it was fascinating to see it mentioned in the 1977 Jubilee *Dollar Chapbook*. That publication also mentioned William's Stone (an erratic boulder named after a school friend) above the Castle and hinted at antiquarian origins. Alas, it was simply one of our regular meeting points before adventuring up the Burn of Sorrow and which we named for our own convenience. I'm sure this is basically how topographical names originate anywhere.

We were always indignant at the Ordnance Survey for the spelling "Ben Clach" instead of Ben Cleuch (they have since corrected it) and Bank Hill was never used: that spur of King's Seat, separated by 'the Valley of Dry Bones', overlooking Castle and Town, was simply Dollar Hill. Castle Gloom/Glowm/Gloum/Glume became Castle Campbell only by Act of Parliament in 1490. I would like to know the origins of the names Burn of Care and the Burn of Sorrow which so effectively guard the Castle with their cliffsteep ravines. Pennant used these names in 1769 and they survived Victorian efforts at deromanticising to be still in use today.

Sometimes we slept clandestinely in the Castle, and in Brewlands when it was left derelict, besides camping and simply sleeping out in all manner of odd places. We learnt the hard way that what appeared sheltered hollows were all too often cold traps which collected the saturating and chilling mists.

When Glendevon Youth Hostel was built it became a regular haunt for some of us. We would tramp through by an endless variety of routes or cycle round by the Yetts o' Muckhart on Saturday and return after church on Sunday by even longer routes. Glendevon church is small and neat with a huge square-set manse. We came to know the glen well and only occasionally would go beyond it by the Borland Glen right-of-way to Auchterarder or on to historic Dunning.

Within our bounds we came to know the hills as shepherds do—by personal experience. We had neither maps nor compass. I cannot recall ever being really lost or even more than slightly mislaid!

I must have been a horror of a youth. As a member of the Cadet Force we sometimes spent Friday afternoons on exercises in the hills. Once, when it was sweltering hot, we secretly made our way to a fine pool in the out-of-bounds glen and enjoyed ourselves there while periodically on the walkie-talkie I would report our mythical manoeuvres on the hills which, of course, I knew far more intimately than the teacher-officer at base.

On another occasion when frost cancelled the Saturday rugby matches we were sent to run up King's Seat. I took the dog and made a day of it. On the mist-clad summit there was a growing gang of the First Fifteen, all lost in the cloud. As the local expert I was grabbed for directions and being in the long-suffering Second Fifteen it was with great delight I sent them all off due northwards. One pair arrived, penniless, in running strip, at Blackford. It was worth the hammering I received on the Monday!

It amazed me even then how a spider dropped onto the page of the Captain of the First could produce a shriek. I was fascinated by all that grew, or flew, or crawled, and took the freedom of the wilds as the natural order of things—but I was very much the odd man out. I can blame my parents for this, of course, and my wandering childhood in a score of countries from Africa to Japan because of my father's work as a banker and the war chasing us from land to land. I was also lucky in the Junior School to have 'Ma' Wilson as class teacher. Nature Study was actually encouraged.

I was lucky, throughout, to have teachers of English who enthused and an art department of wide scope. These influences have remained. The rest was tholed rather than enjoyed. On a day of glorious spring I was away beyond Maddy Moss when I suddenly recalled I was supposed to be playing rugby right then. You can imagine the row that followed! And I never did learn not to ask 'why?'.

The River Devon very clearly defined our self-imposed southern bounds and was equally part of our hill heritage. We swam in its many pools from Dunning Road to Butchart's, floated down it on rafts, skated on it, watched flashing kingfishers, explored its wilds from Cauldron Linn to Rumbling Bridge and Snowdrop Valley.

This last was near a roofless mansion, a woody hollow smothered in snowdrops. Later the big house (as with Cowden or Harvieston) was demolished and the bulldozers shoved the rubble down over the snowdrop slopes in unwitting vandalism (The sequel is told in *The Snowdrop Miracle*).

Vicar's Bridge over the Devon was an historic landmark, recalling Thomas Forest, Vicar of Dollar and one of the first Reformation martyrs. The bridge was crassly demolished some years ago and replaced by a new utilitarian modern one. My first foray into print was a study of this saintly man, who used to smuggle food to his poor parishioners in the sleeves of his gown; but he read the Bible in English so was strangled and burned on the Castle Hill in Edinburgh in 1538.

Vicar's Bridge is more notoriously associated with Joe Bell reputedly the last man publicly hanged in Scotland. He had ambushed and shot a carter on the brae nearby.

Eventually we did break out beyond our childhood country. We made extensive family cycle tours each summer to the north and west. My first Munro was a solo venture up Ben Nevis. When we boys began to outpace our parents they simply sent us off alone. We had learned our craft on the local roads and the hills of home. The rest of Scotland and the wide world were only a widening of experience.

Early loves are apt to linger longest—which is certainly true of the Ochils. How lucky I was to grow up a Hillfoots chiel and, for a lifetime, as W K Holmes wrote:

> ... find,
> Wherever nature's still untamed, unplanned
> The native country of his heart and mind,
> And there his age forget; older than he
> Dewfall and thunder, mountains and the sea.

Ochil Memories

The Ochils now dance gently in the light
Of memory.
        I see them, as long ago,
When a child's eye saw evening's wondrous things,
When a child's feet ran bracken braes on wings
Of thoughtlessness—and longed to keep it so.
        We shall not go again as children there.

Here the grime of the grey and soulless street
Has exiled eyes, the town ensnared our feet.
We see the suburb slopes beyond mist murk
And clink the callous chains that we have made;
Tired men and so sad at heart, who are paid
For our labours with memories that hurt.
        We shall not go again as children there.

Unloved till love cannot the love repair
We shall not go again as children there.

Above the Devil's Elbow

The following was an essay written a long time ago and can have various charges levelled against it. Nevertheless, it demonstrates something which is perhaps missing today in course-catering mountaineering—the ability to rely on one's own judgment, to try and test personally the tenets of the sport, and to experience the challenge of solitude. Never to have known the hills alone is to have missed one of their greatest joys and some of their strictest schooling. As a teenager I often had to go alone or not go at all. Climbing was not so organised then. This is the story of a solitary week-end, written on the Sunday night for school the next day. David failed to keep the rendezvous as he had run into a tree while rushing home and had knocked himself out!

Perhaps I should not write of events so soon after their happening. My body still feels one big bruise. It is still only twenty-four hours since I staggered into my tent above the Devil's Elbow. I had been alone; I had completed twenty-five miles of tough going in nine hours; I had come as near to being exhausted as I had ever been; but now as I sit, stiff and sore, by a window overlooking the soft lowlands, I have only a wild singing within and a clearer, cleaner view of the world without.

This is the glory of the testing times; not victory over the impersonal, unalterable hills, but finding one's own mental and physical peak and walking there and returning home again, conquered—'none but ourselves'. Nothing happened that was not within the compass of expectancy. I could still shout in delight at the intense vista of blue that opened southwards in the storm. I could still thrill at the whirl of white wings as the ptarmigan burst from the corrie below. I made the decisions to go the extra miles, and, weary beyond remembrance, could still check the guy lines before crawling into the storm-tossed tent.

David, a school friend, who was to have come with me, had not turned up, and when the offered lift to Perth arrived I took it, otherwise the week-end would have been lost altogether. This lift connected with a bus, and in no time it seemed I was at Blairgowrie. I had a cup of tea there, for the night was frosty and, eating chips as I went, walked out to the last lamp-post beyond Rattray. The light of a car swept along the raspberry canes above my head. It stopped, and I climbed in beside three Carn

Dearg lads from Dundee, who were heading for Glen Derry and Coire Etchachan. A fox ran up the road in front of the car in Glen Shee. We had a halt at the Spittal before twisting round the Devil's Elbow. I was dropped at the Cairnwell. An icy wind filtered through the pass.

I spent longer than usual pitching the tent in the dark, for I carefully double-pegged it in the windy site. It was not long before I was lying in a cosy sleeping-bag, listening to the noisy flap of canvas.

Dawn came with a shimmer of red clouds and blue skies—far too good to last. As David had intended bringing half the food I had to live off my half, which meant an abundance of some things and the complete absence of others. I had no porridge, nor bread, but could make a double cheese omelette with lashings of bacon. Prunes, biscuits, and marmalade with milkless tea made it a satisfying enough meal.

Then off. Winter garb again; the top half a string vest, a wool one, a rugger jersey and an anorak; below, long johns and windproof trousers. Scarf, balaclava, pullover were in the rucksack along with a torch and first-aid kit and piles of food. Automatically, I checked my pockets—maps, compass, knife, whistle, paper, pencil, sweets, all were there.

There were a few ski-tracks on the way up Meall Odhar (3019 feet), an easy climb from the highest main road in the Highlands. [No tows and lifts and car parks in those days; skiers still had to work for their runs.]

I visualised the day. It would be a long one for I wanted seven Munros to complete my hundred. Why should it not work out? The day was young, the clouds rolled high in a golden conglomeration. I was fit. To the north and west, however, the big hills looked dark under a pall of snow-clouds, and were streaked in the unmistakable Cairngorms pattern. Glas Maol above me was snowy, too. Up on the tops it was winter.

I skirted south on a path, and then stuttered along the shambles to the top of Creag Leacach (3238 feet). The wind suddenly rose. What a world of sound, the wind woofing from Glen Brighty and mixing with the roaring of stags and tumbling waters. Returning, I sheltered at the big cairn, and when I set out again, the tops were in cloud. I went on up to Glas Maol (3502 feet), the highest point of the day. The weather was thick and cold and the wind clawed at cheeks and eyes.

Little Glas Maol followed, and I returned up the snow to the trig point again rather than take my hands out of my pockets. There was a fence marking the county boundary so I raced off along it. Three stags suddenly loomed out of the misty half-light, huge creatures, with wicked-looking antlers. We stood staring at each other for a long second or two, and then they raced off. I breathed again.

At the lowest point the mists cleared and I wandered out to Druim Mor. Two hundred yards before reaching the cairn, the blanket rolled back, and I waited some time 'shivering on the brink', wanting to see into the double amphitheatre. I followed my footprints back again, and went on up Cairn of Claise (3484 feet), the next Munro.

It began to snow; the powdery stuff came racing across the bog and snow and rutted tussocks or shot upwards out of the Kander corrie. It was hard to see at all, and I slipped and stumbled on the loose rock and snow over Carn an Tuirc (3340 feet) for the Allt a' Gharbhchoire. Below the storm level I stopped for a long icy drink and welcome food.

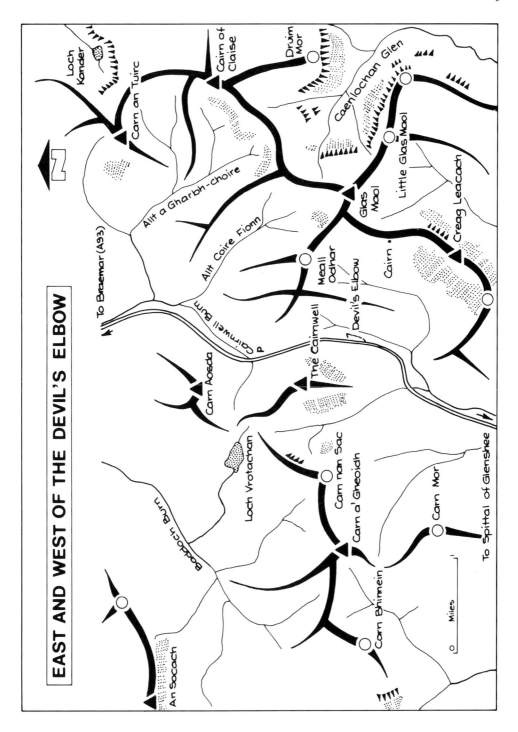

EAST AND WEST OF THE DEVIL'S ELBOW

I was quite weary, for it had been hard going. Already four Munros and three Tops were in the bag. Deer streamed out of the valley, spreading out in ragged lines and vanishing into the mist. The burn was in spate and difficult to cross, its waters pouring down, dirty and dangerous. I crossed back to join a path on the right bank, and this led to a beautiful old bridge which led across to the main road.

The tent was two miles up the road, and it had been a good day. But I wanted my century, and, secretly, wanted to go on.

I began to zig-zag up the shoulder of Carn Aosda (3003 feet) from where I was. I picked up an old antler. Circling the slope I found myself on the wrong summit knoll. Looking back to it, it was easy for weariness to suggest, 'Och, miss it; you're near enough to claim it. It's only fifty yards off.' Only! Those fifty yards were straight into the gale, a dry hell, no snow, just the searing battery of icy fists.

I was soon blown back to the calm of the saddle where I could see the orange patch of tent against the russet hillside. It was very tempting and sensible to descend, but the human animal is very determined. I turned into the western wastes.

As long as I kept a regular rhythm I felt I could go on for ever. I skirted above the lochan, a long, windswept plod, energy coming from a succession of sugary sweets. My eyes ached. The final rise to Carn a' Gheoidh (3194 feet) was only about two hundred feet, but it felt like two thousand.

The clouds were thick again, and I had to use map and compass down to the last silly top, Carn Bhinnein. Only the thought of a special visit for it alone made it worthwhile. It was downhill, too, and the return was wind-borne and erratic. I swept by the cairn of Gheoidh, forgot to check, and suddenly realised I was not on my old track, so had to return—right to the cairn again.

Even simple directions like this took on epic proportions. Again and again there was the temptation to short-cut or take a risk. I recognised the dangers and when least welcome, took double care. Now, indeed, I was being tested.

Going back I kept resolutely to the edge of the corrie—nameless on map or guide— because my lower route had been wet and awkward coming. Every rise seemed a mountain. I would pause for a fix and then head along the bearing. At one place I stood for what seemed an eternity above a short, steep snowslope. 'Charge down!' said the tempter to tired legs. 'Go round, you clot!' argued the voice of experience. I hung irresolute, slowly worked it out, and went round and down by a grassy rake. (I had no ice-axe). By then I felt really weary—as I had never known before.

Well, I had asked for it!

After leaving Carn nan Sac, which formed the west wing of the corrie, the sky cleared in a flash and the whole vibrant south sprang into view. Like the huge welcome of an excited dog, it almost bowled me over. I shouted with wonder.

The clouds had parted, and I seemed to look down a long, long corridor of light. The blues were unbelievable; hills beyond hills, and then the shadow of lower lands; the Lomonds like a crouched, tensed lion ready to spring on Largo Law; then a translucency of waters and the haze of Edinburgh with Arthur's Seat and the Pentlands beyond, all clear and sharp as the wind held its breath a long moment and stillness silenced the wintry tops.

It was one of the most beautiful things I have ever experienced. Its joy hurt like a pain.

Like an omen, a flight of ptarmigan blossomed out of the corrie and wheeled across below my stance. There must have been thirty of them, a white flurry of wings across the purpled air; omen of peace across the ache of a restless world.

With a sigh, I hauled myself to my feet and continued my cold pilgrimage. My whole body cried out in a long ache, every limb and muscle complained unbearably, yet after sliding down to the gap (to the ruination of the seat of my trousers) I never considered not adding the Cairnwell (3059 feet) to the round. My hundredth Munro would be worthy. Whenever I passed over the Devil's Elbow I would be able to look up to its modest summit and remember this day.

Every hundred yards or so I would huddle down for a few minutes' rest, cram in a sweet, then struggle on. All I wanted to do was sleep—if only the wind would stop for just a few minutes . . .

I came up to the cairn and kicked up a stone to add to it. I looked back to the black corrie with its snow rim, I looked, without revelation, to the vanishing south, I looked east to the hills of the morning, cloud-clung, their walk already aeons of experience away. It was a quick glance round the stormy horizon, and I started down with relief.

You could romp up that summit in very little time from the main road, and sometime they will desecrate it with a chairlift; but I had to rest several times going down, and each foot had to be placed on the slippery surface with exaggerated care and willpower. My thoughts were on the orange tent seen below beside the empty ribbon of road. I worked out an order of procedure—and, in fact, carried it out—otherwise I am sure I would have gone to sleep as soon as I crawled inside. I felt very foolish sitting not a hundred feet above, watching the flapping canvas.

Then suddenly I was there, going round checking the guy-lines, opening the sleeve entrance; crawling in I lay for a minute with my feet outside, feeling a great surge of content at having done all and being back. There was the physical content of complete relaxing. Every limb throbbed, and my eyes felt as if on fire. I slowly unlaced my boots.

Then followed the pleasant ritual of making tea—sweet, stewed nectar. I swished down some salt as a cramp preventative. It was anything but nectar! I clumped off in unlaced boots to fill the dixie again, paid a necessary if unpleasant visit, and crawled back in for good.

I had a real climber's meal—odd in its ingredients, filling, satisfying. I had a vegetable soup to which had been added beef cubes, cheese, lemon juice, and macaroni, the whole mess poured over a tin of corned beef. Six cups of coffee followed.

My last memory was of snug comfort under rebellious canvas rattling in the rush of rain, my next of a still world and the near chuckling of grouse. My breath hung in the sharp air when I looked out the entrance. The ground was frosted white and the hills rose boldly against a lemon sky.

I was back home before sunset, and now I write while the memories are still fresh and clear. I feel years older, and yesterday seems an age ago. Tomorrow, as I sit in class, it will be like a dream, sweeter than the reality, until I move and stiff muscles cry out again.

And a confession. I have just looked up my log books and the Munro's Tables to find the week-end brought, not the expected hundred, but only a total of ninety-eight! I had to laugh, but also to speculate. If I had known it up there in the storm, would I, could I . . .?

'Non nostrum inter vos tantas componere lites' (*Not ours to decide such high dispute!*—Virgil): we may go in boldness, but from the mountains, anyway, we come again in humility.

The Snowdrop Miracle

Once upon a time, when I was a boy, I discovered Snowdrop Valley. Boy and dog had followed up the river and off it lay this hollow, this coombe, this small glen which was a mass of snowdrops.

We broke through a brittle screen of rank elderberry bushes, big as trees, and there they were. Snowdrops by the million. There were double ones and single ones and if they amazed by their numbers they were—and remain for me—the purest and most lovely of all flowers when seen singly. Such delicate proportions, such restrained touches of colour among the silken white—a white which outshines any TV commercial even when they burst through in the sourest and most grimy corner of a city.

The rest of that valley lay dead in the dank rump of winter, the hills above were a tired tawny colour, and the river alone seemed to have life. Had we not set a kingfisher flashing fire up its tree-hung darkness? Had a dipper not curtseyed at our passing? Had a heron not cried Good Day to us in his cracked voice? Later explorations showed the river had carried snowdrop seeds far downstream. Areas had been vigorously colonised here and there and the last migratory clump we noticed was five miles away.

We penetrated up into that hollow and discovered its banks were completely white with snowdrops, more even than on the boggy flat by the river. There were old walls and pathways and a crumbled archway. When we panted out above the glen we saw a mansion: gaunt, roofless and already invaded by willowherb.

I was there again the May after the discovery and had the shock of seeing what looked like snowdrops in flower near the house. In May? They were something else of course but puzzling enough that I dug out a clump. The leaf was as rank as a hyacinth, the bulb looked like a daffodil bulb, the flower was rather like a snowdrop.

Nobody helped with identification and one elderly friend even suggested I had created a leg-pull. I sent it to the Edinburgh Botanical Gardens and they said it was Summer Snowflake *Leucojum aestivum*, once popular in Victorian demesnes.

The descendants of that clump run riot still in gardens all over the country—as do successive generations of snowdrops. Every spring I would bring a few home from the abandoned valley, which is illegal now of course. Snowdrop Valley became a very special place for one boy and his old dog. There were few grown-ups, and fewer contemporaries, who were taken to see it in all its glory. It was my 'Secret Garden'.

17

Then disaster struck. As a sensitive teenager I one day found the ruined mansion had been knocked down and the rubble had been bulldozed down the banks of Snowdrop Valley. It was probably a quite unintentional destruction but I wept in sorrow and rage and vowed I would never return to the desecrated valley of youth.

As I was soon off to the far corners of the world doing my National Service it perhaps held more symbolism than I realised. The family also went to live thirty miles away so it was some years before I did return.

We found a miracle, itself perhaps the most symbolic of all. Coming up through the slopes of rubble were the shy, white heads of snowdrops. There were not many but year by year they increased. The rubble too is now invisible. Once the snowdrops, in all their original glory, have finished flowering the banks are rank with nettles—an excellent protection.

This year I went again, an older man with a young dog. It was as if everything between the years of a young boy and his old dog had never been. The banks are a glory of white year by year. It is my snowdrop miracle.

Curiosity had set us exploring in the rubble and what we found was a fantastic lesson in the tenacious strength of life. The snowdrops, even those buried feet deep, did grow and flower—underground! They were long, pale, yellowy, specimens but they grew, and bloomed. Just imagine those delicate white flowers deep in the blackness!

Now the miracle. Instead of the plant's resources returning back into the bulb, a new bulb formed an inch or two up the stem and the original one withered away. Year by year, inch by inch, they fought their way up through the rubble till, in ones and twos, then in tens and scores and eventually in thousands the white heads broke into the open air. No longer cramped, they could spread their petals wide, and drop their seeds, and bring tears to the eyes of a man from the wars returning.

I now make a visit to Snowdrop Valley every year. Since it's a place where a miracle happened I consider it to be a pilgrimage. At the deadest time of year those white spears rising from the dead soil speak boldly of Resurrection and Life.

Memory-haunted

Recently I met a former pupil of mine outside Kirkcaldy railway station. He hailed me tentatively by name, then grinned after our introduction: 'I recognised the nose.' I suppose greyer hair above and below that feature was my main change but John had gone from a tiny fifteen year old to a natty, thirty-plus businessman, quite beyond recognition. In the few minutes before I had to rush off to a dentist appointment we recalled people and places and good times we'd shared a quarter of a century ago.

'Do you remember going off to do the shopping from the bothy at Gorton?' was my first query. This is not Gorton bothy but a one-time linesman's cottage near Gorton railway station, called Rowantree Cottage. Alas, it and Gorton station have gone the way of all brick and mortar. I mourn them both for the late Charles Murray at Gorton was a great friend to the school parties with which I once criss-crossed Rannoch Moor. There was always a cup of tea and a good crack at that remote spot. He'd regale the kids with horror stories of life there in winter. 'Aye, I'd come in frae thawin oot the points and *stand* ma coat behind the door.'

Which MBA worthy was it too who, heading for Ben Alder for Hogmanay, left the train at Gorton, having been informed that he should get off at Rannoch, 'the next station after Bridge of Orchy'? (Trains only stopped at Gorton on request, or to top-up Mr Murray's water supply or deliver his newspapers.)

Rowantree Cottage was about a mile up the line and stood right by the track. British Rail destroyed it, no doubt with the best intentions, but it was the loss of a superb bothy. Staying there with a school gang we were running low on bread so John, who must have been less than 5 feet at the time, was despatched to Tyndrum, the nearest shop, to fill a rucksack with bread—and sweets, lemonade and all the other juvenile essentials.

He caught the Glasgow train from Gorton and had soon completed the messages (the 'shopping' to Sassenachs) and was back up at the station kicking his heels with a long wait for a Fort William train. A heavy goods drew in, a long line of alumina tankers hauled by one of the new-fangled diesel engines, and John was hauled up into the cab and juddered off to Bridge of Orchy and Rannoch Moor.

We heard, and then felt, the train coming from inside the bothy but when it stopped at the door we all tumbled out to see why. There was John grinning from the cab. He was so tiny that when he climbed down the ladder he had to hang from the lowest rung and drop some distance to the trackside. He stood back, gave a regal wave, the goods tooted and slowly went on its way. Yes, John remembered.

'Do you remember the haunted experience at Ben Alder?' John asked in turn.

Much has been written about the happenings and the hauntings at Ben Alder. Most of it is nonsense but our experience was genuine. Hadn't John remembered it over all those years?—after all he'd been scared stiff by what happened.

The school had its own bothy in the Black Wood of Rannoch and enjoyed a tradition of bothying that considerably pre-dated the MBA's creation. Quite a few trips were made to Ben Alder over the years for many of the youngsters were avid Munroists and Ben Alder and Beinn Bheoil of the easy to remember 3333 feet were two more local hills for the bagging. We were actually up as a work-party painting the school bothy but the work was all done in half the time available (ulterior motives?) and a quick raid to Ben Alder was suggested. We set off from the old sawmill one afternoon near the end of April and, having reached the bothy, had a brew and set off for Ben Alder at 6 pm.

We watched the sun set from that high, cornice-edged plateau land and made it back to the Bealach Breabag between Alder and Bheoil in the gloom of night. There we split as some enthusiasts were set on Bheoil ('Because it's there, sur!') but I put my foot down to the extent of sending 'the babes', Bugs David and John, home to the bothy. This had ulterior motives too. They could make the supper. Some of the party who continued were soon to traverse the Cuillin Ridge, climb Mont Blanc and wander to the ends of the earth. Wee Bugs went off to live in Australia (packing his forty-nine Munros), John later joined the RAF and had done his fifteen years in it. When I met him at Kirkcaldy he was just back from sorting out the Omani air force! The bothies and bens have a lot to answer for.

Beinn Bheoil was climbed into a cold-edged night that had the stars yellow-blinking like the lights of Dalwhinnie away up Loch Ericht. We descended by torchlight and when the bay and the bothy came in sight we were delighted to see a light. The bairns would have supper cooked and a brew ready.

A few hundred yards short of the bothy John and Bugs rose at our feet like startled hares. They had been crouching there all the time and had not been in the bothy at all. 'There was a light on Hamish . . . and funny noises . . . It could be anyone . . . After aw the stories you've been tellin us we werna gang ben oorselves . . . It's haunted!'

The 'ghosts' turned out to be a schoolmaster from Rannoch School and his son who had come up for a bit of fishing.

Yes, I remember it, John. What great times we've all had in the bothies and on the bens. If nowt else we are memory-haunted.

Salute to Adventure, without Cars

'Being safely off the hills and steaming for the open seas, the mirth prevailed—the pipes were brought on deck, and the President, in all the splendour of Highland garb, footed it deftly through the Highland fling—and reels were danced—a fitting termination to the Meet.'

Mountaineering is not what it once was; the above being the end of the Scottish Mountaineering Club's 'ever-memorable yachting expedition of Easter 1897'. Mind you the expedition had intended its excursions to be undertaken in Skye but Scavaig proved an inhospitable anchorage and various ploys took place on Rhum and Knoydart instead.

How much more interesting it must have been in the day of tweed: they really were 'expeditions', none of our plastic age's 'trips'. Perhaps as we choke ourselves in cities and burn up the world's fuel we'll see a return to reality: man minus machine.

In my richly-bound SMCJ Vol IV there is also an article entitled 'Mountaineering with Cycles' by Willie Douglas. The 'idea struck that a weekend excursion might be made to embrace the notable mountain of Lurven'. This laudable plan entailed cycling off from Spean Bridge at noon, shoving their 'beasties' over the unridable watershed and fighting to Skiary on Loch Hourn in the dark, a howff where they lived solely on porridge and whisky.

A twelve-hour round bagged the peak and the next day they pedalled back for the Edinburgh trains. In those good old days before there was a West Highland line you had your weekend on the Ben by starting on the Inverness line and then by horse trap, cycle, and foot reached the Allt a' Mhuilinn. No CIC Hut either.

As a teenager I was a madcap cyclist as well as hill basher and years ago, in revolt against vehicles and always being the driver having to return to the starting point, I renewed acquaintance with the beast.

The benefits were seen the first weekend. I made a quick run up into the forests of Strathyre and cached the cycle. After dinner I bivouacked by the Falls of Leny. At dawn I was up Stank Glen and the morning gave a fine traverse of Ben Ledi and Ben Vane. The cycle gave a rapid descent to Loch Lubnaig and while the traffic battled it out on the road we pedalled blissfully along the dead railway track opposite.

Cycling has it own hazards: often forestry or estate roads have surfaces of either jagged rock or clawing sand. You then find why it is called a *push* bike. Going in down

Loch Ericht one winter to Blackburn of Pattock provided another hazard in frozen ruts. Once cycling through from Tilt to Dee I caught a pedal while in a rut and fell down the bank, in alternative bounces with the cycle. I stopped on the edge of the river, the bike went in!

On another occasion I left the folded carcase of bike chained to a tree at the head of Glen Ogle, motored round to Strathyre and enjoyed a Corbett-collecting traverse back to the pass—to discover the vital wing nut to hold the machine together had been left in the car. It is the sort of error you only make once.

A canoe is my impecunious substitute for the yacht. Its baptism in approaching Munros was for the peaks west of Loch Lochy. A gale was forecast for the afternoon but the raid was over by then and we sneaked away from the clawing forests with two more scalps. The good summer of 1984 may never be equalled for canoe-Munros with raids into Knoydart, to Sgurr na Ciche by Loch Quoich, and all the Loch Mullardoch hills. Earlier we'd canoed the Great Glen and on the River Forth.

But to return to ships. A recent bit of reading in old logs has revived memories of The *Captain Scott,* which once plied our waters. It was sold off to the Arabs when sponsors failed and no one would pay the price of quarter of a mile of motorway to buy her.

The courses were sea-borne Outward Bound in character. On one course we climbed and trekked on the Ben, in Arran, and across Cape Wrath from Loch Inchard to Loch Eribol; we sailed from Plockton via the Sound of Sleat, Rhum, Mull, Loch Linnhe, Jura, Kintyre, Northern Ireland, the Minches, Pentland Firth to Invergordon. And I mean *sail.* Sir Hugh Munro and the SMC crew *motored*, it was that sort of ship; ours was the real thing—a t'gallant three-masted schooner with the biggest spread of sail of any British ship while she survived.

The *Captain Scott* really started courses with a bang. Thirty-six innocent trainees yet, three days later, sails reefed, in the dark, battling a gale round Ardnamurchan Point, clinging to the yards (unbelayed 100-foot above the sea), they are a crew sailing a ship. For many the snowy nights in Glen Nevis were the first camping and the Ben the first hill. Arran camping suffered hurricane-force winds in Glen Rosa with Goatfell a memory of frequent flattenings by big gusts.

The Cape Wrath trip gave as wild, yet all trainees, on their own, completed the three day trek in good style. Machines add nothing to adventuring.

I have a picture yet of the last dusk with my Hawke Watch romping about in the rigging, frantically trying to cover the furled square sails with hessian before the month of refit, while the snow fell steadily. They joked and sang, fear and sickness, weariness and discomfort forgotten. 'We would sail her for Everest and climb the bloody mountain,' one of them laughed.

Before turning in that night I climbed out along the jib boom where you could see the whole ship: masts and rigging, white, vanishing aloft in a spread of hazy stars, a faint glow from the chartroom, a quiet sound of singing from the mess deck. Below me the figurehead of Scott, goggles on brow (irreverently referred to as Biggles), peered through the falling snow. He certainly knew nothing of machines when he set off on his march to the pole.

A Day of Glory Given

The romance of the mountains that draws us to the hills is an elusive sort of thing. It comes, out of mystery, and even if never really understood, it is about us all our days. We cannot conjure it up. In C S Lewis's phrase, we are 'surprised by joy'.

'A day of glory given', was the term an old keeper friend of mine used for those odd days which come unexpectedly, without forecasting or likelihood, and present us with splendour. I had one during the run up to Christmas past.

I'd been out at weekends through November into December and had had a reasonable enough time even if there was a lack of snow to upset all my skiing plans. The fieldfare and snowbunting still flew in from the north. Winter had to be somewhere. The week before Christmas the dog and I headed off to the hills for the festive season. We crossed the Cairnwell to Deeside. Not a streak of snow was to be seen on the sorry slopes of the resort.

2 'A Day of Glory Given'.

The next few nights did slowly turn the tops grey, if not white, and then it went from being 'Dreich' to being 'Mayar Dreich'. In Bob Scott's old bothy at Luibeg the rain and hail battered on the roof. The fire went out from lack of wood. I retreated to headphones and watched the candle shadows while discovering the aptness of Bruckner's Fourth Symphony to the situation.

The alarm went off at six but the rattle on the roof meant it could be forgotten. Day just intensified the wet but, surely, it would be snowing higher up? I cycled out to the car at the Linn o' Dee, with many a stag eyeing laden bike and roving dog, then trotting off disdainfully into the pines.

I drove to Ballater for an urgently needed replacement headlamp for the bike. The car radio said milder weather again (it was raining on Deeside) and gave the unexpected news of England actually winning a Test Match.

With an eye on a remote Munro the dog had not climbed I did a repacking for cycling on to another bothy base, then drove over to the valley of the Gairn. It was raining on Gairnside too so it would be warm pedalling with waterproofs on. A mile up the track I remembered I'd not packed candles. Back we went. Two miles on the chain snapped and lay, adder-like, on the track. A half-hour fight (in sleet) followed before that was dealt with. The other five miles went safely but by the time we reached the bothy there was a mix of snow, wind and dusk. Our secure base was very welcome.

We lit a fire after supper and as I'd a good book and music I enjoyed the evening and tried not to notice the clattering and banging on the roof or the white that covered the window and crept in under the door. The hunting winds were loose. The blizzard would probably go on all night, so I did not even set the alarm. If the storm stopped, the silence would wake me. I slept till long after daybreak.

It was only then the silence came: the muffled, breathy, silence of deep snow. I could hear an occasional grouse complaint, a dipper flew past up the river but these were the sounds of belonging, mere accessories to the fancy. When I opened the door a thin wall of blown snow was left standing in the gap. All the wall and the northwest side of every tree was plastered white. There had not been all that much snow but the gale had enjoyed doing things with what it had. The world sparkled with light.

The sun could not reach the bothy because of the shape of the hill across the river but the big hills up the valley and Brown Cow Hill behind the bothy were ice-cream white, melting deliciously in the sun. We let out a yell of glee and dived back inside to hurry up the mundane necessity of breakfast.

I had gone down to the river to brush my teeth when I spotted a Land-Rover coming up. It proved to be two keepers out after hinds (two corpses in the back dripped their blood on to the snow all day) and here they swopped over to a tracked 'snowcat' for the upper-valley reaches.

They had to cull a hundred hinds each year to keep the beasts healthy, they explained, a task often made difficult by the vast scale of the landscape and the weather conditions. 'Aye, its nae a bad day a'ta,' had been their greeting, in resonant Aberdeenshire voices. I hoped their tracks would make cycling out easier the next day. It had been very wet coming in and all water would be ice now.

We set off up the burn from the bothy but soon had to climb out of its depths as the snow had piled in deeply. On a bit we could see the whole southwest flank of Brown Cow Hill and worked out a route to bypass all the deepest drifts. It was heather moorland, loud with grouse and full of charging hares. Poor Storm didn't know where to look. At one time there were five rushing off in different directions. A burn came down a gash direct from the dome of hill and in the hollow where it met the moorland a score of deer were clustered. As it looked deep snow this was puzzling. We were more than a mile away but were seen at once and the deer closed up and filed off round the hill, leaving a dark line on its white sweep.

The hard work of teasing out a route to avoid drifts, bogs and drains kept eyes and mind busy so we were on the plateau edge of this huge sprawl of hill before really looking around. Wow! The whole world was white!

Ben Avon alone loomed higher than we were and its odd warts or tors (here called 'barns') stood up like sword blades in the sun.

Lochnagar lay in the eye of the sun but Mount Keen and Morven were indentikit paps breasting the Dee to the east. We had a good look at the Lecht Road, that Cockbridge to Tomintoul route so familiar from radio announcements as to it being blocked with snow. It wound a black snaky line up through the whites so was probably all right for my escape tomorrow. (It was and we drove to the Dirrie More.)

We went off in search of the cairn of Brown Cow Hill. It proved to be a wee scab of stones on the bare back of the beast. Some would decry this part of the world as 'just heather bumps', 'pudding hills' or, sin of sins for any hills, 'dull'. Such designation usually is a comment on the commentator, not the landscape. Corbetts are nearly always superlative viewpoints.

I sat on top for half an hour, just mesmerised by impressions: the magical sliding scale of the hills, from the wild white panorama itself to the tiny patterns of stars clinging to blades of grass. To be able to sit for that time was also unusual. The freezing temperature felt quite comfortable as there was no wind and the sun shone golden from over Lochnagar.

We circled round to descend by that direct gully we'd seen coming up. Gravels and soil had washed down and on this fan grass grew rather than heather—which was why the deer had been there. The drifts in places had completely levelled over the 10-foot-deep gash and in others had scooped out extraordinary shapes: snow sculptures—undeservedly impermanent for much worse things are shoved, all too permanently, in art galleries.

We stumbled back over the heather moors, the powder snow glittering in sunbursts as we kicked it up while, behind, we left a dark line of track. There were more grouse than I'd seen in years and scores of white hares, some which sat till we were only yards away. It seemed even they called Truce with dog and man in the 'day of glory given'.

A Night Out on Beinn a' Bhuird

That 'day of glory given' was fairly recent but the following piece describes a weekend in the early nineteen-sixties. While equipment has improved since I am interested to see how little my ideas and methods have changed. The BFMC was a club open to staff, pupils and friends of Braehead School where I taught for many years—and not to be confused with the Braes o' Fife club which roams the hills today.

It was one of those weekends which started off badly yet led, in the end, to fun and adventure—all the more delightful because of the initial chaos.

We were a party of the BFMC (politely referred to as the 'BF's') and set off from Fife on a Friday evening in Horace, once described as a 'sort of vehicle', being in fact a home-made car with a body like a horse-box. Enough. He rattled us over the Devil's Elbow to have us in Braemar before midnight. There Mike and I were left while the other carried on for the Linn o' Dee, Glen Derry and the Corrour Bothy. As none of them had been there before and everything was frozen up after a wet autumn they had an eventful passage. They bedded down at four in the morning after their eight mile hike. Our destination was the ruin of Slugain Lodge whose glen we decided to reach by fording the Dee. Innocents abroad in the moonlight. Waist-deep was enough so we dressed again and disentangled ourselves from the high deer-fenced fields all covered in white frost. We stomped moodily down the road for a few miles with our laces trailing. I was ill (with internal pains) and could hardly manage even a light rucksack. In 'the wee sma' 'oors' we lay down under some trees determined to make a start an hour before dawn to regain the lost ground. 'We'll be glad to get off then, we'll be so cold anyway.'

It was cold, too, but it was nine o'clock before either of us confessed to being awake. We crossed Invercauld Bridge and set off into the Cairngorms. We collapsed at Slugain with the deer standing clear round the horizon. We felt decrepit and I was racked with cramps inside. This was our nadir. What now? Our aim had been a winter traverse of Ben Avon, Beinn a' Bhuird and over the great moss to the Coire Etchachan Memorial Hut, with the others possibly coming to meet us to climb in Coire Sputan Dearg of Macdhui; here we were—hardly in the hills even, feeling like death, the hills blotted out and with a mere three hours of daylight left of the short winter day.

3   The granite 'tor' or 'barn' marking the summit of Ben Avon in the Cairngorms.

A little later we were spanking gaily up the path towards the Sneck, Mike chattering away as of old while he raced to keep up. I swear there was nothing stronger than sugar in the tea we brewed. Anyway, our phoenix strength drove us on rejoicing into the world of rock and snow. Ice axes were loosened for their labour of love.

The Cairngorms have a personality of their own; other areas crowd their beauty into small compass, here there is vastness, but a vastness almost equally packed with interest. The wild-life, the old Scots Pine forests, the heathery slopes and the great passes, corries and high plateaux are unique. They require care, for their greater elevation brings Arctic rather than Alpine conditions. Nowhere else have I so often had to fight or crawl to reach summits! They can demand the highest standards in navigation in mist. It is quite an experience to wander over their flat, featureless and invisible miles. Ski parties in particular are often lax at carrying (or understanding) map and compass.

Near the end of the track we crossed the burn and followed up the flow coming down from the Dubh Lochan. Before the steep slope to Coire Lochain there is a smaller loch and from its end we set a canny compass course to skirt under the huge Dividing Buttress into Coire nan Clach where the guide, hopefully rather than helpfully, informed us we would find a howff under 'the second largest boulder'. We had been in deep snow since leaving the path. There had been thick fog also and it was a flounder and barking of shins on granite all the way up to the lochan and into 'The Corrie of the Rocks', which was a nightmare of boulders, dozens the size of buses, covered in snow, slobberly, floury and slippery. We crawled over and round and under them while time sped and no howff could we find. A forced bivvy loomed ahead when, with about half an hour of light left I stumbled on the built-up cave under a boulder. Either the guide places it under the wrong buttress or it is several hundred yards out of place, or it is another cave. But it was sanctuary. Could not such mountain positions and descriptions be given as simple six-figure references on the OS map? At least we could then use dead reckoning and arrive with some certainty. Periodically through the evening there were snorts and giggles and quotes about 'the second largest boulder'. When the mist cleared momentarily our calculated position was correct and we had a glimpse through the half light of grey hills and stark crags and gullies round the boulder wilderness. We settled in for the night.

I crawled in through the narrow opening to level the floor and clear the snow which had drifted in. Mike remained outside cutting snow blocks, some of which were passed inside to serve as water supply, the rest being used to fill gaps in the hostel and reduce the entrance to an even smaller aperture. Snow takes time to melt and putting the dixie on is always the first job. I lit a candle as Mike wiggled his way in and blocked up the entrance with his instant material. Capes were spread on the floor and sleeping bags unrolled. It was cold, but with extra clothes and sitting in our bags we were cosy enough. The only thing we lacked was an air bed, the surface under us being as comfy as any pile of broken bricks. Nevertheless we slept excellently, wearing all our extra woollies (of which we carried many and little else in the clothing line, worn top and bottom they make you look like a Michelin advert but keep you very warm) inside Icelandic sleeping-bags and with a layer of newspapers and our maps insulating from ground-cold. We were about 3300 feet up, which is higher than a great many summits.

For this trip our rucksacks weighed about twenty pounds. We had a light rope, used double for serious climbing, axes, bedding, woollies, food, stove and so on. We believed in being light—from bitter experience. The rules of camping and preconceived notions should all be thrown away—if we had followed the pundits we would never have been there in the first place. Can I plead for experimentation? Question, question and question and try, try, try until you come to the balance for each expedition that will give maximum safety, certainty and enjoyment. Much of my work has been with youngsters who simply cannot carry heavy burdens anyway. Yet last summer we trekked and climbed for weeks with boys as young as 13. They were quite capable of walking from Inverie in Knoydart to Kinlochhourn over Mam Barrisdale—and climbed Ladhar Bheinn on the way. The same boys have crossed and camped on Rannoch Moor summer and winter. Success was often the reward of dealing with the superfluous.

This includes food. Tins should be omitted completely and so can most of the utensils and containers. Our cave-dwelling cuisine was filling, appetising and nourishing—and light. We craved liquid, so first had chicken broth (cubes) and into the half dixie of boiling water left we poured a packet of dehydrated apples. Bread with the broth, and biscuits with the apples, were used. Then more snow was dumped in the dixie along with a packet of 5-minute soup (avoid the long-boilers), dried onions and Surprise (dried) peas. A poke of salt, pepper and spices made it a tasty broth. This was followed by a macaroni-cheese dish with similar vegetables. After that a dixie of tea and biscuits left us replete. The order in which they were eaten was not exactly conventional but then neither was the cafe. We cooked on gas, but the primus is still 'the best buy'. Gas is clean and easy, but it is expensive and keeps running down to burn at an infuriatingly slow pace. We had one dixie and lid, one mug, one spoon, one penknife for the two of us—and lacked nothing.

Such howffs deserve better patronising. There are (as in winter camping) certain differences if not difficulties which are best overcome by experience, as no two expeditions are the same. In winter there is always a water supply, it is dry and crisp, there is no perpetual rain, the midges are absent, the peasants are away till the next summer and the beauty and fun of climbing unsurpassed. The biggest difficulty in winter is condensation and only experience with one's own gear in each circumstance will deal with that. Too much warmth with too little ventilation will soon set things sweating; too much ventilation and you have an icebox. In this grotto we had more than enough air filtering in through side cracks. We were cold, but not enough to leave our pits to stop up the cracks with snow. Comfort is a relative thing.

We settled down at nine o'clock. The moon filtered a tracery of light in the doorway. It was too much—perhaps the full moon was shining from a clear sky and we could be climbing on the glittering magic of night snow. (Another habit not in the pundit's standing routine.) We broke a hole through the snow. Visibility was nil.

We lay back again and watched the candle flicker over the red granite above our heads. The cave was about tent high and about two tents in length and the roof was twice as hard—as our craniums had discovered. Sleep came easily all the same.

Mike pulled the stove over and lit it while still in his sleeping bag. Tea in bed to start the day—I don't get that at home! Mike forgot to place something under the primus for insulation and when he next looked the stove had melted its way down through the snow. My boots had to be thawed out over the stove before I could force my feet inside them. Mike had kept his warm by using them for a pillow. It had been cold certainly. Some prunes left soaking overnight were encased in a cylinder of ice.

Last night had given a glimpse of a nice gully, possibly the Crocus Gully of the guide, well banked up with snow but steep below the rim of the cornice. We contoured round and up in the mist, first one then the other pressing on at top speed. The crust held and we could kick steps. The gully steepened and we began cutting. It then reared up in a shallow chute of snow ice, crusted with the remains of an avalanche. The wind had risen too and the chips flying from the axe stung our faces as they shot about the gully. A short vertical section, a hammering-down of cornice, a wild devil's white of spindrift and we crawled out onto the summit plateau. We stood in stillness while the wind tore out of the corrie with a roar a few steps away. We roped for fear of walking over cornices in the fog, but in fact the edge could always be heard if not seen—a roaring as of surf in the whiteness of the fog.

We followed the edge round to what we took to be a true position on the map and then set off carefully for the cairn. We left a deep track to ease the return. Half a mile later the cairn was suddenly beside us. We fled back along the barely-discernible track, the blizzard full in our faces now. An old team, we wasted no time. The cornice was reached and Mike baled off while I belayed. I soon followed into the inferno and then we moved together. Soon we were sliding and romping down. Back 'home' we unroped and packed. It was only 11 a.m. The visibility cleared slightly and we could make out our steps of the search for the cave. We wondered what anyone would make of their giddy gyrations. Superimposed across their drunken course was the clear trail of a fox.

We followed the Quoich down, first on the path and then through trackless forest until it swung south to the Dee. Groups of stags stood still watching our passing. We turned off to take the line of a fault (a continuation of the Glen Tilt fault) through to Glen Derry, a remarkable, steep-sided trench with a ribbon of frozen water up its length. We picked up an antler, already chewed by the hungry deer. The heather was alive with the elusive music of the tits. It was the Cairngorms as they will always be recalled. We paused before dropping onto the road down to Linn o' Dee and Horace. We were there by 2.45 p.m. and were able to hand out tea to the others an hour later as they arrived, Robert and Alastair (Mike's 13-year-old brother) well ahead of Noddy, Michael and Greig. They had been on Devil's Point and Cairn Toul the day before and learned much of step-cutting, glissading and compass work. By 8 p.m. they were all in their homes along the mining coast of Fife. It was school on Monday as usual—but with more than usual tales to tell.

Snow sets on

The snow sets on
towards the loch. It moans
wind-pains. It limps along
to whiten the Scots pines' bark
with its floury hands.

The blizzard will follow
this first biting and blind night-tapper
but not till dusk sucks the day
of its warm blood. Storm and night
are fellows, drunk with puking power.
They go out, wretchedly, to scream at stars.

This is a night for holding

Wade and Caulfeild, Road Builders to the Nation

Several times recently when people have been discussing the West Highland Way I've heard Wade's road over the Devil's Staircase mentioned. Perhaps West Highland Way walkers feel like echoing the lines attributed to Toby Caulfeild: 'If you'd seen these roads before they were made, you'd lift up your hands and bless General Wade.'

Whatever the means of moving through the Highlands, Wade has a lot to answer for, but, before some readers start reaching for their pens or claymores, let me proclaim that the Devil's Staircase is NOT a Wade road nor are many others which on maps have 'Wade Road' written against them.

The Devil's Staircase is a Caulfeild road—and note the spelling of Caulfeild. Even Inverness, who at least have named a street after him, manage to spell it wrongly. I note this with feeling for in my first book I had it wrong and when this was pointed out I checked a dozen source books and found half of them were wrong too. Caulfeild was Irish of course. So was Wade. Caulfeild succeeded his boss Wade and in fact built almost three times his road mileage but, somehow, Wade receives all the credit.

After the abortive risings of 1715 and 1719 various measures were taken to try to prevent a recurrence. In 1725 General Wade, C-in-C North Britain, who had already made a thorough survey of the Highlands began the construction of roads and forts and barracks (like Ruthven) as part of his vision of controlling the clans.

It took just three summers to link Dunkeld and Inverness more or less on the line of our notorious A9. About two miles north of Dalnacardoch (Wade's headquarters for the A9 job) standing off the south-bound lane, is Wade's Stone, a 7-foot monolith, dated 1729.

His most famous landmark is surely the beautiful bridge he built at Aberfeldy, which was half way along the Crieff–Dalnacardoch road he also built. Crieff was the great cattle tryst through those droving years but the Jacobite unrest saw it shifted to Falkirk and some of the cattle were even marched all the way to London.

In 1725 he raised the Black Watch at Aberfeldy, some 500 men of Clans Campbell, Grant, Fraser, and Munro who were 'loyal' to the crown. They formed a sort of Highland constabulary: disarming the clans, preventing cattle reiving, guiding Sassenach forces and so on. They were drafted in to build his roads. He referred to them as his 'Highwaymen' and they received extra pay, plenty of beer and beef and there were some wild parties (with beasts roasted whole) when any stage was completed.

Before Wade went south to another post (and promotion to Field-marshal) he had constructed about 240 miles of road and twenty-eight bridges, quite a feat in just six years. Between the lines I think Wade comes over as almost a decent bloke. He was still in the field in 1745 when that rebellion broke out and by an ironic twist of fate it was Prince Charlie's army that was the first to cross the Corrieyairack, Wade's most spectacular creation, linking Fort Augustus with the A9 route.

Rising to nearly 2000 feet, it was not the most practical road but it was used until Thomas Telford built the road we still use along by Loch Laggan and Roy Bridge.

The other major Wade road linked Fort William and Inverness, keeping east of the Great Glen lochs, and where this crossed the river Spean at High Bridge the first shots were fired in the 1745 rebellion.

Wade was in England then. Cope's feeble efforts and ignominious defeat at Prestonpans led him to be court-martialled, Field-marshal Wade presiding.

Wade's bridge at Aberfeldy was designed by William Adam, the father of famous architect sons, and it was intended as a showpiece. Most of his bridges are simpler and functional rather than beautiful but my favourite, Garva Bridge on the Corrieyairack, is simple, functional *and* beautiful. Only Dorothy Wordsworth seems to have thought the Aberfeldy bridge ugly.

Just along from Wade's bridge at Aberfeldy there is a statute of a Black Watch soldier, commemorating the raising of that regiment, but the figure is supposed to be the likeness of one particular man. In 1740 a thousand men were mustered near Aberfeldy and marched to London where they were reviewed by Wade. The Government had secretly decided to send them abroad despite promises that they would serve only in Scotland and when wind of this became known there were angry meetings and desertions. The deserters were caught and three, *pour encourager les autres*, were shot, the rest drafted into regiments serving abroad. One of those shot is portrayed in the monument at Aberfeldy.

At Weem just outside Aberfeldy, the hotel bears a picture of Wade like an inn sign. He was based here at one time and it, and many of his bases, were made into stage houses, often 'King's Houses', which is why that name survives in several places today.

Caulfeild was Wade's able assistant and in 1732 he was made Inspector of Roads. He was on active service in the '45 and two years later became deputy to absentee Cumberland as Governor of Inverness Castle. His work on roads continued till his death in 1767—about 700 miles in all. His main routes were in two areas.

The longest began in Angus and went by Braemar and Cockbridge to Fort George with a continuation for Easter Ross through to Poolewe, so when you hear the radio saying the road from Cockbridge to Tomintoul is blocked, blame Caulfeild! He also developed a whole system of roads from central Scotland into Argyll, including one over Rannoch Moor, the Devil's Staircase to Fort William and the Rest and Be Thankful road to Inveraray and Loch Fyne.

The military handed over to the civil in 1785 and the whole system was soon in disrepair. In 1803 Parliament set up a commission and appointed one Thomas Telford

4   Wade's finest bridge. The showpiece of Aberfeldy.

as engineer—but that is another story. There is a stone on top of the Rest and Be Thankful which commemorates the repairing of Caulfeild's original road. The line wends up below the present sweep of the A83.

We began with a quote about Wade, so perhaps we can end with another, a stanza which is part of Britain's national anthem. In 1745 at the Drury Lane Theatre this new stanza was sung, which leaves Wade's name enshrined in the anthem. (Ironically the tune could have Jacobite origins!) The audience pleaded:

> God grant that Marshal Wade
> May by thy mighty aid Victory bring,
> May he sedition hush,
> And like a torrent rush,
> Rebellious Scots to crush,
> God save the King.

When you pech over the Devil's Staircase on the West Highland Way you can bless Caulfeild, not Wade, and ponder on the ghost-haunted historic route you follow. Rest, and be thankful you are not a redcoat marching up that brae in full gear, and that there's still a King's House to wet the whistle.

Game of the Name

That most lively and diverse Glasgow poet Edwin Morgan calls his poem Canedolia an 'off-concrete scotch fantasia'. It is a cornucopia of Scottish place names and a reading has them bouncing around with snooker ball colourfulness.

It was the first 'encore' he was asked for at a reading I heard him give at the Pitlochry Theatre. My hand was up to ask for it as well. I made sure it was in my anthology, *Poems of the Scottish Hills*.

In its imaginative conversation the following occurs:

> *What is the best of the country?*
> blinkbonny! airgold! thundergay!
> *and the worst?*
> scrishven, shiskine, scrabster, and snizort

Walking across Scotland each spring on the Ultimate Challenge has a tremendous fascination in the constantly changing landscape. Part of the interest is in the diversity of place names. There is no likelihood of meeting Tipperty, Dillivaird, or Corsebauld west of the Great Glen, nor of meeting hill names like Bidean a' Choire Sheasgaich or Sgurr nan Ceathreamhnan on the Braes of Angus.

Walking down the River Avon in the Cairngorms we stopped at Faindouran Bothy. In the bothy book stalkers mentioned going after hinds by the Spion rocks. Now Spion Kop is in South Africa.

An old tin trunk of musty books had an engraved label on its lid: 'O Haig. 7th Hussars.' Now, if my link is correct, they were in the Boer War and as the Haigs once owned that estate, the *kopje* name could have come to describe a tor in the Cairngorms.

A copy of Maxwell's *Memories of the Months* which we found in the box had articles on the fascination of names. He was emphasising the simple solution in looking for derivations, rather than the fanciful.

The part of Kinghorn where I live is Pettycur, the old port for crossing the Forth, which some suggest comes from the French *petit coeur*, little heart, but is simply one of the *petty/pit* names deriving from the Gaelic/Pictish term for a 'portion of land'. You can still find old cast-iron milestones in Fife with the puzzling name Pettycur on them.

In those days the port of Pettycur and the village of Kinghorn were quite separate. Our house stands on 'Crying-oot Hill'. No doubt when the ferry came in some youth would scramble up to yell to the village so passengers could then leave the pub!

The harbour has only one arm and the old Scots word for this is *hynd*. Along the coast is Buckhaven. None of the locals there would ever call the town anything but Buckhynd. And if you look back at old maps or manuscripts that is what you will find, or even Hynd of Buck.

As a Dollar lad I knew the River Devon well, the 'clear-winding Devon' of Rabbie Burns, but earlier yet it was Dowan or Dovan, far lovelier names than the usurping one.

5   One of the old iron milestones across Fife naming Pettycur, the old ferry to Edinburgh.

Names go on changing, too. The Cairngorms were once the Monadh Ruadh, and the Lairig Ghru not so long ago was Lairig Grumach. Much seems to have been altered in Victorian times. Devil's Point is a prudish translation of the Gaelic and, balancing it, has sprung up an Angel's Peak, a name which seems to be winning over the original, apt, Sgurr an Lochain Uaine, *peak of the green lochan*.

Loch an Nid, *loch of the nest*, led me, as a bird watcher, to one of my first eyries. And once, planning a cross-country walk over new country, I chose a line over a *ridge of the cows* on the assumption the going would be easy—cows do not climb crags—and so it proved. Teasing at names can be great fun.

Maxwell in his book was quoting some headland in Galloway still called Bhuidhe, *yellow*, though Gaelic has not been spoken there for hundreds of years. He suggests it is evidence that it once was.

In Munro's Tables the commonest mountain name is Ghabhar, *goat*, but there is not a sheep to be found, perhaps testimony to a change in status. The sheep came late to the Munros (that could be taken in more ways than one).

English writers sometimes complain that Gaelic has six ways of saying white. There are more in fact and this is simply due to the richness of Gaelic vocabulary—or the paucity of English.

Many names leave riddles. Why a *smallpox peak* in the Cuillin? What tale is lost in the *ridge of the sword*? Growing up in the Ochils my gang was not averse to naming things. With hindsight now I can see this is exactly how it was in the beginning. Features and activities had to be pinpointed.

Walking across Scotland gives a cross-section of accents too. From Speyside I phoned Cock Bridge to book accommodation and the accent I heard was resonant of the east, a real spur to the journey from far Achnashellach *the field of the willows*, where the accents had been as soft as the weather.

From Cock Bridge it was all couthy eastern names, with hardly a Gaelic name in sight. But don't they ring splendidly, names like Shank of Cardowan, Glensaugh, Tipperweir, Tillybreak, Kirktown of Fetteresso.

Some leave one as bewildered as intrigued: Wairds of Alpity, Temple of Fiddes, Stankeye, Snob Cottage, Bogjurgan, Feathers . . .

The Bogbraes, Stony Muirs, Hillheads are safer, if duller, and cannot have changed in centuries.

No doubt it was some Lancashire Redcoat who turned Loch Ba on Rannoch Moor into 'Loch Ball'. The notorious sportsman Thornton managed to make Crianlarich into 'Cree in La Roche'.

That rainy night in Faindouran bothy we pored (poured?) over our map, choosing good names. How would you like to farm at Pendicles of Collymoon, Goosecruives, Balnakettle, Backside of Garden, Whistlebare, or Stock o' Broom?

And as for Blinkbonny—our next Ultimate Challenge route has a kink in it near the end in order that we can pass Blinkbonny on our tramp down to the North Sea.

Rounding up Round Towers

Scotland and Ireland have connections which go back to the beginnings of our known history. The original 'Scots' flitted from Ireland into Argyll and the west and, quite how we will probably never know, ended up ruling a Scot–Pictish kingdom. The Irish have been infiltrating Scotland ever since!

Jokes apart, Glasgow and the west do have a large number of Irish-born or Irish-descended inhabitants, surely one of the contributions to making the city miles better. Ireland and Scotland have a great deal in common, not just racially but in culture, literature, and folklore. Ireland even shares with Scotland her unique contribution to architecture, the Irish round tower.

Wherever you wander in Ireland you soon come to notice these marks of the early church—the round towers. Visit the magnificent Rock of Cashel (one of Europe's great sites), or Conmacnoise by the River Shannon, or Glendalough in the Wicklows south of Dublin, or Kildare or Kilkenny Cathedrals, or scores of other places—and there are round towers. There are about sixty-five remaining in Ireland in recognisable form.

Some soar to more than 100 feet (Kildare is one), others are just circles of stone at ground level (like Liathmore, which, oddly, has the deepest foundations of all), but two of the best of Irish round towers, to be a bit Irish myself, are found at Brechin and Abernethy in Scotland.

Most towers seem to have had six or so storeys and become more slender with height, rather like factory chimneys. There is a stump of a tower on Iona and there is also a half-sized tower at Peel on the Isle of Man, though this was given fake battlements by Victorian 'improvers'. These are the only towers found outside Ireland. It is a form of architecture found nowhere else, as individualistic a feature as the stave kirks of Norway or our own brochs.

Most if not all the towers once had conical roofs, but many of these were destroyed by lightning or man's destructive hand. Some have had the conical roofs restored, like Glendalough (1876) or Brechin, the latter not being strictly conical, but faceted and somewhat pseudo gothic.

One of the delights of collecting round towers is that no two are the same: Kilkenny has six, not the usual four, windows on its top storey; Scattery has the only door at ground level; Kildare has a triangular hood moulding over its door; Brechin and

6 The old market cross and Round Tower at Abernethy.

Donaghmore have crucifixions carved over the door; Tinahoe has a series of Romanesque arches, one sunk inside the other, finely carved and decorative.

One evening we drove many interesting rural miles to find this particular tower. The door was 18 feet above the ground and on the shadow side, so no photograph was possible. Next time we decided to visit in the morning and bring along a fireman's extendable ladder.

Kinneigh was one tower we could actually climb up. A ladder led to the high doorway and then a whole series of them led up from one floor to the next. Some of the rungs had rusted through with neglect and no rock climb could equal the exposure of our perch on the brick-width open rim of the top. A waving foot for the last heave caught the bell and it sent a mournful toll across the quiet countryside.

Kinneigh's unusual feature (there is usually one) was having the first 18 feet up to the door built in a hexagonal rather than a round shape. Ardmore in the far south, Devenish on an island in Lower Lough Erne in the north, Kilkenny and Clondalkin in Dublin, and Abernethy near Perth, are towers which have safe access to the top of them, if you can find a key or a custodian to enter at all.

The Irish Gaelic for a round tower is 'cloigtheach' and simply means bell house, but no one is quite sure why. Perhaps a saint's bell (and other treasures) were stored there. Perhaps the monks rang hand bells from the top, or after the twelfth century (when many towers were restored and real bells first hung) they were proper belfries. All towers were built free-standing, though later on, as at Cashel or Brechin, subsequent building incorporated them.

The doorways were always placed inconveniently high up the walls, indicating their use as places of refuge in the unsettled times of the Celtic church. Once you were inside and hauled in your ladder, security must have been sure. Gunpowder was still to be invented.

I think many have survived because, when you pinch stones from some building to build another, you take them from the top first. A round tower, with its interior fallen in, is hardly easy picking.

They must have had some canny builders in the first place. Brechin's tower survived a Viking raid in 1012, illustrating the defensive role. The stone steps up to the very low-set doorway at Abernethy are a modern addition, as is the clockface higher up on the side facing the market cross.

Abernethy was almost certainly rebuilt as its lowest twelve courses are built of a differing stone. It is 72 feet in height. Brechin is 87 feet, and positioned at the corner of the nave of the old cathedral, itself mainly a thirteenth-century construction with a chequered history. Some Irish towers go back to about AD 900, for the one at Castledermot was built by a man known to have died in 919.

Brechin has one of the finest doorways of all, originally about 12 feet from the ground, highly decorative, and gaining from the rich texture of the red sandstone. Above the door the carved crucifix figure has its leg uncrossed in the traditional Irish manner.

Left and right of the door are carved figures of bishops and at the foot are two grotesque beasts. At the top are two blanks which presumably were intended for further carving. At Kells, traditionally founded by Saint Columba, there is a head carved on one jamb and an uncarved block on the other. We are left to speculate what bloody intervention stopped the masons at their work.

Our Scottish towers must have been very much the outliers of the tower building, intruding really into what was unsettled Pictland. The reconstruction at Abernethy incorporated early Norman touches, so it was no doubt among the last.

Plenty of churches have copied round towers for their belfries. Last time in Ireland we saw one in Donegal Town and one under Errigal Mountain, I've seen them as near as Dunfermline and on remote Canna. These don't count and neither apparently does the old Viking round tower of St Magnus's Church on Egilsay in Orkney. The experts lump these all together as 'bastard' round towers.

The Seasons

SPRING
wears a plastic green
which would normally
be very bad taste
but, being trim and young,
she gets off with it.
More! she flaunts it
among the tweedy tones
of jaded winter
Spring is a flirt;
which is why she wears
that bright green skirt.

SUMMER
is a mature gentleman
out for a gentle stroll
round the park.
Summer is all rounds,
bald-headed,
with outsize waist.
Summer has consumed
strawberries and cream,
cream teas, sparkling wine,
which is why he walks
gently
to coronary time.

AUTUMN
is the grey face
I see in the mirror
so is no topic
for any gossip.
With 2.4 kids and a wife
cast a cold eye on average life—
the seasons lie,
summer passed by.

WINTER
is two people in one:
—an old man, frosted
and iced, and tucked into bed
till he meets the dead,
—a young lad, white as snow,
finding a book on sex
not knowing what it's about
but sure it will be fun.
Under their blankets of snow,
too soon, too soon, they'll know.

Clouty Wells

The first well I can remember was the Maiden Well on the old hill track that led through the Ochils from Dollar to Glendevon. It was the writer and poet W K Holmes (whose work appeared in many magazines before and after the war) who told me it had a legend. A beautiful maiden could be summoned from its depths by any bold adventurer who came to drink of its cold waters on the dark nights of winter. With a twinkle W K H cooled any youthful notions I might entertain. The truth of the story could not be verified. All such visitors were invariably found dead on the path the following day.

W K H regularly cleaned out the well, for it was only a couple of feet in diameter, but however choked it became the water never ceased flowing, even in the driest summer drought. W K H was very much the voluntary caretaker of the well and on more than one occasion I accompanied him when he went up to clean it out. When he died I took on the task, but then went to live elsewhere and did not see the well for some time. When I did eventually return, the well was almost hidden in boggy growth. I cleaned it out and, of course, had a drink of its delectable, unchlorinated water.

The well has now been made better known and with many more people walking for recreation it will probably be kept clear in future. On a recent walk I found visitors had thrown two empty soft-drink cans into it. That struck me as rather ironic. Someone had carried those artificial, heavy cans of chemically contrived liquids miles into the hills only to dump them in a well of pure, delicious, natural water. But, before we think all old values and appreciations are rejected by modern people, there is this odd fact that the well frequently has coins left in it and quite a proportion of passers-by pause to drink, make a wish, pray for some benefit, or just tidy the little spring. The late twentieth century sees people as superstitious as ever. Wells have occupied this position for centuries.

One of the most extraordinary visual signs of this continuing superstition is what, in Scotland, are called *clouty wells*. On these, whatever other beliefs or rituals are involved, the visitor leaves some item of cloth behind, and fences, trees, everywhere within reach is festooned with bits of cloth. The result is hardly pretty, but judging by the amount of colourful *new* bits and pieces the habit is very much alive today. As nylon and other almost-indestructible materials are hung up it shows a certain ignorance of traditions, for it was believed that a sufferer symbolically hanging up a bit of himself would recover health in proportion to the rotting away of his offering. *Clout* (pronounced *cloot*) is just cloth, as in *dishclout* for dishcloth.

Wells have importance throughout these islands, but I have not come upon clouty wells in the south. There are two close to Inverness and, as that is very much a tourist centre, it is worth pinpointing them. One is at Culloden and one across the new bridge on the Black Isle.

The road to Culloden battlefield is well signposted from Inverness. The National Trust for Scotland have now felled trees and rebuilt the interpretive centre to restore the site nearer to what it must have been in 1746. The Culloden Wishing Well is strictly St Mary's Well (grid ref. 723453) but also has the Gaelic names Well of Youth and Blue Well. At one time the wall-enclosed well had a female guardian and pre-war, on the first of May, a dozen coaches would run to the site. Those who made wishes threw coins into the water (which were later recovered for local charities) and those who believed in its curative powers hung their rags on the nearest trees.

The well should not be confused with the Well of the Dead which is just across the grass from the Trust's centre. It has no powers attributed to it and lies beside the grave mounds of the clans. It is strange how some wells are left as quite natural and ordinary, while others accumulate legends and rites and superstitions.

The curative effect of some well water is well acknowledged in the growth of spas, both in England and Scotland. Strathpeffer, not far from Dingwall on the other side of the Black Isle, is one such, though its glory has now departed, and there is nothing to see except the old buildings. Nearer, and one of the most extraordinary sights is the Munlochy Clouty Well—St Boniface's Well (grid ref. 640537).

To reach it, leave Inverness over the new A9 bridge onto the Black Isle (which is neither black nor an isle, but a rich, green peninsula) and at the first roundabout turn right (A832) for Munlochy and Fortrose. The well is on the right about 2 ½ miles on— and can hardly be missed. The locals would be more than happy if it could be lost. It is regarded as an eyesore, but superstition has it that anyone removing any offering will have bad luck or incur the ailment of the donor. The well remains—and the rag collection is spreading rapidly. At least recent additions are colourful. The great age of this site is emphasised by the solid thickness of grey-green rags that completely cover the fence behind the spout of water. I did a quick estimate and reckon there are something like 50,000 bits of rag quite apart from those which have quite crumbled away.

The way wells have acquired saint's names is an indication of their age. They were probably venerated long before Christianity arrived and, as with many pagan customs and beliefs, were simply incorporated by the church. One classic example is St Maelrubha's Well on one of the islands in Loch Maree. This well was once powerful in the cure of insanity, but the ceremony involved was drastic. As the boat with the sufferer rowed (sunwise of course) round Isle Maree, he was thrice thrown into the loch, then landed and drank of the well, a process which could be repeated indefinitely, till a cure (or despair) resulted.

In the case of Isle Maree, coins rather than rags were left and these were hammered, edge-on, into a tree. In time the whole tree trunk took on a scaly, reptilian look. The well eventually dried out, its power gone, when a shepherd tried to cure his mad dog at it.

Birds of the Mountain

If you were to ask people to name one Scottish mountain bird the majority would answer golden eagle. It is the image-creature of the wild Highlands. I would hazard that few enough visitors north of the Highland line have actually seen an eagle.

Too often it is just a big, gawked-at specimen in safari park or zoo—and it sets more than just heaven in a rage to see the most free of creation in a cage. It is pre-eminently the bird of the mountains, of the wild and lonely places where not many humans dare.

All too often its presence is simply noted as a speck in the sky. Sometimes the speck will grow or become two and these will thrill our earth-bound imaginations as they possess the skies in display flights. It is how I most appreciate them.

Returning from Mallaig by train on one occasion, a friend and I were sitting in that sadness of being homeward-bound after grand days of camping in the isles when we spotted a pair of eagles performing over the hillslopes. We sat entranced as the twisty railway route swung them in and out of view. Our compartment was shared by two whining females from the deep south who had nothing good to say about their holiday. Their continuous complaint had been souring our sad-pleasure until the eagles swung into view. We watched them and perforce listened to the west being castigated. 'And as far as wildlife, it's a big con. D'ye see any deer? You do not! Big con. And what about golden eagles then? I bet they don't even exist.' We exchanged glances. My friend opened his mouth to speak—and then shut it again. We watched the eagles.

Another friend and I once did a climb on a crag in the far north and in the middle of the last pitch I found myself climbing into a huge five foot deep eyrie. It was largely composed of old fence posts carried down from the summit ridge of the hill above. An eyrie in the west was discovered because we came on a naturalist's hide—so simply looked where it was aimed. We had reached the hide by a scramble up a burn and my partner lost his grip on the top slab and slithered back down the rock into the pool below. While I was declaiming about eagles he was, simultaneously, trying to plaster bloody finger tips, change clothes and swipe at midges.

I once almost jumped onto an eagle while romping down a ridge. I was actually airborne, in mid-leap, when I realised the bird was below me. It seemed like slow motion: the twist upwards of an enquiring gaze followed by a dignified launch into space. It must have taken a second but the memory is photographically sharp for ever.

For sheer verve and style the peregrine is my favourite mountain raptor. I camped in a blizzard once and it was only next morning that I discovered peregrines were nesting in a crag above the tent. I woke to that keek-ing racket which, there, shot the lovely dawn with fire. On another occasion walking through a narrow pass I watched two warning a buzzard off their territory. One swoop raised the feathers on the buzzard's flank as the tiercel shot past. The buzzard, a picture of hurt dignity, was only too glad to take himself off. Buzzards are often gregarious, perch on telegraph poles, mew like gulls and do all sorts of things to spoil the beginner's desired first sighting of an eagle. Once, and only once, have I seen a gyr falcon in the far north. I live in the hills and take what comes. The 'twitching' mania has no place in the wilds.

I saw the gyr falcon at the time when the snowy owls were breeding on the Shetland moors. Does it count as a mountain bird? Where does a mountain begin? If you take an arbitrary figure like a thousand feet then some tens of thousands of Boreray gannets are mountain birds. A place like Rhum is mountainous even at sea level but it is at over 2000 feet the Manx shearwaters burrow. Birds, thank goodness, break all the rules and thereby entertain us the better. By mountain bird I'll simply keep to what is commonly seen in the wild country that takes over where field cultivation fizzles out: a world too harsh for men—but not for the fiery mite of wren.

Probably the commonest hill bird is the ill-named 'meadow' pipit. Its pipiting is simply the background noise of summer. Like unto it, until soaring upwards in song, is the skylark, the bird of the poets which no amount of cliches can overstate. No other British bird song so delights the moorland hiker. Poets, not politicians, usually have the right of it, though both are apt to shut eyes to what they do not want to see.

St Kilda is romantic enough and when I took a group onto the puffin island of Dun there was a shock delivered by a great skua. The bonxie grabbed a puffin and, in full view of the audience, proceeded to duck it under the water until it drowned, then plucked and ate it. In only a few minutes the bonxie was off, a drift of puffin feathers alone left to tell the tale.

Is the bonxie a hill bird? It nests high enough on St Kilda or in the northern isles. They can make walking over the moors exciting as they crash dive at the heads of intruders. My dog has long learnt to be kind to all living creatures. I have a picture of him and a baby skua, nose to beak, quite friendly but adult skuas who rip at him out of the air just cannot be tolerated. He goes daft over them. Like squirrels—they cheat.

The ubiquitous pipit has its problems too. Twice I have had one snatched a few feet in front of my face by sparrow hawks which have been beating round their woods. Once was in the Cairngorms, once was in the Fannichs. In neither case did I see or hear the predator. One moment a pipit was flitting before me, the next it was grabbed and gone. Merlins we used to see working up the alder burn of 'Camusfearna', Gavin Maxwell's home made famous in *Ring of Bright Water*. Seeing my first hen harrier was a joy: instant recognition from long expectation. Remote bothies make good hides. Last summer in the gloaming at one I was sitting in a 'dwam', gazing out of the window, when the pale shape came banking over the rushes to pass about ten feet away.

Sitting outside a Galloway bothy, on a midge-free, yellow spring evening, with dram, coffee and book suddenly there was a bang above my head and a wren fell on my lap. The window must have appeared a tunnel and it had flown straight into it. After a few minutes cupped in my hands it came to and flew off. I was much relieved. How do you go about giving the kiss of life to a wren?

I have a special affection for these effervescent midgets: such quantities of sound from such a small creature, such cockney wit from such rural good manners. They could charm the witches of their brooms!

They often seem to be ubiquitous too, adaptable and happy to co-exist with man—when the latter allows. (The superstitious persecution of wrens has not entirely died out.) In 1904 the sub-species of wren on St Kilda had a special act of parliament passed in order to protect it from visiting collectors or souvenir hunters. Now, with snipe and oystercatchers, it is one of the common background sounds in Village Bay on Hirta. This mouse-like wall-scurrying miniature has the resounding Latin tag *Troglodytes troglodytes hirtensis*.

If St Kilda has its sub-species of wren, Scotland as a whole has a heather moorland sub-species in the red grouse, which for many years was given full, proud, separate status. It has been reduced to the ranks. It has also been sadly reduced in numbers, the reason still a puzzle despite a great deal of research. It is very much the bird of the heathery acres and how many miles of *Caluna vulgaris* one has to tramp before chancing on its nest.

A dog helps with this. The grouse is one of the many birds which performs a distraction display to lure danger from its brood. It flaps about as if it has broken a wing, a display convincing enough even for a marauding fox never mind my innocent Sheltie. A grouse rocketing off from underfoot is a common enought experience for walkers. 'That . . . bird just about gave me heart failure' is the likely comment when this happens.

More alarming yet is the eruption and escape of a capercaillie, for it is the size of a turkey, and crashes off through the pines with all the grace of a jet-propelled bulldozer. We came to know these big brutes well through many visits to the Black Wood of Rannoch. They gather in a communal display area where the noise is indescribable: rattles and pops, glugging and scarting. The cock can be quite aggressive and for several years one notorious bird in the Black Wood used to chase alarmed visitors from the local picnic site.

The navy maintained a hut base near where we used to stay with school parties and one day while the kids were playing by the lochside there was a great shattering of glass. We dashed up to see who was responsible and were on 'the scene of the crime' within seconds. There was no one to be seen. We found windows had been smashed on both sides of the building. Closer inspection showed one had smashed in (the glass was scattered all over the floor inside) and one had smashed outwards (the glass lay on the ground) so something had gone right through the building. No missile could be found and suddenly we knew the culprit—a caper had simply flown through the building. The outcome of its hitting the windows was rather different from the bothy wren. I sent the boys along to explain what had happened to the local bobby; otherwise I knew who would be likely to come under suspicion!

At Rothiemurchus I once heard an amusing tale. A party of ornithologists was staying at a hotel and while most were always rushing off to watch crossbills, crested tits or ospreys, one lad always remained behind. On the last day he passed on the news, in strict confidence, to the proprietrix, that there was a capercaillie nesting among the rhododendron bushes. She promptly went through to the kitchen to let the staff know that yet another bird watcher had been watching their broody turkey all week.

The blackcock is a close relative of the caper and has a communal display 'lek' which is not difficult to see—if you happen to be up at four o'clock in the morning. For years I had heard about this extraordinary performance without coming on it. A heatwave walk across Scotland had me rising at that unearthly hour and on several successive days finding I was actually camped in the middle of a lek. The sound carries for many miles: a weird, warbling, bubble-and-squeak effect. The males bow and parade, showing off white pants and black lyre-shaped tail feathers. The duller grey hens sit by and watch the commotion, the scuffles and fights of their punk woo-ers.

The most mountainy bird of all is also one of this family: the ptarmigan (from the Gaelic *tarmachan*). It just does not come down from the upper barren limits of the mountains, surviving through the seasons. It turns white in winter (as does the mountain hare) and has a fluff of feathers round its feet to act as snowshoes. This adaption can break down in some circumstances and you see white ptarmigan (or white hares) perching in full view against a snowless background, happily convinced their camouflage makes them invisible.

It can be equally well disguised in summer when mother crouches, granite-grey on the Cairngorm summits. You can walk past only a couple of yards off and the bird sits unnoticed. Sometimes its presence is only betrayed through the blinking of an eye.

The dotterel sits even more firmly on its eggs. It is suggested the name derives from the bird being so dottily innocent. You can lift one from its nest and it still does not desert. (The Gaelic translates as 'peat-bog fool'). Dotterel once bred in the low eastern parts of England but now survive only on remote mountains.

Ptarmigan and dotterel are both birds of the highest landscape. There are few others, but, loveliest of all, is the snow bunting, which is also called the snowflake. When a shiver-voiced party blows over the summits the latter name is perfect. This is one of our rarest British nesting birds and its nest is not easy to find. Man took something like twenty years of searching for the first-ever nest to be discovered (still in the British Museum to prove it) and it has never resided in large numbers. In winter many Scandinavian migrants fly in and they have become as nimble as sparrows as they hop about the ski-resort car parks after crumbs of bread. Birds even nest near the summit of Ben Nevis where the snow may scarcely vanish in a summer and were the hill four hundred feet higher there would be a glacier. Brave bird.

If the snowflake has the sweetest song of the high places the saddest I think belongs to the golden plover. The plaintive call is full of northland space. It's a Sibelius bird. Its weeping on the heights however does mean spring has come. In the straths the equivalent bird is the curlew, or, northwarding, the divers. A curlew calling across an ochrous glen can tingle the hairs on your neck while a diver, beating like concorde, across a sky, can call out such longings for the empty places. These are the birds for dreamers.

Many of the wader family invade the hills to a surprising extent, whether dunlin above Glen Affric, oyster catchers at the head of the Tilt or greenshanks in Sutherland. The drumming and chipping of snipe (*heather-bleater*) is a common enough Grampian sound. Drumming, or bleating, is the whirring sound as the bird slices down the sky in its display flight and is caused by wind rushing over two feathers which protrude outwards from the base of the tail. It is not easy to see, for there is a ventriloquist effect, but the knack is soon mastered. (Have you noticed how we always tend to look too high when trying to find the singing lark?) It is a sound for the dusky hours, as the rip of peewit wings is the sound for dewy mornings.

The woodcock is marginally a hill bird but where deciduous trees reach up past the thousand feet its evening beating-the-bounds with its limping squeak-grunt, squawk-grunt will still be heard. I have my favourites among the waders. The trim pied piper is one. Oystercatcher seems a daft name for a bird nesting as far from the sea as can be. On my last two visits to Blair Castle I have even seen them nesting in the visitors' car park; one sitting tight mere inches from passing wheels, its mate strutting and calling like an offended waiter.

The pre-eminent herald of spring is not the monotonous, crass, cuckoo but the hyperactive, excitable summer sandpiper—nothing 'common' about it at all. As it flickers up the rivers into the hills the days of summer sun and flowers cannot be far behind. It cries *willie-needy, willie-needy* and in Orkney has the charming name of watery 'pleeps', though this is used of the next bird as well.

The redshank I have come to enjoy in other countries so any sighting—or hearing—is a delight. 'Ebb-cock' is a Shetland name I like.

> I was mid-city, mid-winter
> Miles from the sea
> When suddenly the mist overhead
> Cried *pwee-wee-wee*
> *Pwee-wee-wee*
> It was an echo
> Of that ghost bird
> Lives in me.

Hearing is surprisingly important in noticing birds: so many things may confuse the mere watcher, whereas the listener is not distracted. One of our school gangs once ran into Tom Weir at Loch Mullardoch and his cheery chat with the lads was frequently interrupted by comments such as: 'Hear that? Hunting cry of a kestrel.' When walking up to Derry Lodge with another gang we met Syd Scroggie who is blind but in the ten minutes we stood chatting together he pointed out more birds than the boys had seen any day before. Voices are a surer register than sight.

Oddly enough some hints can be gained from our maps, especially if the Gaelic is understood. Loch an Nid is *loch of the nest* and once did have an eyrie above it. Loch nan Eun is *loch of the bird* which, if it's the one west of the Devil's Elbow, has gulls nesting on its islets. North of there, under Beinn Bhrotain, is Lochan nan Stuirteag the *loch of the black-headed gulls,* but either the person giving the name was no ornithologist or nature has changed—now it is the nesting site for common gulls. The word Iolaire (*eagle*) is probably commoner now on the map than in reality. Many go up to the Lairig Ghru by the Chalamain Gap—*the pigeon's pass*. Carn a' Chlamain above Glen Tilt was Queen Victoria's first Munro—*the cairn of the kite*. We even borrow from Norse with the 'erne' (*sea eagle*) now being reintroduced on Rhum or the tidy 'tystie', *the black guillemot.*

There are some delightful Gaelic descriptive names for birds. The grouse is a *heather cock*, the snipe *goat of the air*. The chacking wheatear is *smith of the stones.* The name in

English is an inane Victorian side-stepping of its old, apt Anglo-Saxon name *white arse*. Years ago one of our kids explained this in a BBC programme we were doing about birds and it was cut from the recording! The wheatear is another of those cheery visitors which flees the country for winter. Most springs I see them in Morocco and I often wonder, a few weeks later, if I am seeing the same birds as they leap and chip and flash their geometrical white rumps in some high glen in Scotland.

The stonechat is another smart fellow whose voice is unmistakable: a rasping chack from the heathery slopes while its cousin the whinchat has to wear tweedier tones and skulks in the bushes that name it. Many of the former stay over winter, the latter have more sense and migrate. The French like eating them both.

If the cuckoo is not the favourite harbinger of spring it still is very much a bird of the Highlands. I have seen one at a summit cairn at over 3000 feet and nearly a hundred years ago one was found dead outside the Ben Nevis' Observatory.

A cuckoo which lays in a blackbird's nest will lay blue eggs to match. A cuckoo which lays eggs in a pipit's nest will lay mottled buff eggs to match. The parent flies away after laying, yet the next generation will dutifully pillage blackbird or pipit in their turn. We can only marvel at, and not explain, so many things to do with birds.

One gain in the Highlands with its sparse cover is the ease with which one may *see* cuckoos as well as hear them. As they tend to start calling at first light and go on all day they soon become a tedious presence. Sharing a wooded camp site with a cuckoo is nerve-wearing. I've seen the kids reduced to throwing stones at the blighters and yell 'Go away you . . .!' Even the twittery pipits will gang up on the bullies and chase them 'hell-for-feather' off their patch of hillside.

Last June I saw several pipits so chase a cuckoo while I was motoring down Glen Roy. I nearly left the road watching them. They zoomed across the Parallel Roads car park, and so deep in newspapers or thermos flasks were people that no one noticed. As the season wears on the cuckoos' voices turn 'rusty', managing only a strained 'Cuck, cuck' with no 'ooh'. Then they are silent and another summer reaches its peak.

The fieldfare is both a seasonal and a temporary mountain bird but in late autumn when the colours have faded from the hills and the landscape is at best tinted like a musselshell, they come sweeping in with the breeziness of blowing snow, bustling and busy, then, an hour later, they have moved on, the world the emptier for their passing. I have seen them crossing over the Cairngorms which have 4000-feet summits. A mountain bird, certainly.

But we have to draw the line somewhere. Do we count the crested tits working the trees that signpost up to the Lairig Ghru? And all the other birds peculiar to the forests of the Cairngorms? Much of Speyside is over the thousand feet which some use as the measure of a mountain.

If the fieldfare is a passing thrush of the mountains the badly-named ring ouzel is very much a real mountain thrush. I prefer the name mountain blackbird, which is what it is. It may not have such a trained and theatrical voice as the garden blackie but the plainer notes ring out on a sparser, harsher stage. They are shy and nest in high scree slopes so are the more rewarding to encounter: in smart black with white crescent bibs. They fly off, wildly complaining, like any blackbird and when they land, they bang down and twitch their tails up for balance, as does any blackbird.

The 'other black bird with a white bib' is equally mountainy but ranges up and down from small streams to mighty rivers like Dee or Tweed. The dipper is loved by all. To the commoner abilities of floating or diving under water, or swimming above or below it, the bobbing dipper can walk on the bottom. The bird shaped so the water's flow pushes it downwards but the dipper is also super-buoyant. Few creatures show themselves so at one with their peculiar surroundings. They are a watery wren— and share many a stream with that other dumpy, tail-cocking character.

All black is one other of the really high-living mountain birds, the raven, which, as the biggest of our crow family, is the one least maligned by man. Their acrobatic displays high above cliffs and corries can match anything of the eagle. And they seem to enjoy it!

Most birds are flying simply to survive. The raven will fly for fun. Watching a family of young ravens following father as he puts them through their paces can be a breath-taking experience and often amusing. I once saw one fail in some manoeuvre, stall and tumble with loud cries (fear and/or cursing) only to be made to try again. Maybe anthropomorphic—and so what?

When ravens soar into display flights you see a verve and style nothing can equal. They will even roll over to clasp talons, tumbling down the sky in loving embrace, only to split and soar again in effortless ease. An aircraft trying anything half as stressful would simply disintegrate. If the eagle has to be the king of mountain birds let him be so for the red suits. The black suits belong to the raven. His double *kwack-kwack* echoing through the clouds is all of mountain pride and mountain peaks.

Were I never to climb a hill again in my life, regret would be overlaid and lost under magic memories. When I consciously think of it I realise just how much the pleasant memories are concerned, not with our vain-glorious doings, but with this wholly gratuitous, unmerited, bitter-sweet world of birds. They help boost us with wonder and humility and set us, singing, up life's mountainy path.

Fieldfares: November's Vikings

They come in over the hills,
 rags torn from the grey gown
 of patchwork clouds;
 they stutter through the leaves
 of the gorge like hailstones
 that melt in an hour.
 They are such an obvious invasion—
 November's Vikings,
 battling south into the country of
 strangers.
 A month later they have vanished,
 absorbed, like other arrivals,
 into the stolid security of the safe south.
 Now and then we see one, solitary
 in a field edge, a shadow in the
 shade . . .
 It's like a child noticing
 the white hair of a schoolmate
 and saying 'Mummy, there's one girl
 at school has such pale hair and blue
 eyes.'
 'Yes dear, she probably had an ancestor
 who was a Viking.' It shows thus,
 occasionally. So, too,
 with these many-tinted wanderers;
 only, later, they vanish completely,
 not absorbed at all.
 They have gone home.

The Open Door

THE JUBILEE OF THE SCOTTISH YOUTH HOSTELS ASSOCIATION, 1981

Recently I was saying to someone how glad I was to be my age, for I can just remember the Highlands before the tourists came. Then the Sabbath really kept its calm, the roads were yet to be tarred, the Forestry and Hydro had not re-written the landscape. And youth hostels were a shilling a night, for a lad revelling in the discovery of a rich heritage. It is a bit of a shock now to realise the Scottish Youth Hostels Association is celebrating its fiftieth birthday.

As a lad I accepted its presence as if it had always been there; ageless and as much part of the hills as the heather. It was, in truth, only a big brother in years to me. This was not just youthful lack of insight. The SYHA was remarkably established in just a few years, and the popular movement, despite the trauma of war, was in no way diminished. It was a child of its time and has grown up. Social history was being made then, whether we careless users knew it or not.

The objective of the Association was clearly proclaimed: 'To help all, but especially young people of limited means living and working in industrial and other areas to know, use, and appreciate the Scottish countryside and places of historic and cultural interest in Scotland, and to promote their health, recreation, and education, particularly by providing simple hostel accommodation for them on their travels.'

My first subscription was a shilling for the year, and a later twenty-first birthday present of a life membership at £5 must be one of the best investments I've made.

In the autumn of 1930 George Lansbury made a speech in which he said he hoped to see 'hostels for hikers' established throughout the country. The report of this in the press led to letters and meetings, to contacts with the newly formed Association in England and with the Glasgow and West of Scotland Ramblers' Federation (who says long titles are a new habit?) whose offspring the Rucksack Club, had two walkers' huts at Arrochar and Kinlochard. It was decided to set up a Scottish Association rather than become part of a British one based on Welwyn Garden City, and in the spring of 1931 a public meeting was held in the capital. Lord Salvesen was in the chair and A Fothergill was elected the first Honorary Secretary.

Alan Fothergill had been injured in the war but disability did not inhibit his enthusiasm. The first office was set up in his house! Things moved fast with the

Edinburgh District Committee being formed two weeks later, and Glasgow soon followed. Sir John Stirling-Maxwell became the first Honorary President and as Chairman of the Forestry Commission was able to make a link there that led to several hostels being sited on Commission land. The first council met in April so in just a few weeks the pattern of administration was evolved which has lasted ever since. The SYHA is a body of enthusiasts who very much run their own affairs. Only the scale has changed.

The first youth hostel, Broadmeadows, was opened on 2 May—and is still in use. By August there was a chain of five in the Borders. Sir John donated, and enlarged, his boathouse on Loch Ossian; Inverbeg was custom-built; and the Rucksack Club's huts incorporated sites, if not identical hostels, which have stood the test of time. Carn Dearg, near Gairloch, was also gifted in that first halcyon year and in 1932 topped the bed-night figures—the North West had been discovered!

By the end of the first year there were nine buildings and a membership of just over a thousand. A couple of years later there were thirty-two hostels and a membership of over 7000. A really staggering expansion when you think of the economies of the period and the little leisure time available. Clova, Glen Nevis and Glen Brittle were added to the hostel map then.

7   Craig, Scotland's remotest youth hostel.

The Second World War could have been a disaster and began badly, but the reaction was startling; it became a boom period. In 1941 the millionth bed-night was registered and, in three years, 10,000 juniors joined. New hostels were opened at Kirk Yetholm (no Pennine Way in those days), Alltsaigh on Loch Ness, Kingussie, Killin, and three on Arran. It is an extraordinary story. Our whole family 'joined up' then and mother, father and three boys would cycle off for holidays in the west and north; or the lads would go off on separate ways. My first bed-nights are remembered almost like a litany: Creag Dhu, Creag Dhu, Killin, Killin, Strathtummel, Kirkmichael . . . We revelled in it all.

We youngsters practically lived off Army war-time emergency food packs and with ration coupons still operating we had to send parcels ahead. Meat, vegetables, eggs and milk were always available locally. Going off with a jug for milk was always one of the rituals. Few roads in the country beyond the Great Glen had surfaces, so it was vital to carry spare tyres and spokes. At Kylesku the road workers were allowed time off, officially, when the midges became unbearable. What memories we stored away then—nostalgia tinged with a certain sadness when we recall old friends no longer with us: Feughside (I had a girl-friend in Aberdeen), Opinan, Inveralligin, Barns, Loch Eck, Auchmithie, Phesdo . . . But we saw birth too, tramping through the Ochils from home in Dollar to help raise 'our' hostel in Glendevon; or paying odd tanners towards the youth hostel bridge over the Nevis. I had to paddle that river to climb my first Munro. Years later, as the first teacher to be appointed in a State school to take youngsters into the wilds, we sometimes ran up a hundred bed-nights in a year. Once at Glen Nevis I went in to rouse my girls from bed—which I did with much yelling and pulling from bed. When the third girl bounded on the floor I suddenly realised I had gone into the wrong dormitory . . .

My widening interests owe much to the SYHA. A Hamish MacInnes Winter Climbing Course at Glen Coe added new dimensions to the hill game. Since then the association has branched out to add pony trekking, sailing, canoeing and ski holidays to its programme—usually based on one of the larger hostels, which are often splendid old shooting lodges like Loch Morlich or Rowardennan on Loch Lomond. Instruction is provided and the accommodation is luxurious.

Possibly because of the changed world many value even more the quieter, remote, less posh hostels; like Loch Ossian or Glen Affric or Craig, which still can only be reached on foot. The boom in bothy-ing points to their need. Adventure's call to young people (of all ages) is still not to be denied. A Jubilee appeal is aimed especially at their preservation.

I remember a gang of us arriving at Loch Ossian over the hills and discovering the warden was Hari Dang, an Indian climber, who was recovering from frostbite on Everest. He was a writer of poetic prose and a grand teller of tales. Some places often cast their spell on the wardens. Tom Rigg has kept returning to Loch Ossian, and once the season was over he simply shifts along the loch to act as ghillie.

Loch Lochy in the Great Glen was another I have used for many years while canoeing or climbing in the area or as a stage on coast-to-coast treks. The Frasers seem to have been welcoming stravaigers there as long as I can recall. If there is nostalgia for hostels gone, there is also sadness at the retiral of great warden characters. There will be folk now I suppose who do not remember kilted Dom Capaldi of Ratagan in Kintail, or Ingrid and Jim Feeney in Glen Coe, or Mrs Ewan at Braemar . . .

There is something catching about figures, anniversaries, and celebrations. I think we use them to try, briefly, to stop thieving time. It has been a very quick first fifty years of the SYHA.

There can be few organisations so completely dedicated to such useful work and creating such marvellous pleasures. Whether it is in the great mansion of Carbisdale Castle or the tiny Coigach cottage of Achininver, the Norwegian timber-built climbers' centre of Glenbrittle or the modern concrete cubes of Kirkwall, the game goes merrily on. As every youthful spirit is a member (44,000 at present) perhaps I'll meet you in one of them one day.

Silent Stones

It was interesting to have tea with friends near Brora in Sutherland and hear them complaining about the distance it is to Glasgow. It is usually the other way round.

Which is why, having reached those places, I was loath to come home. I lingered on to photograph, or simply visit, some of the prehistoric sites. Caithness and Sutherland are covered with old brochs, hut circles, burial cairns, burnt mounds, clearance cairns, standing stones, alignments, and so on. How completely those people, our ancestors, baffle us with the silence of their monuments.

Loch Hakel lies under Ben Loyal, and in a corner of the loch is an islet-held *dun* (fort)

8 Ben Loyal seen across Loch Hakel.

which is neighboured by a hunk of rock covered in cup and ring marks—just one of the unexplained remainders. Ben Loyal itself is a monumental mountain, the frenzied chiselling of the eerie north.

By Loch Hakel, not long before Culloden, Prince Charlie lost the bullion he so desperately needed. Some of it was thrown into the loch and 'once in a blue moon a coin turns up on the sandy spit'. Having seen a blue moon I hopefully paddled along but had no luck with dubloons.

Brochs are peculiar to Scotland, and their largest concentration is in the Northeast. Sadly few are more than walled circlets among the grass. One is spoilt with Glenelg, Mousa, and Carloway. Many in Caithness or Sutherland have cliff or promontory settings which makes them spectacular as well as sepeculative. The one I liked best this time was Dun Kilphedir, above the Strath of Kildonan.

There is enough left to see the entrance passage and a chamber/stair in the back wall, but its real fascination is the vast earthworks of dykes and ditches that encircle it as it perches high on a heather slope above the glen.

Across a stream from the broch are a cluster of hut circles. There were probably more people in the Strath of Kildonan then than there are now. The Sutherland Clearances made sure of that.

The two sites which most fascinated lie inland a bit from the A9 but they are signposted and well worth the detours. The Hill o' Mony Stanes is a grid of 250 small stones set on a gentle slope. There is speculation enough as to their reason, with astronomical observations advocated by some. I found it a decidedly atmospheric place.

Up a long straight road (a Caithness speciality), lie the Grey Cairns of Camster, a round cairn and a long cairn, the most complete and impressive burial 'buildings' in the country. Thousands and thousands of tons of stones have been brought and piled up in these monuments to the dead. They have been carefully restored and you can crawl through the tunnels to stand in the central chamber (lit by skylights; twentieth century), and let your imaginations yeast back to those years.

Culture and imaginative craftsmanship are as old as the human race. I wonder, if someone returned from the grave on Camster hill, would we, today, be humble enough to make contact?

Pictish symbol stones I just cannot resist. Their meaning may be lost but the artistic flair is clear. The meaning of Z-rods, crescents, 'tuning forks' beat our best guesswork, but the simple line-drawings of eagles, fish, dear, or boar, simply astonish. But what of the creature with the long snout? Is this an imaginary beast? If not, what on earth is it?

These were some of the thoughts that ran through my head as I stood in the museum at Dunrobin Castle. The season for visitors was over but they had very kindly arranged a private viewing of the dozen symbol stones brought together there.

What a monument to vanity Dunrobin is. In the days of the Dunrobin Dukes of Sutherland there can have been few people in the north who were not affected by their presence. In Golspie I was told 'they meant well' (the rudest of all praise, I often think), and Dunrobin is certainly a must for the tourist gawker, or the person interested in social history. It must have been fun to have been a Duke or Duchess of Sutherland last century.

9   Silent stones—a pictish symbol stone at Abernethy.

The weather coming south turned mild so I turned off up the Kyle of Sutherland to have a night at Carbisdale Castle Youth Hostel. Perhaps it was an unconscious move after Dunrobin, for it is a similar sort of extravagant, misplaced chateau. You walk in to a huge gallery of marble statues, the walls covered with what appear to be millions of pounds worth of paintings by Raphael, Rubens, and the like. But it's all fake: the building has no history and the paintings are copies.

Carbisdale stands south of the River Oykel and therefore just outside Sutherland—and for reason.

The details escape me, but there was some family disagreement and the offended widow, to spite the family, built this rival to the Dunrobin family seat. It lies just outside the county which, in those day, was virtually the family estate. The spite went to the extent of placing clockfaces on just three faces of the tower. The fourth, facing Sutherland, is blank. Now Carbisdale is a youth hostel, and no doubt overdue for being used for some TV serial!

The setting is superb, for it stands high above the river. I set off to the west, but with gale force 11 raging from Rockall to Shannon, I decided the Torridon hills were best left for another day. I motored down to Gairloch and on to Red Point, packed my rucksack, and set off along the five miles of coast to Craig Youth Hostel. I believe in contrasts.

It was a good-going storm, off the sea, and at times I was knocked over by the gale. As my boots were beyond repair I went in bare feet. That got some odd looks from some local kids out playing on their super bikes. Yet, their grandfathers never went any other way. Carbisdale and Craig, Castle and cottage, crazy contrasts of our crazy world, which seems hell-bent on the castles at any cost.

The cottage-hostel, Craig, is much loved by those who seek peace and atmosphere, and the SYHA has invested some of its small hostels fund in renovating the hostel. It stands very much in the tradition of the older monuments. May it last a thousand years.

Peaceful Places, Caithness

They knew rain on their faces
and the whipping Caithness wind.
Something of their loving, living, clings
to the honeyed moors. Their stones
mystify our cleverness for we
(who reach, proudly, to the stars)
cannot read the blessing of *Grey Cairns*
or *The Hill o Mony Stanes*.
Stemster Loch laps, laps (or laughs, laughs)
against the silly centuries.

The skies are the same
whether gruel-grey or golden.
Now we come, the clever-blind,
who swopped wind and stars and stone
for micro chips. We call it progress
but we pause as strangers
in these peace-grown places.

Munro of the Munros

Ten years ago, even five years ago, if one mentioned climbing Munros, one would have had to explain that these were Scotland's 3000-foot mountains.

Now half of Scotland seems to be ticking them off and we even have articles and guide books misappropriating the term, so that we read of Irish 'munros' and such like. Who was Munro then, that a whole pastime has been named after him?

Mountaineering was developed by the Victorian leisured classes. In mid-century the Alpine Club was founded and in 1889 the Scottish Mountaineering Club followed, the membership of the two having a considerable overlap. The wilds of Scotland were as little known as the alps and when the 1891 SMC *Journal* produced Sir Hugh Munro's 'Tables of Heights over 3000 feet' it came as a shock to many.

Ben Nevis had only recently displaced Ben Macdhui as Scotland's highest summit and far from there being only about 30 peaks over the 3000-feet plimsol line, Munro's 'Tables' listed nearly 300. There were no trains and few roads then so the SMC had a marvellous feel of original exploration in its early years.

In 1901 the Rev A E Robertson completed the ascent of all the 'Munros' as they had already come to be called. Munro himself never completed them and before the Second World War only eight people had done what is still a considerable feat. Since that war the numbers going to the wilds have increased by leaps and bounds. What would Munro think of it all?

Hugh Munro was born in London in 1856 and spent his time either there or on the family estate near Kirriemuir. He eventually became Sir Hugh Munro, Bart, of Lindertis. As a child he was a magpie collector of fossils, shells, eggs, butterflies, pastimes of the open air, and the braes of Angus. Even as a young man, after a spell in South Africa, he returned with a collection of Basuto curios, antelope heads, a monkey, as well as an African servant.

As a student in Stuttgart he was bitten by the mountaineering bug and though never a leading climber his vast experience under all conditions rendered him a powerful mountaineer. He was a great enthusiast with a warm personality and something of a dancer and musician. He would have been good company in a mountain hut.

He had a business training and held various public appointments at home and abroad (including the Basuto War); he stood as a parliamentary candidate for Kirkcaldy Burghs as forlorn a Tory hope then as now.

In all this he still found time for the Scottish hills. The SMC *Journal* was to carry eighty articles and notes of his over the years. Weather was not allowed to interfere with plans and we hear of him having his ice-frozen clothes chipped off his back after a 'tussle' on Beinn a' Ghlo. He would make long traverses through remote areas and enthusiastically used few-fangled aids like trains and cars. Why then was he not the first to complete the Munros?

Sheer bad luck is probably the answer. He had kept an easy one for the last (Carn Clioch Mhuillin) and apart from that only had the Inaccessible Pinnacle in the Cuillin of Skye to climb. I know quite a few people who have 'done all the Munros except the In Pin'. It was not called that for nothing, only losing its virginity in 1880 and still proving the end of many a Munroist's dream.

Munro tried often enough but he was driven out of Skye by atrocious weather in 1895; in 1897 a Meet based on a yacht could not even anchor safely; in 1905 arrangements with Harold Raeburn (the MacInnes of his day) fell through. He was last there in 1915.

Though past military age he went out to Malta to work and in 1918 he organised a canteen in the town of Tarascon in the south of France. There he caught a chill which developed into pneumonia and he died, aged sixty-three, still without the Inaccessible Pinnacle. A laird of parts you might say and if a name has to be attached to the esoteric pastime of scaling Scotland's 3000-ders, whose could be better?

The first person to manage all the Munros was the Rev A E Robertson, once minister at Rannoch, who basically romped round them in four long summer expeditions which were meticulously planned and executed. He was very much the gentleman climber but he also spoke Gaelic and was welcome to the humblest cottage in the wilds.

One sad thing on reading of these pioneering exploits in the old journals is how much more empty the glens have become since their time. Steall (Glen Nevis), Carnoch (Loch Nevis), and a dozen other keepers' homes are now ruins or under hydro scheme waters. Forestry planting was unheard of then. Roads, if any, were unsurfaced and the hills approached by trap or cart.

How successful would the hundreds who have completed the Munros since the war have been under those circumstances?

Whatever the changes since Munro's days the thrills and spills of the game have not changed. Munro, in Inverness cape, Balmoral bunnet, and knickerbockers would be quite at home with a thermal-clad bothy lad of today. We drink the same clean waters and sleep well under the same circling stars.

A Highland Lament

I am writing this sitting in a Berber village high in the Atlas Mountains of Morocco. It is one of the most breathtakingly beautiful spots I know with a wall of snowy mountains soaring up behind a rich frieze of almond and cherry blossom.

The valley is a vivid green of stepped terraces. The song of a goatherd floats down on the fresh morning air. It is that most pleasing of views: a loved and lived-in mountain landscape.

In Corsica the bergeries are being abandoned, in Switzerland high Alps are deserted, in Scotland the summer shielings are rickles of stones among the heather, yet here, in conditions of extreme toughness, by mattock alone, new fields are being won back from the wasteland. It is very impressive but it makes me so sad when I consider my own Scottish mountains—abandoned, played-with, and pillaged.

The 'quality' of the land depends on people and what they do or do not do. Generations of misuse have reduced vast areas of the Highlands to wet desert. Much of it could be restored under the application of the scarce commodities: cash, hard work, and genuine governmental commitment. Trying to do anything in Scotland is so frustratingly fraught with bureaucracy and nothing much will happen until the will from above is real and applied.

A lived-in landscape is far more beautiful than a deserted one. The Irish hills are more attractive than ours because they do rise from green fields, stitched together with furzy hedges, and dotted with farmhouses. A whiff of turf reek (peat to us) on top of Galtymore was a bitter reminder of our own empty glens.

Conservationists are frequently slated as 'being against everything' which is symptomatic of the petty bickering that keeps delaying any hope of real improvements. The Scottish landscape, even in its present sub-standard state is *sans pareil* and attracts visitors from all over the world. It is a treasure: fragile, but all too open to vandalism and theft.

One would expect the powers that be would understand this. A Constable painting say, the mere copy of landscape, is given a status beyond the reality. There would be an outcry if someone suggested painting in this and that on the Constable but apparently it is all right to daub the real special settings with (last year alone) unimaginative forestry and ski lifts and walking ways and bulldozed tracks and pylons and ugly hydro works.

There are certain areas of Scotland which are outstanding. They should be inviolate and safe from any and every risk of spoliation. This again can only come from the top, when there is genuine 'legislation with teeth' that puts the land first.

Do I seem to be advocating both development and the opposite? Of course I am. Truth never lies in extremes but extreme measures are needed to safeguard the extremes when they are exceptional. Perhaps it is a case of 'where there is no vision the people perish'.

It should be inconceivable that the approaches to Creag Mheagaidh could be ploughed and planted or a bit of Nature Reserve mechanised for skiing. Selfish materialism has blinded our vision. Lacking national identity or vision the people of Scotland basically don't care.

For a long time I have been crying out that it is a sad—but necessary—waste of time fighting case by case as inane development schemes crop up. Money power can only be stopped by legislation, by people-power. With the continuing ridiculous state of so-called democracy in Scotland I don't see much hope ahead. All along conservationists have tried 'to keep politics out of it', which is precisely why they go around in circles.

Politics is at the heart of the Highland situation. What is done on Ben More is basically at the dictate of a government based in London, *against* whom the people of Scotland have emphatically voted (a situation which arose two centuries ago when our then masters took the cash and handed Scotland over—does nothing change?) People, just ordinary people, have been powerless in the Highlands for generations.

Originally 'the boss', the chief, was just that. He owned a people, not the earth and all it contained. In the breakdown of the system (itself a London ploy) the chiefs looked to their own ends at the cost of their people. They grabbed 'rights', they produced law-given 'title deeds' (easy as they were the law-makers), they packed off their people to the ends of the earth. The great betrayal was the reward for great devotion. That was the real death of the Highlands.

Cleared of people, over-grazed by sheep and deer, burnt, allowed to revert to waste, it is a continuing saga of misuse. What so many don't realise is that this situation is here and now. It is not history (last year's politics), it is present reality (this year's politics).

If I want to build a garden shed I have to get planning permission and officials will see I comply with every jot and tittle of legislation, yet in the Highlands a landowner can bulldoze horrible scars of tracks across superb scenery without any let or hindrance. Oh yes, I know there is now legislation forbidding this above a certain height—it came in *after* the main damage was done.

Upper Deeside is typical of the wasteful system. There are dozens of fine buildings, boarded-up for 20 years and rotting away, simply to preserve the exclusiveness of an owner—not even British, never mind Scottish. This surely deserves to be a criminal offence, the destruction, by inaction, of any property or land.

It could be stopped easily enough. Let a building stand empty of people for two years and it is confiscated! Let taxation of estates be quite separate from their being part of any business concern (many are useful loss-makers to offset against profits) and let the taxation be in inverse ratio to the developments within that estate! (i.e., those estates where the population is growing, because plenty is being done, are exempted, but where population falls penalties are applied).

Let ownership be qualified by residence not absenteeism, with swingeing fines if owners are not resident for 50 per cent of the time! Of course this is all political and until political weapons are used, the fight is merely a game.

I think there is a rising groundswell of discontent at the Highland situation and if the owners do not change their ways the reaction may be the sharper when it comes. Certainly the finest scenic areas should be taken into public ownership and really declared inviolate—not in the NTS sense where commercial exploitation has made that a joke—but really *left alone*.

To leave anything alone seems almost impossible for anybody yet this, above all else, is what the areas of outstanding beauty require: utter, complete protection against all invasive and intrusive works of man.

Tom Weir's first book *Highland Days* has been republished and should be read by all who enjoy the Highlands. It tells of his enthusiastic and youthful pre-war wanderings. He shows a very different Scotland to the one we know.

Most people do not realise the continual nibbling-away effect of development.

In my lifetime the demeaning of the landscape has been a continuous process, which is why the resistance by the imaginative is so constant. The developer, after all, is only concerned with his own particular ploy. But it is only one of scores and hundreds, of which only a few hit the headlines or go to inquiries or end up on the desk of the Secretary of State for/against Scotland.

One example. It used to be possible to walk any glen from the Great Glen to the western sea by routes free of ugly man-made intrusions. In my lifetime every one of those routes has been defaced. Hydro, with ugly tidelines, did for the Loch Quoich area, regimented forestry mars beyond Loch Arkaig, and the power line to Skye was carefully routed along where it now scars 'because there was nothing there'. The newcomer today takes this lesser landscape as the normal. What will it be like a hundred years hence, when it will be all the more desperately needed?

I don't have a hundred years and neither do you. We don't have to pass on the sins of our fathers upon their children's children. I have seen success carved into barren landscapes like Iceland or the wild valleys of arctic Norway. I look, as I write, at the vibrant Berber life existing between the snows and the desert. These are successes against overwhelming odds but then they are all the work of proud, old, unconquered peoples. Maybe it is too late for subservient Scotland. We have sold our birthright for a mess of (EEC defined) porridge.

Extinction

There was a flower once near the mountain top
Till all the world came to marvel at it—
As notices bade them do, while books
All praised it. But countless feet can wear hard
Rock away; no chance then for fragile flowers.
Perhaps the flowers of stars are similar
And earth's pale blink will be extinguished yet
By rush of visitors from 'empty' space.

II   Ranging Scotland

If the preceeding section ranged through various topics this one ranges geographically. One of the riches of Scotland is its compact, concentrated contrasts. In some countries one can drive all day and the scenery hardly alters. Scotland offers a kaleidoscope of colourful contrasts.

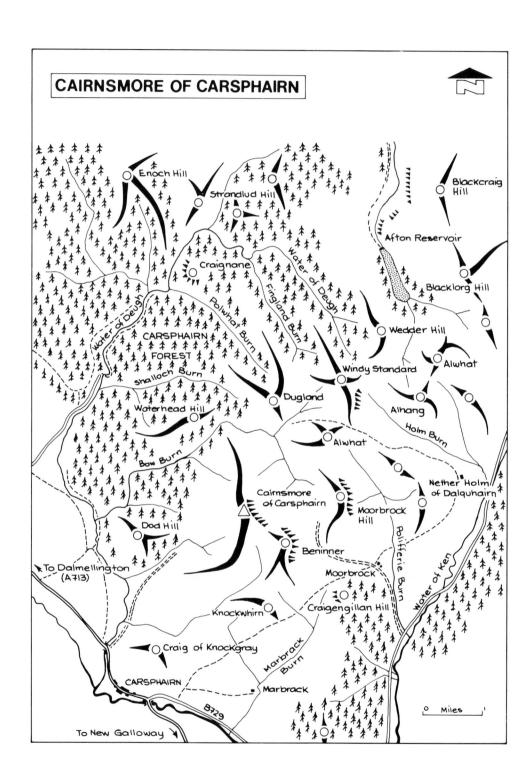

CAIRNSMORE OF CARSPHAIRN

N

Enoch Hill

Strandlud Hill

Blackcraig Hill

Craignane

Afton Reservoir

Water of Deugh

Polwhat Burn

Fingland Burn

Blacklorg Hill

Water of Deugh

CARSPHAIRN FOREST

Shalloch Burn

Wedder Hill

Windy Standard

Alwhat

Dugland

Alhang

Holm Burn

Waterhead Hill

Bow Burn

Alwhat

Cairnsmore of Carsphairn

Moorbrock Hill

Nether Holm of Dalquhairn

Dod Hill

Beninner

Poilfferie Burn

Water of Ken

To Dalmellington (A713)

Moorbrock

Knockwhirn

Craigengillan Hill

Craig of Knockgray

Marbrack Burn

CARSPHAIRN

Marbrack

B729

0   Miles   1

To New Galloway

Cairnsmore, the Highest of the Three

> There's Cairnsmore of Fleet,
> And Cairnsmore of Dee;
> But Cairnsmore of Carsphairn
> Is the highest of the three.

Not quite high enough to be a Munro (though a Corbett) so this remains a quiet spot, gentler than the wild country of the Merrick. On my first visit I thought the ochrous domes a bit like the Ochils.

Having abandoned a planned day on the Kells range I found the weather had improved so I simply parked by the Water of Ken and headed up the Craigengillan Burn to reach Cairnsmore over Beninner. That rather casual walk would need some re-routing now as vast areas up the Water of Ken are a strangle of conifers. The farm road from Craigengillan Bridge up to Moorbrock is the obvious line of access.

From Knockgray (east of the village) the path to Moorbrock and the Ken can be followed and Cairnsmore reached over or round Beninner.

What I saw on my first visit made me plan a proper visit to the hills. There was a bothy right in the hills which would be fun for a night out and, besides, Carsphairn has a cluster of 'Donalds', those Lowland 2000 feet hills of the third list in Munro's Tables, which I'd been pecking away at while motoring to and from the south. The next visit came on my return from a trip to Morocco and Corsica and I'll just quote from my account written at the time. (1978)

> . . . from friendly Dumfries I motored up to Thornhill and Penpont and then by the wee road up Scaur Water where we lunched and packed under some big trees. The bird life was varied: bullfinch, sandpiper, warbler, blackbird, kestrel, cuckoo. A shepherd with two dogs stopped for an hour's blether then I continued along the twisty upper glen. The trees finish and a grassy sweep of hills was about me when I parked at the road end.
>
> During the rest of the day only one other car came up, turned and went off without stopping so they missed hearing the curlews, thrushes, pipits, redshanks, snipe and hoasty sheep. It rained most of the time but I was able to keep the sliding door open and drink in the sounds and scents of 'my ain countrie'. A contrast to Peakirk and the Fens two days ago and even more to the Atlas or jagged Corsica. The glen is almost a mirror of our geographical history: ruined castles, holiday homes, forestry plantings, hills of sheep and the grey sadness of rain, but, oh! it is home to me.

Thursday 22 June: A good day and delighting to be on home hills once more. I was stiff by the day's end. Departure was at 8 a.m., up by Polskeoch Rig. All day I was stopping to add new features on the map.

Forestry workers drove up and set off to work on Fortypenny Hill opposite. I skirted by Ryegrain Rig to reach outliers Blacklorg Hill and Blackcraig which lie above the Afton Water, 'Sweet Afton' of Burns's song. Donalds of course. Curlews down below and skylarks up above made the day's *continuo*. There was a spacious feel to the tawny hills with little sign of cultivation, other than an invasion of forestry and fences everywhere.

Back at my rucker I had tea and while fetching water found a meteorological balloon. As I was going up Meikledodd Hill a loud bang made me jump and, looking back, I saw a pillar of smoke rise from the Kello Water glen—a good route *not* to be on! Between Alwhat and Alhang I passed the source of the Afton. The Holm Burn leading south to the Ken had an amazing array of little bumps like moraines, but are more likely to be old mining tips, and beyond the Ken, were ugly blanketing trees again.

A col led to the second block of hills, higher and rougher than where we'd been. Windy Standard had a stark trig point. The vast Carsphairn Forest rolled away beyond. The outlier Trostan Hill had such spongy grass that it was tiring to walk on, like soft snow. Dugland was the last Donald addition and then it was brutally down to Clennoch, an old shepherd's house now saved as a primitive bothy. It was only 2.30 but the rest of the day went with a book while rain on top of rain rattled on the flat roof.

Friday 23 June: An early start (6.15) to use the grey but dry morning, a wise move as the afternoon broke down again and was 'gey weet'. We wandered up the Bow Burn and some rocks on the watershed made a recognisable spot to leave the rucksack. We set off up into the saturated mist (soaked from the knees down already) and a fence did likewise but then sloped off southwards.

The ground steepened but we were almost disappointed to find the huge cliffs marked were simply small crags and scree. We scrambled straight up to the summit of Cairnsmore.

The summit was left on a bearing of 600 paces and at that precise spot there was a big cairn. My second bearing led me down and up onto Beninner. (I wasn't sure if I'd come over it on the previous occasion.)

In thicker cloud I went up the other side to find Moorbrock Hill and carefully, with map, compass, altimeter and dead-reckoning made my way over its NW Top, a col, another Alwhat and Keoch Rigg (not named) the last of the dotty Donalds. I'd worked back to be almost above Clennoch again and planned to exit by the path that crossed the hills from it down to the Holm-Ken valley. I paced off what it should have been and began to go uphill. No path. So we followed the compass down the Bawnhead ridge and never did see a path anywhere.

Nether Holm of Dalquhairn was still lived in and had sheep and cows pastured round it.

The tarmac was reduced to two strips, the grass between making a kind surface for feet, then it was just a footpath—until new forestry works cut it. Their activities up the Polvaddoch Burn were responsible for the muddy Ken. The gentlest of watersheds led us back to Polskeoch and the dormobile.

An hour of tidying up and we drove off, singing with content, back to Thornhill and on for the Dalveen Pass and Moffat where John Cairney did his 'Robert Burns' presentation. He is a good look-alike. The show nicely done, sad in a way, but not sentimental and the poetry was treated as it deserves. What a grand 'welcome home' day.

Hermitage Castle

Apart from being all a Scottish castle should be to look at, Hermitage Castle has romantic associations with that unchancy queen, Mary Queen of Scots.

James Hepburn, Fourth Earl of Bothwell and something of a political maverick, had become the queen's lover and when he was lying wounded at his castle of Hermitage following a Border fracas the queen made a dash from Jedburgh to be by his side. That 50-mile round trip over wild moorland and boggy valleys was no mean feat of horsewomanship but the day's ride brought on a fever and it was the queen who came near to dying. Her demise then would have raised one of those intriguing IFs of history. As she recovered, it was the scandal that remained, and so did Bothwell. Her infatuation and marriage to Bothwell ultimately cost her the throne.

Hermitage had been handed over to the Bothwells when James IV became aware of the double-dealings of the Earl of Angus but there was probably little to choose between the Douglases and the Hepburns for loyalty. The fifth earl, in 1594, finally lost the castle, being attained after years of misconduct and the Lordship of Liddesdale reverted to the Crown. As James VI soon flitted south the castle played little part in history thereafter and gradually fell into ruin. It was 'repaired' in 1820 by the Duke of Buccleuch and in 1930 was placed in the care of the state.

Hermitage was so well known from pictures that I made a special diversion to visit it when motoring from England, which, I suppose, is how many a raiding party or tramping army came to it. Liddesdale, like no other Border valley, lies along the old national frontier (today it is armies of ranked conifers that face each other across the Border!) so has an eventful history. I decided my approach would be in this older fashion, on foot. Just driving up in a car seemed much too prosaic.

Cauldcleuch Head was the highest hill locally so after a run up Teviotdale and a branch road east I was dropped at the highest pass, between Tudhope Hill and Georgie's Hill. The road continued down to Hermitage Water and the castle. An owl came and flew about the dog's head as we walked up a forestry track to outflank Tudhope Hill into the Billhope Burn.

Down in the glen there were *round* sheep shelters, very much a mark of the Borders (both sides), and the hill opposite was Pennygant—which is nearly the same as the well-kent Penyghent.

The hills reminded me of my boyhood Ochils: 'creased elephant skin lumps' as I once heard them called. The names were all of the Borders however. I descended by Windy Edge (which it was that autumn day) to Crip Burn and on by the Braidley Burn to join Hermitage Water below Gorrenberry Bridge. Other names caught my eye on the map: Skelfhill, Maiden Paps, Thiefsike, Crossbow Hill, Holy Den, Twislehope, Headless Knowe, Butter Hill, Crummiecleuch—names for a novelist of the Tranter ilk.

Hermitage Castle only came into view from quarter of a mile away, its stark, bald shape rising in fearsome geometry behind the undisciplined burnside trees. The western side is a completely bare sandstone rectangle, the only major feature being a huge arched doorway several stories high, only it is not a doorway but an arched support over the gap between corner towers. At one time a wooden balcony, or war-head, ran right round the castle near the top, hence all the odd-looking doors below the corbelled parapet (which was reconstructed in the nineteenth century 'restoration'). This gallery allowed things to be dropped on top of anyone approaching the walls. There is a similar flying arch on the east side. The overall effect is one of impregnability.

Though it looks so complete as it stands and indeed has only had minor changes in 600 years it had quite a hectic evolution before that. The present doorway leads into the small courtyard of the original English-styled fortification, certainly the work of the Dacre family. The remains of this (destroyed in the time of Richard II) were incorporated in a more typical keep built by the Douglases.

10   Hermitage Castle, one of the most dramatic castles in the Borders.

Their entrance was in the SW corner, on the first floor level and defended by two portcullis gates. By 1400 corner towers had been added and we have the castle we see today.

I walked across to the castle over several mounds and hollows which were probably earthworks for cannon though some may be earlier than the castle itself. There was an earlier castle (upstream) and just up from the bridge across to the site lie the remains of a thirteenth-century chapel. Some day the archaeologists may have the cash and manpower needed to dig into the mysteries.

Mystery, legend, folklore, and historical fact exist in plenty at Hermitage. Built by de Soulis before the War of Independence it had a chequered history through those bloody days. A ballad about the last Lord Soulis has him as a seducer and extortioner in league with the devil and finally meeting his fate on Nine Stane Rigg (a mile east of the castle) by being wrapped in lead and boiled to death in a cauldron.

Sir William Douglas, Bruce's champion, the 'Fair Knight of Liddesdale', did not hesitate to starve a rival to death in the castle dungeons. After the collapse of the Black Douglas family the Red Douglases possessed it till they too overreached themselves, when it went to the Bothwells. The Scotts of Buccleuch followed them. Quite a parcel of rogues in the nation when you think of it.

I was quite sorry when I was picked up again and headed home up Liddesdale. Pleasingly there seems to be a growing awareness of our historical buildings like Hermitage Castle. Many are in the caring hands of the National Trust for Scotland or the Historic Buildings and Monuments Department. The latter in the last few years has taken on a greater involvement with the public and has produced a good range of publications. You can now become a 'Friend of the Scottish Monuments', which is greatly to be recommended, not only for entry to *everything* in state care in the UK but for various additional benefits. When I visit the likes of Hermitage now I have a greater feeling of association with its past. I'm involved. History, after all, is our story.

Information on Friends of the Scottish Monuments can be obtained from the SDD, PO Box 157, Edinburgh EH3 7QD.

An Eastern Iona

Edinburgh (as one example) is 'the Athens of the North'. It is strange how we make these geographic comparisons. One of the oldest described is 'the Iona of the East' a place which may have been one of Columba's bases while on missions among the Picts and which certainly had a religious settlement when a king's life was succoured. The thanksgiving foundation was given St Columba's name instead of its original Aemonia.

Recognise it? It uses the Gaelic *Colm* rather than the anglicised Columba. Yes, Inchcolm. If there are almost as many Inches in the Forth as there are in Loch Lomond then Inchcolm is certainly the most beautiful of them.

The sun was shining as I drove down into South Queensferry. The narrow main street and the old houses always make a visit a step back in time. It would be difficult to drive fast through South Queensferry. I parked opposite the historic Hawes Inn with its Stevenson connections and almost under the Forth Bridge spidering over to Fife, a view of this marvel that gives it an unusual slim gracefulness.

One forgets the bridge is so long and though its main supports could take a train inside their tubes the proportions are so right that the scale is lost—until a train chatters across.

It is a big bridge and, with its centenary now past, a historic one. A few minutes later I was splashing under the bridge on *Maid of the Forth,* a friendly cruising launch which operates regular sailings throughout the summer.

It was a sparkling day, with a strong enough breeze to set white horses galloping down the river and bring out scores of yachts which made their colourful, butterfly progress in all directions. On the pontoon of the first navigation light a seal had hauled out to bask in the sun. I collected a coffee from the wee bar and perched at the back where I could watch the two bridges and the Ochils beyond.

A commentary pointed out the features to be seen on the half-hour cruise. When we landed at Inchcolm the crew helped ashore anyone who was elderly. In this day of cursory service, full marks to the *Maid's* crew who were welcoming and friendly.

After the brief appearance of the witches, Shakespeare's play *Macbeth* begins with emissaries staggering in with news of Macbeth and Banquo fighting successive—and successful—battles in defence of King Duncan's realm. At the Battle of Kinghorn he defeated the Danes and they petitioned the victor for a truce to bury their dead on Inchcolm. Shakespeare puts it:

11   Inchcolm, in the Firth of Forth

Sweno, the Norway's King, craves composition;
Nor would we deign him burial of his men
Till he disbursed at Saint Colme's Inch
Ten thousand dollars to our general use.

It cost you to land on the island even then. 'It takes a lang spoon tae sup wi a Fifer.' On a knoll above the monastery there is a Scandinavian-type hogbacked tombstone and any digging in that area turns up skeletons. That start is about as far as historic truth goes with Shakespeare.

It is interesting that burial in a holy place was important, even in the middle of a war, and this really did make Inchcolm the 'Iona of the East'.

Other large-scale burials have been found on the island but these are probably dating from the periods when Inchcolm was used as a quarantine station. There are some grisly stories of disease-ridden ships left there so long that the ships rotted and everyone died. Last century, restoration in the abbot's house uncovered a skeleton, not in a cupboard, but hidden, vertically in the thickness of the wall.

Such grim history was hardly in the minds of the visitors. It was a sunny Saturday afternoon and there had not been too many of those last summer. The island has a narrow waist between two curving sandy bays, with the main pier on the north-easterly bay, facing Fife. Technically the island is part of the parish of Aberdour and there is a ferry from there too.

The monastery tucks in under the higher western part and the landscape of manicured grass, trees, and bright flowers gives it a feeling of being in an Edinburgh park. I say Edinburgh because the lettuce-crisp day and snell breeze were of the east rather than the west. Besides, all the landmarks of that city stood out with a clarity that in the west would have presaged rain.

As everyone streamed off to the monastery I went the other way. From up the hill there was a sweeping all-round view out of all proportion to the 100 foot ascent. The monastery is surprisingly big and well preserved. It is in fact one of the most complete early buildings in Scotland to have survived and is very impressive. The only visual disappointment is the array of twentieth century fortifications that litter the island.

When the roof of the tower had cleared of figures I wended down the slopes of silvery buckthorn and across the neck of land to the monastery. The tower has a very narrow stair in its wall: a fat person would simply not manage up and there is no way you could pass anyone—hence my waiting till the press of visitors had eased.

The stair only makes one or two circuits to the next floor and then steep companionways lead on. (Originally the tower had several floors, linked by ladders.) The top half of the tower was honeycombed with alcoves for nesting pigeons: a unique doocot! The low parapet made it an exposed viewpoint and a good spot to study the layout of the buildings below. The architectural style could best be described as 'sturdy'.

The church is the least showy part for it was much extended in the fifteenth century and while the extension has all but vanished the original twelfth century church was turned into living quarters and vaulting filled its interior to create an upper floor. The extension was the work of a bishop of Dunkeld (who footed the bill) and he requested his heart be buried there while his body was interred at Dunkeld.

A recess in the north wall was discovered as the spot where his heart was said to have been immured. While investigations were being made another recess was discovered and this, the tomb of some VIP, had a mural of seven figures in procession, some swinging censers. It is the only thirteenth-century painting of its kind in the country.

The figures, alas, are decapitated, but the flowing, colourful lines of the garments are as sparkling as a Pre-Raphaelite work.

The Chapter House is the dominant building of the monastery and it has been built with an upper room called 'the warming house' which is reached from the *dorter* (dormitory) by a low doorway and an awkward stair. (Any monk over five foot was likely to be tonsured by the lintel!) The warming house was the only communal fire in the monastery. Also leading from the *dorter* was a stair direct to the church. Monks went to bed early but at midnight were summoned to church—and an internal entrance was usually made somehow to cater for such night manouevres.

The *frater* or refectory is in good condition, with a sea-view landladies would envy, and a small stair leads to a platform (pulpit) in the wall's thickness where readings were given during mealtimes. Hands were washed at an alcove and the lavatory lay so it drained down to a cell at sea level which had arched entrances so it was flushed twice a day by the tides.

At the reformation the island began a chequered history but it eventually became a possession of the Earls of Moray. That 'braw gallant' of the song, the bonnie Earl of Moray, who may have caught Anne of Denmark's eye to an indiscreet extent, inherited Inchcolm and had a home at Donibristle, on the Fife shore nearby, and it was there he was brutally murdered by the Earl of Huntly.

An hour and a half had seemed plenty of time for seeing everything on this small island but it proved quite inadequate. A big LPG tanker *Hermion* was 'inched' round the island by tugs into the terminal at Braefoot across Mortimer's Deep. She was flying a Norwegian flag and as we passed inshore of the Hound Point terminal an even bigger tanker *Abant* was being chivvied by its tugs to that mooring.

The ship flew a red flag and was registered in Instanbul. They were a bit of a contrast. It will take three or four days to fill the *Abant* and her bridge was considerably higher than the tower of the monastery which we could see looking back to Inchcolm.

Inchcolm's original name of Aemonia vanished when the monastery was founded in 1123 and dedicated to St Columba. The romantic story is probably true. The king was crossing the Queensferry passage on a wild day and the south-westerly drove the craft to Inchcolm where the party was marooned for some considerable time.

The only resident was a poor anchorite (heir of an older, even St Columban settlement perhaps) who lived in an unpretentious cell, supported by one cow and such shellfish as he could gather. He provided as best he could for the visitors and the king vowed, if he survived, that in gratitude for his help he would found a monastery on Aemonia, which he duly did.

Inchcolm grew, through troubled history, and its island position perhaps stopped it being utterly pillaged and quarried as so many were, to leave it now as one of the great sites of Scottish history.

I'm glad the name was changed. Aemonia sounds a bit like something contagious—but then the present Inchcolm could be quite catching. As we landed at South Queensferry a skitter of uniformed cubs were demanding their leader to fix another visit.

12   Loch Lomond. The *Maid of the Loch* at Inversnaid.

Ben Lomond, Eventually

Seldom have I been so glad to be plodding up a hill as I was a while back on Ben Lomond, for seldom had the chance of scaling it (or any hill that day) seemed more remote.

Ernst, a friend from London, had come up for the AGM of the Scottish Wild Land Group in Edinburgh and the next day we hoped to have a walk together somewhere. Ben Lomond was near, had none of the early-October access problems, and Ernst had not been up it before. As a long-range Munro-bagger he was all for the idea. The dog approved too.

The meeting was held in an Edinburgh hotel which proved very difficult to find. I drove up and down the street several times before spotting its inadequate sign. This probably threw my sense of direction out of focus and as I was late and had to show slides with an unknown machine I was no doubt a bit under pressure, especially as I was trying out something different—a presentation of largely abstract slides of the wilds with a mixture of poems to go with them.

It could not have gone too badly. Several people asked me for copies of *Poems of the Scottish Hills* afterwards.

I met Ernst after the performance and we staggered out with slides, books, and baggage to the car. Only there was no car!

This was a stunning shock. I could take the theft of the old dormobile (vital as it is to my lifestyle) but the dog Storm, treasured beyond all else, had been in it. It was back to the hotel and a telephone. A policeman was on the doorstep five minutes later. The dog has a name tag and the house telephone number so, as it was 11.50 and the last train was gone, we had double reason for an expensive taxi ride home.

As soon as we walked in the door the telephone rang. It was the hotel, to inform me the dormobile had been found, just a couple of streets away, intact, and with a ferocious dog inside! I had simply gone to the wrong place to collect it. Ah well I suppose the police were glad to have an idiot rather than a criminal wasting their time.

Ernst was staggered at the visual similiarity of where it actually was and where I'd wrongly thought it was. My comments on the New Town's crescents earlier in the day had mentioned this. In every way I had made a glorious ass of myself: the expert mountain navigator who couldn't find his car two streets away. It was two o'clock when I fell into bed utterly exhausted, but with Storm cosy in his usual corner.

Ben Lomond, however, roused us from bed (plus the help of two alarms and a mad-keen dog) and with the snell air of autumn we battled across into a strong wind to reach the bonnie banks of Loch Lomond.

We set off through the forest at 11.30 a.m., the latest start in years. But there was no hurry. It was one of those golden days to be comfortably savoured: sipped like a good malt in pleasurable relaxation.

Whichever way you aim for Ben Lomond you will have to face trees. The tourist path route is perhaps the best, a conjunction that certainly doesn't always apply (think of Ben Nevis!). This is a very old, popular route up, and to this day Ben Lomond is one of the most-climbed hills in Scotland. Judging by the accents Ernst and I heard it is very much Glasgow's mountain.

It is a fairly safe mountain, for the path runs from lochside to summit with the thorough markings of millions of feet. The path does not stick out as does the hideous scar of bulldozed track and is in a fair state considering the heavy use. It is a long time since I have been on such a busy mountain.

The mixture of people making the climb was a delight. It was obviously a new or perhaps a once-only adventure to many and if clothes and footwear were not always up to the dream-standards of the gear touts, the right spirit was very much in evidence. People were climbing the Ben for fun.

There was a strong wind but with the sun coming and going in a sky of churning clouds we enjoyed fresh walking: no sweat and little effort. The inches lay like scattered pieces of a jigsaw puzzle, with the loch water polished silver beyond all clichés. Great beams of light played over the hills to the west. It was great, just great. Why on earth don't more people do this sort of thing?

A constant stream of youngsters seemed to be going up and down the hill. They proved to be on some cub-sponsored exploit. They were obviously enjoying themselves. I don't think I saw one of the scores of them looking less than cheery. They certainly found it less of a pech than some of the adults. Two-thirds of the way up you come on a vast tawny moorland with the final upthrust of hill away ahead. One jaunty youngster on the way down paused long enough to greet a red-faced adult: 'Hi paw! You're nae up yet. There's aw that tae dae yet. But ah think ye'll manage it.' Ah! the glad strength of being a twelve-year-old on a windy hill on a sunny day.

That final upthrust is a crest that edges the big eastern corrie, a cliff-black hollow that seems to leer down on the farm below. Oddly there was less wind on the top than on the lower slopes, but the clouds had darkened and it looked as if a storm could strike. We had a quick look-round, a ritual naming of peaks, nibbled our Kendal Mint Cake—and retreated, fast. It stayed dry and the clouds regained their silver linings.

There is a gap on this summit edge of ridge and when on top a few years ago with Storm during our *Groats End Walk* I was wanting a photograph to mark the occasion for we had just tramped from Ben Hope (most northerly of Munros) to Ben Lomond (the most southerly) and it had also been the last Munro of a sixth round of those enslaving heights.

We sat on the summit for an hour and nobody came, despite it being a peak summer holiday weekend. The mist did not clear anyway so we went on—and found scores of people at, or arriving and descending from, the next bump along. Someone had taken it for the summit and everyone else followed suit.

The dog had done much since then and was now nearing *his* Munro tally. It is hard work being owned by a Munro-bagging dog.

13　Ben Lomond seen from the top of Duncryne at the south end of the loch.

At the end of the *Groats End Walk* his previous owner saw the book on that trip which has Storm in all his glory on the cover. She showed it to someone else with the words 'You'd never know he'd had a broken leg as a young dog, would you?' I had not been told that when buying the dog! [Munros done, Storm is now on the Corbetts.]

Back at the car, brew in hand, we were approached by one of the rangers who'd been keeping an eye on the cubs. 'You must be Hamish Brown?' he queried. I grunted some acknowledgement. 'I was sure you were. I recognised the dog.'

Fame at last—in the dog's reflected glory! He, loyal creature, never even laughed at my daftness the night before. On any Ben Lomond we were all equal.

The Blackmount and Rannoch Moor

The friendly hotel at Bridge of Orchy always seems to mark a change in atmosphere on a drive northwards on the road to Glen Coe. It is as if the white building was a milestone which suddenly says 'Almost there!' The pull up on to the Blackmount I have always regarded as the portal to the enchanted regions beyond; I am quite unashamedly a romantic in spirit but surely everyone must get a twitch of feeling in passing Loch Tulla and sweeping up onto Rannoch Moor—the Blackmount. The curve as the road swings up the brae beyond Loch Tulla is a mathematically-precise sweep. If you drive into it smoothly you can hold the steering wheel absolutely still right through the curve. The view is then down to Loch Tulla—a panorama of great beauty. As the road reaches the height of the Blackmount, give your greeting to the Rannoch Rowan.

This has become almost a superstition with some of us, who first discovered a tiny rowan growing in the cleft of a big boulder just west of the roadside when we were young. Now it is a full-sized tree while we grow old apace.

14 Looking down from the Blackmount hills to Loch Tulla and the hills of Bridge of Orchy.

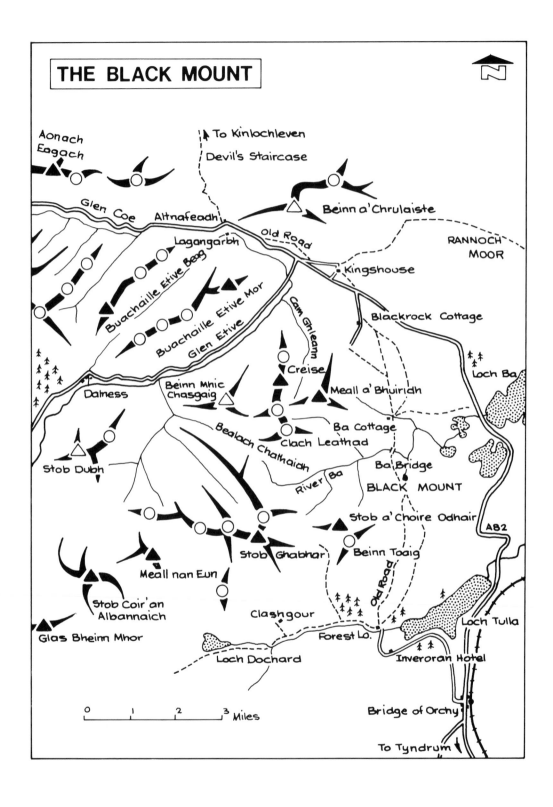

THE BLACK MOUNT

Aonach Eagach

To Kinlochleven
Devil's Staircase

Glen Coe
Altnafeadh

Beinn a' Chrulaiste

Old Road

RANNOCH MOOR

Lagangarbh

Kingshouse

Buachaille Etive Beag

Blackrock Cottage

Buachaille Etive Mor

Glen Etive

Cam Ghleann

Loch Ba

Creise

Dalness

Beinn Mhic Chasgaig

Meall a' Bhuiridh

Ba Cottage

Bealach Chathaidh

Clach Leathad

River Ba

Ba Bridge

BLACK MOUNT

Stob Dubh

Stob a' Choire Odhair

A82

Beinn Toaig

Stob Ghabhar

Meall nan Eun

Stob Coir' an Albannaich

Clashgour

Old Road

Loch Tulla

Glas Bheinn Mhor

Forest Lo.

Inveroran Hotel

Loch Dochard

0   1   2   3 Miles

Bridge of Orchy

To Tyndrum

The pattern of water on Rannoch Moor is complex (as we discovered canoeing and skating about on it) but if you look west you are instantly aware of a great encircling wall of mountain summits. All here drains into the River Ba which flows through Loch Ba to Loch Laidon. This in turn leads away east right across Rannoch Moor to Loch Rannoch and the Tay, which eventually flows into the North Sea as a big estuary. That rim of mountains lies above Glen Etive and the western sea, the Atlantic if you like, so the Scottish watershed does a most peculiar bend to the west here. You could symbolically throw a stone into the North Sea or the Atlantic from the same spot.

The Blackmount is this area of Rannoch Moor and the barrier of hills westward round Coire Ba. The Breadalbane fortunes have long ago dwindled but it is still stalking country, and still as rough as ever, though certain man-made additions have altered the landscape since the Marchioness tramped across it and wrote a fascinating book *The High Tops of the Blackmount* (1907).

The road in her day passed over the eighteenth-century bridge at Bridge of Orchy, then rounded the west end of Loch Tulla (Victoria Bridge) before pulling up onto the Blackmount. It then dropped to Ba Bridge, rose again and finally angled down to the old inn at Kingshouse. My father, on home leave from the Far East, in the year before I was born, hired a car for a Highland Tour and crossed Rannoch Moor by the 'newly-opened' road—which still proves adequate for today's traffic. In the early 1930s you can imagine what a futuristic bit of engineering it appeared. Following the old route is still attractive as a low-level walk. The route can even be cycled if you are a rough-stuff enthusiast.

One of the finest of historical novels is set here and further north on the Corrieyairack Pass from Fort Augustus to Speyside. The latter is *The New Road* of the Neil Munro title, but the tale follows up this road as well. There are some superb word pictures, describing Rannoch Moor for instance, but I'll leave you to find them for yourself. Under a pseudonym Neil Munro was also the creator of the *Para Handy* stories.

With the present road keeping a couple of miles east of the old, Coire Ba gained back something of its original wildness. From Forest and Black Mount Lodges, on Loch Tulla, to the old 'black' Milehouse on the ski road there is no building at all and the only people likely to be met are stalkers, fishermen or walkers. Visitors are however well provided with accommodation, quite apart from the delights of camping in unrestricted areas. Camping does have its drawbacks in the midge or monsoon season. As these often coincide with the tourist season, a roof over the walker's head becomes no luxury but sometimes a matter of survival. Glen Coe Youth Hostel and other alternatives are a bit remote for the Blackmount though within easy range with a car. Two 'huts' exist right on the edge of these hills, however.

Blackrock, on the Meall a' Bhuiridh ski road opposite Kingshouse, is a very old building with walls six feet thick. It seems sunk into the moor as if it had been there, like some erratic boulder, since the last ice age. For many years it has been leased by the Ladies Scottish Climbing Club who have thankfully not over-modernised it—it retains some feeling for the past under its black tin roof.

At the other end of the range is the Glasgow University Mountaineering Club's

Clashgour—about a mile west of Forest Lodge on the Loch Dochard track. It is not the Clashgour named on the map, which is an occupied house. The 'hut' is literally that, unlike most in Scotland which are often rather fine old cottages like Blackrock.

Lagangarbh, an SMC Hut, lies near Alltnafeidh where the Devil's Staircase joins the modern A82, and Kingshouse Hotel has been a well-used base since the earliest mountaineering days. Inbhirfhaolain near Dalness in Glen Etive is a Grampian Club Hut. Bridge of Orchy and Inveroran Hotels lie south of Loch Tulla, the former is open all year—and has its own Bridge of Orchy malt, an attraction in itself. The Glasgow Ski Club has a custom-build modern 'hut' at Invereigh, three-quarters of a mile south west of Bridge of Orchy. If this all adds up to a considerable number of beds, they are all needed.

Clashgour allows foot access both to the Starav group and to Stob Ghabhar, the chief of the southern Blackmount hills. Stob Ghabhar is almost like a starfish in shape, with long legs of ridges which enclose deep, often cliff-girt corries. The Upper Couloir was one of the early classic winter climbs and I am sure there are routes as yet undiscovered. The walker will find ridges of the finest quality in traversing Stob Ghabhar, in any direction. Stob a' Choire Odhair is a secondary peak east of Stob Ghabhar but, being a Munro, is dutifully ascended by those working through the list.

From the Clashgour hut a good stalkers' path goes up the east bank of the Allt Toaig towards the col between the Munros. A branch path breaks off and ascends the wide spur on Stob a' Choire Odhair's south slopes—it lies roughly up between the two streams shown. These paths are missing on the map but are very welcome, either to start or finish the day, especially if all the hills are being traversed.

The group splits naturally into northern and southern sections at the Bealach Chathaid which is about 2300 feet. It is here that the North Sea–Atlantic drainage systems most nearly meet. Actually the systems overlap, for if Coire Ba and Rannoch Moor drain away to the east, Loch Tulla is fed not only from Loch Dochard in the west but by the Water of Tulla which comes from far in the east—draining the southern edge of Rannoch Moor and the Achalladair-Chreachain hills. These waters eventually escape from Loch Tulla as the River Orchy which flows into Loch Awe and thus to outer Loch Etive. Nothing seems to flow in the expected direction.

Meall a' Bhuiridh, at 3636 feet, is the highest of the Blackmount summits and has suffered the indignity of ski development, but the mess of the development is far less here than anywhere else in Scotland. The astute choice of setting helps to ensure it is unobtrusive. Someone must have known their mountains for the site chosen catches and holds snow naturally, so there is a minimum of fencing and gouged hollows.

Meall a' Bhuiridh forms an outlier and gains scenically from its isolation. Look down and marvel at Loch an Easain in the Glen draining its southern slopes—one of the steepest gradients of any British hill that is not simply cliff—look down the Cam Gleann, which is a deep-set lost world of its own, and then teeter off for the bridging col suspended between Meall a' Bhuiridh and Creise.

There is almost a plateau feel to the wide, gentle ridges that run from Sron na Creise to Clach Leathad (Clachlet). Resurveys have changed the various altitudes over the years with resultant alterations to Munro's Tables. Clachlet has gone, its crown passed to Creise, which is not even named though its nose (sron) is indicated.

The descent off Clachlet to the south west drops over 1300 feet, the major dip in the traverse of all the Munros: Meall a' Bhuiridh—Creise—Stob Ghabhar—Stob a' Choire Odhair. That is the normal direction they are taken in. A friend or partner who does not go on the hill and is willing to act as chauffeur is an asset. You can start at the top of the ski road, a useful 1350 feet, and end at Victoria Bridge, 600 feet. If without a car, start at Blackrock Cottage and descend off Stob a' Choire Odhair or Beinn Toaig to the old road for the tramp home via Ba Bridge.

Above the highest point of this old road you will see a monument built in memory of Peter Fleming, the traveller and author whose books were among those which fascinated me many years ago and ensured my feet were to find many a foreign wilderness. He was the brother of Ian Fleming, the creator of James Bond—as unlikely a pair of writing brothers as Lawrence and Gerald Durrell. The Blackmount belongs to the Fleming family (the ancient Breadalbane interest has gone completely though in the powerful days of these Campbells their domains reached from here to Aberfeldy on the Tay).

Rannoch Moor has one large loch (Laidon) and a whole host of smaller ones right down to the tiny sequins that glitter on a summer's day and make the Moor more silver than any other colour to look at. The lochs are studded with islets—which have their own lochans. The way grazing deer contribute to denuding the landscape of vegetation is seen in many of these islets being jungles of growth, compared to the rest of the moor. You can see the same thing on the banks of ravines which are impenetrable to animals, a mixture of holly, Scots pine, oak, rowan, birch, hazel, alder, honeysuckle and hanging gardens of flowers—another attraction for the game of 'burning up' such gorges. They are also a regular source of antlers for deer will try to browse the tempting growth but, as in the Garden of Eden, the forbidden fruit is apt to lead to a fall.

A comment on antlers. The stags have to grow new ones every year (which differentiates them from antelope, which simply add to what they have) and the old antlers they have dropped are largely eaten, presumably for the chemicals which can be recycled into the new growth. This explains why so many antlers walkers find are only partially complete and look a bit chewed up—this is exactly what they are. As the antlers naturally loosen and eventually wobble off you will seldom, if ever, find a good *pair*. Those nice sets you see on the walls of baronial halls or above garage doors have come from beasts which have been shot or have died with their antlers still attached.

The Glasgow–Fort William railway skirts the southern edge of the Moor, then rounds it on the eastern fringe, where Rannoch Station is a remarkably lonely spot. It is linked to Loch Rannoch by road but few tourists go out to such a dead-end. From the station, a path of sorts runs to the Kingshouse Hotel across the northern borders of the Moor. At the Rannoch Station end there is some planting so there is a forestry road and in the west a rough vehicle track leads to Black Corries beyond Kingshouse. A walking tour from Bridge of Orchy Hotel to Rannoch Station to Kinghouse Hotel and back to Bridge of Orchy Hotel beats the bounds very effectively—and will ensure you want to come back some day for a traverse right through the middle. A central traverse of the moor gives a feeling of loneliness hard to match anywhere in Britain.

Glen Tilt and its Hills

Braigh Coire Chruinn-bhalgain is a contender for the largest mouthful of any Scottish Munro. To mention it (with a quite false but effective rolling authority of voice) causes two reactions, one being the blank look of complete bewilderment, the other usually a smile. If you have climbed Braigh Coire Chruinn-bhalgain you will never forget the name. The world is divided into people who have climbed Braigh Coire Chruinn-bhalgain and those who have not.

If you have yet to tilt at it then perhaps a survey of the Blair Atholl hills will be of use. Braigh What's-its-Name is of the clan Beinn a' Ghlo in the country of Atholl.

It took me three attempts to reach the summit Two of us left a deeply frozen camp at Blair Atholl one early December and battled up Cairn Liath, the cone which shows so well to the A9 mobsters, but the blizzard beat us there. A week later we were back and again made Carn Liath but the fight up through deep snow had exhausted both us and the daylight. We came back next May and did all three Munros that are handily, if incorrectly, lumped under the heading Beinn a' Ghlo (Ben-y-Gloe). Midsummer did not make it easier for us. I have slides which non-hillgoers think are the result of trick photography. We are all walking at impossible angles. It was windy!

When we came back for a winter round again it was a Christmas Day traverse of cold, clear perfection. Pertinacity has its rewards. Other visits followed but last summer it gave a day of hot, clear perfection for one man and his dog. All the years came crowding back as I gazed about from the cairn: the tussles and rewards, the thrashings, and the increased regard. Beinn a' Ghlo is not an easy hill group. Only Lochnagar, a pap visible away in the east, is higher among the hills of the rear-defence of the Mounth. Being clear of other big hills it is always an obvious landmark and for the same reason gives big views—and catches or creates its own big weather. Beinn a' Ghlo means *hill of the mist*.

How comparatively less exciting are the hills on the north side of Glen Tilt, yet they have rewards of a different kind. Head north from upper Glen Tilt and you will have to go clean through the Mounth Minigaig *and* the Cairngorms before you hit a tarred road. It is one of the largest, toughest, emptiest tracts of country in these islands. In poor conditions the navigation is challenging and in deep snow the ski-touring is incomparable.

'Less exciting' is not really correct. They are just different—as Glen Tilt itself is

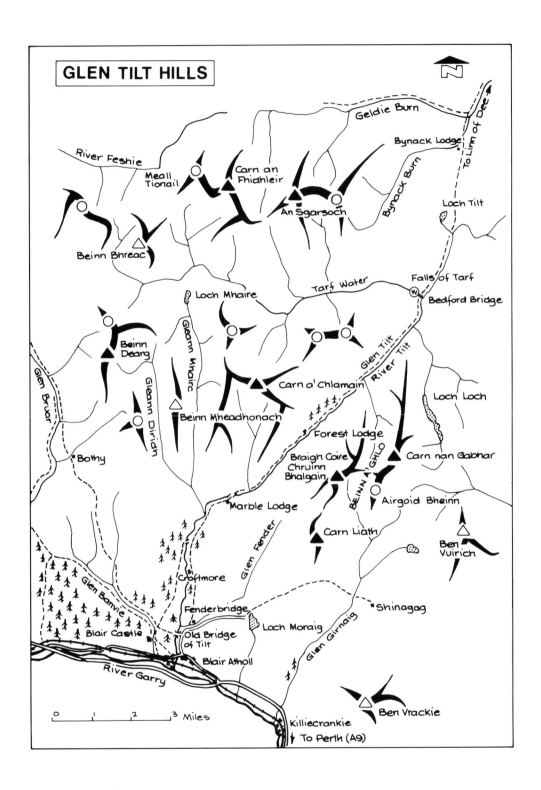

GLEN TILT HILLS

different from any other glen of its size in the Highlands. A walk through glen Tilt is one of the notable hill days—and certainly worth swopping for some Munros or Corbetts I could name.

Blair Atholl is the centre for these hills and as it is on the main Perth–Inverness railway you can explore without the restriction of having to return to a car—explore the hills and finish by walking through to Deeside perhaps. There are several hotels and B&B establishments, shops, tea rooms (one in a working mill and one in Blair Castle, the historic home of the Dukes of Atholl) and a luxurious campsite—so it can be a base for most styles. Not far down the road is Pitlochry with its famous theatre—reached through the Pass of Killiecrankie, where the battle of 1689 was fought: a royalist victory but Bonnie Dundee fell in it and was buried in Old Blair. In the castle his breast plate (with two holes in it) is one intriguing exhibition. The castle is worth a visit for itself—the building—and for what one sees displayed. Nothing though can beat the long avenue of bee-loud lime trees by which one approaches the castle: a magic passage in the fresh-leaved colours of spring. The campsite is in the castle grounds.

For several hundreds of years the Atholl estates have been keen tree-planters so the area now looks much less desolate than some. Robert Burns visited the Bruar Falls (still worth a look though partly Hydro-pinched) and wrote a poem, tongue-in-cheek, to the then Duke, in which the falls plead to be given a surrounding of trees. The Duke obliged. Nothing could be a bigger contrast than wandering up by these falls, or Glen Banvie, or Tilt itself on to the northern plateau. Here it is all peat and heather where six steps in a straight line would be a relief. In winter it looks like the Greenland ice-cap: its frozen state assisting walkers rather than the opposite.

Heading up the Tilt or up Glen Fender for Beinn a' Ghlo, the eye is caught by the unusual greens set among the ling-browns. This is from various richer soils being present so gives a flora far more varied than the usual acid wastes. Glen Tilt has marble and several areas of limestone. The Tarf–Tilt waters at one time flowed into the Geldie–Dee but they now elbow back following changes from the Ice Ages.

Glen Tilt and its hills have been famous as deer ground for hundreds of years. James V, Mary Queen of Scots, and Queen Victoria all paid visits. The last actually went up Carn a' Chlamain, the first of her modest tally of Munros. She returned to Balmoral through Glen Tilt. There was no Bedford Bridge then and though the ford was waist deep, the royal pipers crossed still playing, the Queen perched on her pony. That was in 1861. A couple of decades earlier the Duke of Atholl had tried to close the glen as a public through route—and lost the resulting case.

The glen is private for vehicles, though permission may be granted to drive up. The redoubtable keeper at Forest Lodge keeps a stern eye on motorists. On one occasion we were parked by the Tilt having a brew when the Land Rover drew up. Had we permission? We had—but I had loaded on board some fine pink granite boulders for my rockery at home. These got the comment: 'Aye some folks just climb the hills, ithers must tak them hame wi them!'

To me, Glen Tilt is just too long with too much hard-surfaced track to be really enjoyed. It is a perfect glen for cycling, giving a reasonable ration of rough-stuff at its head, but not the crazy discomfort of routes like the Lairig Ghru. When not made estate track, it is clear footpath.

The right-of-way is well signposted and runs up from Fenderbridge to Croftmore, a rich, tree country. Forest Lodge is the only habitation. An hour on from it the estate track scars off left by Dun Mor to end at a stable on the mighty Tarf; the Dee track keeps on up the minor Tilt (the Tarf produces 75 per cent of the joint flow). The Bedford Bridge, 1886, was built following a drowning one August, and is a period piece of Victorian engineering. From it you look at the lower Falls of Tarf and it is worth going up the gorge to see the upper falls too. The Tarf drains that great wilderness which is rimmed by a handful of remote Munros and Corbetts, called *The Ring of Tarf*—which deserves a score by some McWagner.

The Tilt is now much reduced and called the Allt Garbh Bhuidhe—*the rough yellow burn*. The watershed is hardly noticeable and Loch Tilt invisible on a shelf above. After a couple of miles the ruin of Bynack Lodge is reached. A few years ago when camping nearby we found and used some rhubarb from it. If the Bynack Burn is in spate, cross the Seilich instead. The bridge over the big Geldie does not exist—and in 1983 at least one Ultimate Challenge participant went for a ducking trying to cross. There is a rotten bridge across the Geldie beside the Dee's White Bridge or, if that goes, the south bank of the Dee is followed to the Linn. Blair Atholl to Braemar must be 30 miles: Old Blair to Linn o' Dee, the minimal distance between public roads is 22 miles. (For comparison, Keswick to Windermere is also 22 miles.) It is a good day's hike.

If Glen Tilt and the hills bounding it all give big days, one summit of note can be done in a morning. Ben Vrackie is only 2760 feet, but like so many Corbetts has a solitary state often lacking in the proletarian Munros. (A Corbett is that second list in Munro's tables: peaks over 2500 feet. They are neither a soft option nor a soft succession.) Ben Vrackie dominates the view up the River Garry and Blair Atholl but is very much Pitlochry's private property. A path from Moulin, above Pitlochry, leads to it, or it can be reached across the moors from the Pitlochry–Kirkmichael road. It gives a grandstand view across to the Beinn a' Ghlo triumvirate.

This trio are almost always approached from Blair Atholl though, with a bike, the south-east Fearnaid glen is recommended. Secretive Loch Loch is as surprising and glittering as a lost brooch on a refuse tip. Let us go as I went last summer, up from Old Bridge to Tilt to Loch Moraig by car, the end of the public motor road. The loch was a cacophony of black-headed gulls and calling curlews. Even at eight o'clock that June morning the sun was already hot. I felt the heat on the first mile. There are huts where one sets off over a line of butts and an old wall which aims at the symmetrical blunted triangle of Carn Laith, *the grey hill* (pronounced *Lee-ah.*) There is a path most of the way up but it vanishes when the grey screes are reached. Be warned: the trig point is not the summit which lies further on at a large cairn.

I had been followed, so trig point and figure gave foreground for the view downwards. The other way Braigh Coire Chruinn-bhalgain and Carn nan Gabhar stood side by side close enough that a wide-angled lens was needed to photograph them together. Lawers looked fine (Schiehallion lost in front of it), Lochnagar was clear and the Lairig Ghru–Feshie hills looked startlingly near. Dearg and Chlamain were grey shapes. Tilt, Feshie—these big passes—had just vanished. The great block of the Mounth plateau dominated, the weathered glens were lost to view. It was a prehistoric landscape.

The girl who had arrived had hurried on and it only struck me later that we had met two weeks before on top of Ben Alder. This was a week day so the odds on such a meeting are interesting. There is a long snaking ridge leading to the col before the Braigh and I cut some corners and then traversed left to a burn and followed it up to near the summit. I had quite a few drinks and splashed water over myself to cool off. There was a salvation breeze so conditions felt reasonable but I still wore a light vest to protect shoulders, and a brimmed hat to cover my neck and ears. I was in shorts and tied my shirt round my waist so it hung down on the sunny side. The British have a mania for stripping off and burning themselves—which I don't share.

An old story says there are nineteen corries on Beinn a' Ghlo in any of which a gun could be fired and not heard in another. There are more than that! Even on the map the jigsaw shape of these hills stands out as different from other hills. They are a huge sprawled pile of domes and spurs; heather-skirted, grassy-pullovered and topped with stones. Braigh Coire Chruinn-bhalgain lacks much of the stoniness on top and as the central of the three has a paternal air to it. Carn Liath is the baby, to the south, while east is Carn nan Gabhar, slightly higher as sons are apt to be.

This mouthful translates *brae of the round, bag-shaped corrie* or *brae of the round little blisters*. *Bh* is always a *V*-sound so bhalgain is *valgan* or *valigan*. Carn nan Gabhar (*Gower*) is *goat's cairn*.

I could see no sign of my fellow-walker though I had a clear view down and up the bealach (*balloch*) separating the Braigh from Beinn a' Ghlo—which is just the collective name for all these hills. The dog and I chuntered down, keeping left, to find some water below the summer snow edge, then angling up towards a prominent cairn—which is not the summit, and then the trig point—which is not the summit, and then a cairn which is the summit—nearly seven miles from the car. There was no sign of anyone. I went along a few hundred yards to look down on Loch Loch; a dizzy view for all these hills are big and steep.

Wandering back a figure popped up. We said hello again. Did I know I'd left my radio on in the car? No, but I had realised I'd come away wearing my Bogtrotters which I'd put on for dewy dawn and forgotten to change. That I went through this day with comfortable feet (no round little blisters) testifies to these, my normal British damp-walking footwear.

Dog and I cut down to the col again and took the corrie south, the lassie went off to view Loch Loch and off south over the Top and spur of Airgoid Bhein, *the silver hill*. Several deer went off ahead of us and we were lying back with feet in the burn when the dog noticed the figure descending. We hailed each other again.

The return to the cars presented some miles of circling the base of the hills on deer tracks and heather, hot work now we were off the breezy tops. Storm put up a roe deer and a family of grouse flapped away with the parents doing a fine broken-wing act at a rather disinterested dog. The last two miles were on hot, hard track. As I neared the car I though I heard people talking, but nobody was in sight. It was eerie for a moment before I realised it was the radio.

We had some tea together and parted. I stayed to cook a meal (we were in at five o'clock) before going down to hotter levels for the night. The Ring of Tarf was planned for the morrow, after the briefest night of the year gave its welcome dews.

That Ring of Tarf day was interesting enough: going up the initial miles of Glen

Tilt with the dog in the rucksack and the pair of us on a folding bike. It was a stinking hot day which built up towering thunder clouds that had us running in fear off Beinn Dearg. We escaped being struck by lightning but not being soaked by the rain. For that I reduced to shorts only on the theory of not having garments to dry. After all, humans are waterproof.

However it is an earlier round I most treasure. I've made several circuits of these four or split them with a night at the Tarf bothy, besides having pecked away one by one in various shorter visits. It is the miles up the Tilt that are the worst; five or six miles out which also have to be added at the end as well, on top of whatever is done on the hill. A cycle becomes very much its Scottish legal definition—an aid to pedestrianism.

It was near the end of one February that Mike and I grabbed the chance for a ski tour. We had a bitter cold night in the dormobile in Blair Atholl and were off early up those miles of Glen Tilt to Gilbert's Bridge. Scores of deer were down below the snowline.

On the hillside we found a whole ruined village which is not shown on the map, though this shows many other odd ruins. Later, I could not find out anything from reading up the area. The bridge shown on the map on the stream which is the union of the Allt Diridh and the Allt Mhairc is a sturdy, stone structure but small in span as the gorge leans in to make almost a natural bridge. The lonely bridge appeared as incongruous as a ship left in a field.

When there was snow enough we put on our skis: Mike had 'skinny skis' (Norwegian touring skis) and I had 'mountain skis'—shorter skis, which used skins strapped on the sole to go uphill where Mike used waxes. His were lighter but I had the edge for being able to descend steeper slopes. Both involved alterations whenever we changed from going uphill or downhill and at the end of several hours we would arrive more or less at the same time. Neither was a convert to the other's style.

We both zig-zagged up Sron a' Chro at the maximum angle possible; concentrated work with our packs so when the angle eased off and we rested the change of scene was dramatic. We had a dark trench below us, Glen Tilt, while all around lay a world of Polar whiteness. The humps of Beinn a' Ghlo looked like the ermine pelts of huge beasts.

This way up was chosen so we could use our skis as quickly as possible. Walkers generally go on past Marble Lodge and up the Balaneasie ridge, or the stream before it. A stalker's path leads up from Forest Lodge. Our route had been the descent route when Queen Victoria climbed up Carn a' Chlamain. We had nearly three miles of rolling plateau round to the summit where we sat below the crest, out of the wind, to admire the unique view.

The reward of uphill effort is the run down and we had three miles of that to step out of our bindings at the Tarf Bothy. Later we sat outside enjoying tea, in the sun. The bothy was still in good state then but vandalism has almost destroyed it now. An AA Hotel sign hung on a gable! There were actually beds (no mattresses) and we had a comfortable night snug in our sleeping bags. Mike had what was then a new idea in stoves, a Trangia, and, keeping up his eastern interests, a Russian panoramic camera. A picture of the bothy taken with it is pinned to my study door.

It was taken the next day after we had crossed the Tarf and bagged An Sgarsoch and

15 Above Glen Tilt—on the great ski day described.

Carn an Fhidhleir (*Eeler*), the two Munros that rim the Tarf on the north and beyond which lies the moat of the bridgeless Feshie–Geldie rivers. Most ascents are made from the Dee–Geldie track. At one time the ruin of Geldie Lodge had a tiny upper 'room' which acted as a howff (shelter)—very useful for these remote hills. On one occasion a gang of us camped by the Geldie, after walking in from the Linn o' Dee, and discovered we had left all pots and cutlery behind. I remember cutting up meat with my compass. The meat was then skewered on tent pegs and grilled.

How gentle these summits are can be seen in An Sgarsoch at one time having a cattle/horse fair on its summit. Carn an Fhidhleir's summit is the meeting place of the old counties of Perth, Inverness and Aberdeen. A surface of ling, berry and moss makes them a treat for skiing. Which is why we were back at the bothy for lunch and floundering about still on skis, taking photographs.

In summer wet the going within this ring is unusually hard. The map does not show the peat, the wet, the roughness, the impossibility of rhythm or the short hours that come with difficult miles. Yet the Tarf sanctuary has a lure that takes one back again. It rings with the wild calling of curlews and waders—and they only choose the wild and lonely places to nest. We saw many ptarmigan, wild cat and foxes on several occasions. One fox crossed just fifteen yards ahead of our ski tracks. We then had the crazy idea of going for Beinn Dearg, traversing it and staying the night in a bothy by Glen Bruar. This we did: curving up by the Tarf, skiing across a frozen and hidden Loch Mhairc and steadily up to *the red hill* which, for once, belied its name. (It is a vast carbuncle of pink granite breaking through the brown skin of ling.) We skied right to the summit.

From it we could look to familiar neighbours—Schiehallion the nearest. The fangs of Cruachan seemed to be gnawing a bloody sunset. The cold came pulsing in as day ebbed. We rasped a route down into the shadows of the west, eventually linking runnels among the ling but ending once more at the door of a welcome bothy. The aches of a ten-hour day were forgotten in huge eating and much drinking of tea. We were abed by 8.30 p.m.—and slept for ten hours.

The next day we walked down by the ancient Minigaig track to Old Blair. A walk-out at the end of any tour, in any land, has a sorrow in it. Few rounds have been as satisfying however—or proved the value of skis. On foot in that deep snow coverage it would have taken two long days to struggle for the one done on ski. We had hard work, but pleasurable. On another occasion some of us climbed Chlamain and a friend Jim and I (plus the dog) went on to add Dearg. It proved an epic flounder. I had to carry the dog (thank goodness he was a small Sheltie and not an Alsation) as he was balling up so badly he could not walk at all. We ran out of daylight and fought bogs, blizzard and night down Gleann Diridh to reach Glen Tilt utterly exhausted.

There are many valleys, ridges and paths radiating from Beinn Dearg so it would take many repeat visits to need to duplicate a route. Beinn Mheadhonach between Dearg and Glen Tilt is a Corbett and so is Beinn Bhreac between Dearg and Carn an Fhidhleir so these can be added to a 'rim' round. They also help explain the uniform, plateau-like appearance to the view north from Beinn a' Ghlo. There is nothing notable or eye-catching but we do not need the spectacular to find our enjoyment. Even if Braigh Coire Chruinn-bhalgain is the last of your Munros, there are the Corbetts as well—and there you can try tongue and toes on Sgurr Cos na Breachd-laoidh, Beinn Liath Mhor a' Ghuibhais Li or Meallan Liath Coire Mhic Dhughaill.

Summit Search

Some go tripping with the evening air
Round a clipped edge of lawn
But I would trace the many-graced
Subtleties of dawn.
I would climb into gold wildernesses
Up black screes of soul,
Through cloud-inverted dreams, to a quartz cairn.
I am sure to find my summit, worn, torn, but
Made warm with dawn.

Storm Joins the Munroists

My hill-doings on a recent Hogmanay were dictated largely by Storm, my enthusiastic Shetland collie. He had come within striking distance of completing his Munros and, as anyone will know, or guess, that is a serious matter. Munroitis is a bad enough condition in biped companions but a single-minded canine has twice the zeal and ethusiasm, though fortunately none of man's hang-ups or, being Hogmanay, hang-overs. It is very hard to live up to Storm on the hill.

We had made an erratic journey north via the Cairngorms, taken a hammering on the Fannichs, had Torridon gracefully submit and enjoyed one day above Glen Shiel before the local club arrived for Hogmanay. The last day of the year saw Dave, dog and this gangrel out on The Saddle; the first of January saw only Storm and his slave on the ridge of the Five Sisters—which was Kintail tidied up in a few good days. We moved south of the Great Glen for the last missing Munros: that quartet strung along on the other side of the Bealach Dubh from Ben Alder.

These hills have no obvious group name and the highest of them is not named on the Ordnance Survey map (despite many pleadings) and even if it were, it is a Geal Charn in an area of many Geal Charns. The OS does give Aonach Beag in massive type so they are sometimes called the Aonach Beag range. I've always thought of them as the Bealach Dubh hills for it is hard to visit the one without the other. It's a politer term than one I heard as I left the others in Kintail. 'Oh, Storm is taking Hamish off to the Laggan lot.'

The limited hours of daylight available rather detracted from doing them as a day trip from the car by Loch Laggan. Perhaps we could go in to Culra Bothy and then back out over the four the next day? Carn Dearg could even be done after arriving at the bothy to save a bit the next day. This was more or less what happened.

We spent the night at 'Fasgadh', Nancy Smith's private hostel at the end of the Fersit road. Her Hogmanay invasion had departed. A few of us enjoyed the crack by the fire, along with Baillies and black bun. (Hogmanay was only just past after all.) At frosty first light, Storm and I were crossing the Moy cutting and wended up and round to Lochan na h-Earba. We had a break and I drummed-up on a sluggish stove. The first golden sunrays lit up Ardverikie Wall across the water.

As the ground was hard from several days of frost I had abandoned my usual Bogtrotters for the heavy pair of boots I reserve for winter climbing. These have 'Yeti

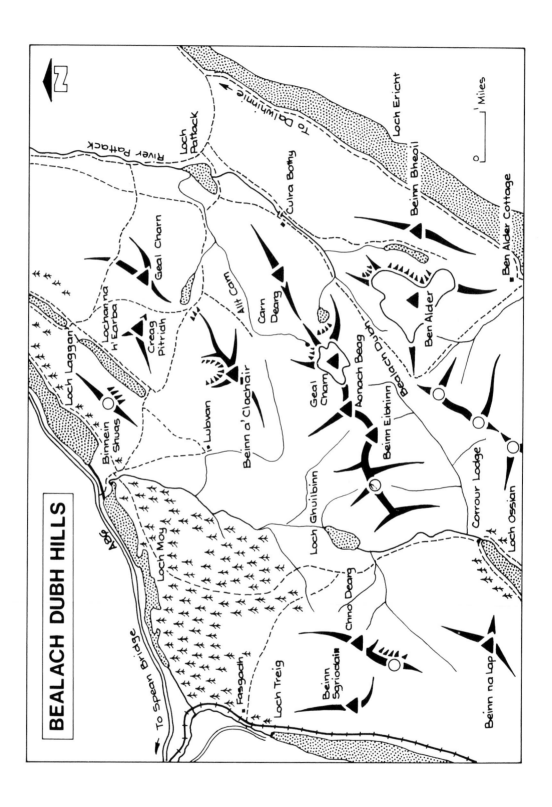

BEALACH DUBH HILLS

16 Storm beside the Cross Stone above Tarfside.

Gaiters' permanently attached so it is possible to splash across knee-deep rivers without taking boots off or having everything soaked as in the bad old days. Alas, the hard boots were hurting. Over our second breakfast I had to plaster blistering heels.

We then went on by a pleasant stalker's path, rather than feet-damaging estate road, and this led up to a pass in the Ardverikie Forest hills, with Munros to right and left. The temptation was too much. We dumped the rucksack and drifted up the bouldery ridge on to the high plateau miles of Beinn a' Chlachair. It took us into the clouds and soon we were silvered with frost. Storm turned into an arctic fox look-alike.

We returned to my rucksack and went down by a deep-set corrie lochan to the river which had been the cause of my donning the heavy boots. I was limping on both feet. This Allt Cam river can often be a desperately dangerous one to cross but it was mercifully low and we splashed across no bother—and dry—thanks to the magic gaiters. Rather than go round the end of Carn Dearg and up to the bothy on the hard road, we cut up direct on to this needed Munro. Which was one in the bag. Three to go.

We dropped down directly to the bothy, with a scattering of deer, the only ones of the day.

The bothy was dank and raw inside and it was pleasanter to stand outside in the moonlight. There were four lads from Fife and two solitary lads. I noted, as we stood on our knoll chatting, that all but one present had on Yeti gaiters. Just occasionally a new item of equipment really is effective. All I want now is a redesigned body that does not sweat and feet to fit any make of boots. My last Christmas pudding of the season boiled dry while we talked and burnt badly enought that we smelt the disaster. We were all abed early as it proved impossible to kindle a fire from the damp wood available. The big moon almost made candles unnecessary.

We set out an hour before dawn with the snow falling and some worries as to the day ahead. We were flanking along the southern side of two ranges that now lay between us and the car. If things went wrong there could be real problems. We tried not to think too much about it. Ice on the path lay under a dusting of snow and could not always be distinguished by torchlight. We had an unscheduled slide or two. Grey dawn found us below the steep pull up to the Bealach Dubh. The pass itself, a link between Loch Ossian and Dalwhinnie, has the remains of aircraft wreckage on it, which goes back to wartime. It was a bleak place in the cloud and snow.

We had intended just wandering up on to Geal Charn from there but navigating would not be easy and the drifted snow made the going slow, hard work. We cut up by the pass edge instead for it was blown clear of snow and led to a distinctive top. Below the pass we had heard grouse go-backing at us; above we were in the world of white ptarmigan.

We found our Top, Lancet Edge, and from it navigated with extreme care for Gael Charn, a mile away across acres of flat ground which merged with the sky in a white visual vacuum. The cairn is small and when it appeared just 10 yards off our port bow I was both pleased and relieved.

After that we were on well-defined ridges so navigation was easy. We could just see enough to follow the crest, down and up to Aonach Beag, then a longer down to run up and round a deep corrie for Beinn Eibhinn (*Beautiful Hill*), Storm's last Munro.

We turned down northwards and as we lost height the ground became steadily more rough, a roughness exaggerated by everything being frozen solid, so we were glad to pick up another path round the west end of Beinn a' Chlachair. Once on it we were safely through. By the ruins of an old house we had another brew and I plastered my plasters before limping on. It was much easier on the tops! Our homeward track merged with our outward one and we were soon back to the road, the car, and the warmth of Nancy's hostel.

17   Geal Charn from Aonach Beag—the peaks of Storm's last Munro.

The Glen of Rowans

I am always sorry when the green extravagance of May slips past. It is as if the year had been given a new coat of paint, which now must mellow, wear thin and peel off as the year progresses. May is the month for the straths and glens, and Glenesk was my choice for a walk this year.

The start was in Glen Clova for the headwaters of Glenesk rise on the peat moors just above Glendoll. We were an international trio: Claudia a German girl, Sandy an Irish lassie, and I was showing them my native Scotland the hard way—on foot.

You could almost gather the type of country from names on the map: Benty Roads, Long Shank, Watery Knowe, Wolf Hill, Burn of Slidderies. For an hour I followed the compass through the silvering mists till I was sure we had crossed the watershed and knew all water safely drained to Glenesk.

We nearly died of heart failure when a grouse rose from the heather, but it pointed us to its hidden nest. Better still was the five minutes we stood stock still and watched a vixen cross our paths only 20 yards away.

We had a leg-numbing paddle across the Water of Unich (any deeper and I would have been a eunuch!) for it was running high from the melting snow that still patched the brown shanks.

The Falls of Damff plunged our river down into a great gorge. It seemed no paths could descend there, but a lonely pony path for stalkers had been cunningly threaded down the crags. Before the green lawns of Glen Lee were reached the Falls of Unich waved a white flag of life in the still, misty world.

We joined a farm track for the two miles along Loch Lee: a dark water which seemed to shiver with the chill weather. This always seems a sad spot for once it was a thriving place of people; but they were replaced by deer last century and the church at the loch end is roofless now.

We stopped there to re-patch Claudia's blister and look at some of the old gravestones. Some are dated 1733 and have evocative carvings of symbols of death or the departed one's trade.

Here we were back to trees: birches in their greenest of greens, dark pines and quivering rowans. This is the Glen of the Rowan Trees and already we could see the Hill of Rowan with its cairn on top. 'The Parsonage is just the other side of it,' I remarked. 'Just another hour.'

Invermark Castle stood like a pepper-pot between road and river, a typical sixteenth-century tower, belonging originally to the Lindsays of Edzell. Sandy noted the castle doorway stood eight feet above ground—'just like an Irish Round Tower'.

Beyond the castle we merged with Glen Mark, another crystal-clear river that rises in the black bogs that lead over to Glen Muick and Deeside. Mount Keen, the most easterly Munro, lies up the glen so is better known. Even Queen Victoria climbed Mount Keen and her brewing-spot is marked by the Queen's Well—a 15-foot granite crown over a bubbling spring.

We escaped the punishing walking surface of the tarred road by cutting over behind the Hill of Rowan—which was the original road anyway.

The Hill of Rowan has scores of prehistoric sites but the antiquity I like is the wayside cross carved on a schisty boulder. It must have been carved 1300 years ago. Its very simplicity is its appeal.

> The hill of Rowan has a cross on its heart
> cut in grey stone
> on a purple tweed of ling.
> Up there, as the old years stotter by,
> the young birds sing.

We were tired and footsore after nine hours of tramping so did not climb to the conical cairn on top of the hill.

I was able to quote (more or less) the odd reason for it. It was erected in 1866 by the then Earl of Dalhousie 'in memory of seven of his family already dead, and of himself and two others when it shall please God to call them hence'.

Claudia ended our day's darg with a comment that left us all laughing. 'Do you know what my name means?' When we shook our heads she said, with some feeling: 'The lame!'

It is marvellous what a cup of tea and a bath can do and the supper that followed will not be forgotten. The Parsonage does not advertise itself but lucky gangrels know it is one of the friendliest of B&B establishments; so much so that on this May's Ultimate Challenge coast-to-coast walk, Mrs Guthrie provided three sittings for dinner and there were thirteen tents on the lawn because the house was full. We toasted before the fire and were deliciously spoilt. Even Claudia's blister gave up the fight and, well-padded, gave no bother the next day when we walked down and out the glen.

The Firmounth and the Fungle drove roads come over to Tarfside from the Dee and continue over the hills southwards by the Clash of Wirren. More than beasts went that way. This was a famous whisky area as the score of ruined houses at Arsallary indicate.

Next morning we walked all the way to Edzell on the south bank of the river. It was a morning of dappled sunshine. Coming out of the tight pass with its water-carved rocks (called 'The Stones of Solitude') was like shutting a door. Behind lay the Mounth, with some of the wildest and emptiest and most difficult hills in the country to travel in, ahead lay the bountiful farmlands of Angus and the bustle of towns. There were even American airmen in uniform who stared at our weatherburnt features, big boots, and rucksacks.

'You folks been walking far?'

That ended the trip for us. We had followed the Esk from its birth to it lowland meanderings. Next May we will walk another glen but I doubt if there is any fairer than the Glen of the Rown Trees.

Blizzard '78

January 1978 will be remembered in many parts of Scotland as the month of the Great Storm. I was made to realise my age during it because of the comparisons with 1947. People either knew that earlier epic or they did not. It does show how far back we had to go to find like conditions.

I was just a laddie in 1947. Going through to the Alloa Baths on a Saturday morning from Dollar, I remember sitting on the top deck of a double-decker and just being able to look over the edge of the canyon of snow. What skating we seemed to have then! They did not salt the roads in those days, and it packed down so hard that I actually skated down for the rolls and papers before breakfast: *down* was the operative word, and a right pech it was back *up* the Muckhart Road home!

Perhaps the most enjoyable skating I have ever had was one winter on Rannoch Moor. We were staying at Blackrock, the Ladies Scottish Climbing Club Hut on the edge of the moor, and three of us had optimistically brought skates. Our faith was rewarded with a deep freeze, followed by a sprinkling of snow. Through this powder we scored our fancy patterns against a superb background of the hills of Coire Ba. That night the storms came lashing back and the ice vanished under drifts. We packed up and went home.

In 1978 it was not as simple as that. Whole areas were cut off for days. When even trains cannot make it you know it is bad. I was in Speyside—and there I had to stay. The week of blockage and tragedy was the result of a 24-hour blizzard; seldom can such chaos have come from so seemingly short a storm.

I had had a dress rehearsal just ten days previously. Coming back from the Northwest after five weeks of mountaineering activities over Christmas and Hogmanay, I was still managing day after day on the hill—hard work, as the snow was deep and powdery. When I left Loch Duich the roads north of there were blocked. I left Glen Garry with the hill road closing behind me, Glenfinnan was feet deep in snow, but at Glencoe the barriers were up. Superb day as it was at sea level, a wind had sprung up and the moor was blasted in drift. An articulated lorry jack-knifed, blocking the road for fifty cars which the snow soon engulfed.

I spent the night in my dormobile at Carnoch—snug enough, though icicles dangled from bumpers and mirrors. Work went on through the night, and by next afternoon it was just possible to squeeze through. Though only wanting to go to Bridge of Orchy, I drove on to Crianlarich in order to take photographs of the white-washed hills. Two days later you would hardly have known it had snowed, so sudden was the thaw.

Then, in January, I drove north one Friday morning. The road was fine, though in Drumochter a wind was sending the drift driving along the new A9. After a few calls I went to Glenmore Lodge to visit friends. The forecast was pretty wild, so I needed little persuasion to stay. However, Saturday morning was promised fair and as the ski road was open and I had a 10 a.m. rendezvous to teach a ski class, I went up. None of my class turned up, so I bought a day ticket and made the most of it. Slopes were quieter than usual as the A9 had been blocked. My clients had had car trouble and only reached Grantown at 3 a.m. And Grantown was to be cut off completely for many days.

I had a good day's ski-ing, but after lunch I went down to the dormobile to change into ski-climbing rig. It had been snowing for hours, and cars all carried roof blankets of white. In the Scottish Ski Club Hut I met the Langmuir family: Eric was for many years Principal at Glenmore Lodge. At the last tow my ticket was punched by Molly Porter, leader of the local mountain rescue team. We were all glad the weather had not deteriorated as expected.

18   The Buachaille

With skins I was able to ski straight up through the glare to the top of Cairngorm. Ski-touring is enjoying something of a vogue just now, but is rather a misleading term as there are two very different ways of touring.

The Scandinavian *langlauf* uses long, thin, light skis and soft, light boots, the uphill grip being provided by waxes applied to the soles of the ski. The other system uses more normal skis and boots, but with adjustable bindings allowing heel-lift. Artificial skin is attached to the soles (or even special crampons if icy) and this grips the snow. There is something odd in seeing either system at work—people calmly going *up* slopes which normal skis could not manage.

The Scandinavian system is having a boom just now but, as the tops are often too wild or icy, the slopes too steep and the valleys too snowless, it is not really suitable for Scotland, though you do have the occasional memorable day. Skis and skins are used much more in the Alps and elsewhere when the object is to climb mountains in winter. As our Scottish winters are unreliable, this, too, is only rewarding sporadically.

Like piste ski-ing ('penguining' to tourers) when Scotland 'gives it good', it is very, very good, but we have to wait and work for it. Too often we have to put up with days of steady snow and visibility almost down to zero.

In the lee of the weather station I took off my skins, adjusted the settings, and crept down again. The only thing visible was the faint shadow line of my own up-track and it was rapidly vanishing in drift. The wind was rising. Perhaps the storm was coming after all.

Back at the car I toasted cheese sandwiches and drank coffee till the general exodus was over, and then went in to Aviemore. I left there at 5 p.m. It was snowing and there was a bit of wind. By Newtonmore I was thankful to stop. In that brief run the full fury had been unleashed and I'd had my share of excitement. Near Kincraig a car ahead of me suddenly went careering up the bank and then fell on its side. I pulled in beyond him, set the emergency flashers going, then raced back to see if anyone was hurt. The sole occupant climbed out of a door which had become a hatch, shaken but unhurt. Others joined in, and we bounced the car out and on to its wheels again. As I was blocking the way, I had to drive on. It took ten minutes in the warm car to stop my shivering, for I had gone out without a windproof.

At times the drift was swirling up so that visibility went completely. I don't think I have ever seen such wildness. It was tempting just to pull into a layby and sit it out. After all, I was in a well-stocked dormobile. But I had promised to look in on a friend at Newtonmore. I pushed on slowly, groping through the flying clouds of snow or battering into drifts already laid across the road. Just before Newtonmore a car coming the other way began to waltz all over the road and went skidding past, missing me by a hair's breadth. I drove down to the station and parked where I was near my friend's house, but out of the way of snow-ploughs operating.

My friend Dave Morris was not in. He worked for the Nature Conservancy Council, and I knew he had been to Deeside for a meeting, so I was not surprised. At ten o'clock I had just turned off the Tilley in the van, when he knocked me up. He had got through, but his car was stuck just a quarter of a mile outside Newtonmore. Few other people were to arrive anywhere that night. Dave had just gone in when the police called him out to try to go through to Laggan; a climber was missing on Creag

Meagaidh. They tried, but even Land-Rovers could not make it far out of the village. The climber had been left in a bivvy by his companions when he became exhausted and nobody gave much chance for his survival.

Dave Gowans battered down in his Land-Rover at midday on the Sunday and we all went up to the village. Hardly a soul was to be seen. When a friend opened his door, only his head could be seen over the drifts. A fine fin of snow neatly concealed a car. The trees beyond the village were snapping under the grasping weight of snow. Dick Balharry joined us and we walked along a wall and over bare fields rather than the high, deep drifts of road. Cows came bellowing up to us hopefully. A lorry was snow to its roof, the policeman's car next to it was half-covered, and beyond, where we knew there was a break-down vehicle, a road works pick-up and Dave's car, not a thing was to be seen.

We poked with broom handles and could not even hit a roof. The brooms were left marking the likely spot, and Dave returned home to dream of the big blower ploughing into his car and flinging it like confetti into the field. The storm died down, the 24-hour blast leaving incredible chaos in its wake. It took weeks in the end to return to normal. We all sat glued to the radio.

Speyside was cut off: Newtonmore, Kingussie, Aviemore, Grantown—there was no link between them. To the north, Caithness and Sutherland had been overwhelmed, a bus was missing on the Ullapool road, Glen Shiel was impassable, Glencoe blocked— yet when I rang home I was told Fife was snowless. It was fortunate the storm came on the Saturday night: Friday night or Sunday night would have seen thousands of skiers on the roads and one shudders at the possible consequences. The toll of life was to be surprisingly small.

Monday morning was clear and still. I fished out my *langlauf* skis and with a shovel set off ahead of Dave to where his car lay buried. There was a digger already biting its was forward—carving out a twelve-foot canyon. People had just located Dave's car under the broom markers. I threw my spade over and it was grabbed and used by a relay of willing workers. I spent a few minutes taking pictures. Several children went by, pulling bakers' trays of bread and pies as if they were toboggans. Helicopters passed frequently on their vital missions, perhaps the greatest boon of all—there had been little such quick help in 1947. At one stage I had car, digger, the Chief Constable's helicopter and the first train to win through Drumochter all in my view finder—only to run out of film.

The Chief Constable, Mr Donald Henderson, had landed by helicopter to check on the activity. He was relieved to be assured that no people were in the buried cars. The train was a welcome sight, opening up at least one exit route from Speyside. Farther north the radio had announced the odd fact that a train had 'gone missing'—vanished, as if someone had slipped it in their pocket and walked off. It had hit drifts and been derailed many miles from any road, and a relief train suffered the same fate. In the end helicopters air-lifted seventy people from it.

The canyon was cut through to Dave's car and the one beside it, and after a bit of digging round they were pulled out like a couple of loose teeth. Inside, the engine was filled with snow, yet it still went. By evening Newtonmore and Kingussie were linked.

The bad news began to come through; rescue parties were finding bodies in cars. But there were odd miracles. The climber on Creag Meagaidh was found alive after his night under the snow.

Tuesday saw the exodus begin. People from Newtonmore were taking the train north to Aviemore in order to ensure a seat south to Perth. The Slochd was still blocked so Aviemore was the temporary beginning of the line.

A busload had made it to Aultguish Inn, whose walls bear pictures of past storms, which must have been much commented on by the refugees. Slowly this and that road was opened. The helicopters still flew—long into the night, dropping food and medicine, lifting a heart case from a distant glen. Dave drove to Aviemore and found more helicopters than cars in its main street.

One tall tale was going the rounds. A helicopter had spied a puff of smoke coming from a big drift and investigation revealed a house, completely overwhelmed. They dug away and were eventually able to bellow down the chimney. A voice from inside replied, 'Who is that outside?' The rescuers shouted back 'This is the Red Cross' only to hear, 'Ach, go away. We gave last week.'

On Tuesday night the last known missing person was found. Willie Sutherland, in his sixties, had spent eighty hours under the snow yet was able to *walk* into hospital: a fine case of morale seeing a man through. To keep warm he wrapped himself in women's tights (he was a sales rep. with boxes of tights in the car). A wedding reception near Inverness went on into the fifth day as Wednesday dawned. No doubt a merry time was had by all.

The radio said there was little chance of the A9 opening before Friday so, having a meeting at home that day, I joined the exodus by train. Four engines pulled the *Clansman* and one passenger commented that, on the Slochd, the drifts had been as high as the train. The only break in the white scene was the colourful clutch of blowers and ploughs at work on the A9. Deer floundered across the slopes and sheep stood forlornly in the corners. There must have been a heavy toll of wildlife.

Some good came out of the disastrous spell of blizzards. People helped and worked for each other in a way that seldom happens normally—and there is the residual awareness of just what can happen. Motorists and lonely households will have a greater respect for winter when they remember the blizzard of '78, just as we old stagers have always remembered the winter of '47.

Behind the Ranges

A glimpse at the map to find some of Scotland's really remote Munros would lead the searcher to some splendid 'wilderness areas': rugged, isolated and often exceptionally beautiful.

By *really remote* I mean areas which are perhaps climbed with a night or two away from roads and civilisation. Any and every Munro could be done and back in a day; but there are some defended by terrain and time, which would make this more of an endurance test than a pleasure. This is the criterion then.

My glimpse at the map brings to memory the head of Glen Affric, the 'Rough Bounds' of Knoydart, Ben Alder, parts of the Cairngorms and three groups in the North West: Seana Bhraigh, A 'Mhaighdean and Lurg Mhor—a golden triptych.

Seana Bhraigh, to begin. Impecunious student days saw us first exploring this direction. Malcolm and I were based on a tent by Loch Droma between the Fannichs and the Beinn Dearg hills, over the dam from the road which runs across westwards to Ullapool—or past An Teallach of the sunset spires. We used cycles, ranging widely east and west. But as our time ran on, Seana Bhraigh still remained unreached. It took nineteen miles of cycling and eighteen on foot to secure it.

It is hidden away behind the Beinn Dearg hills which are rocky and steep and grand themselves. It is surrounded by great expanses of wild country with no public roads. From Strathoykell or Ullapool it would be a marathon. So we tried a left-flanking approach from Inverlael, setting out at 1 p.m., happy in the long summer light.

There are paths on the OS map and these existed, leading us along a string of lochans up to the empty heights, a convulsed landscape, deep-bitten by corries. The deer seemed quite unafraid. Another Munro, Eididh nan Clach Geala, lies to the south and was added on the way back. We ran down the Lael in the gloaming and at a farm stopped for long glasses of milk (at fourpence a pint). How we slept that night!

Recently I've returned there again in successive June visits: halcyon days. Endless sunshine and stars at night; camping on the Diridh Mor with gentle strokes of wind over the back of Scotland to keep the midges away.

We were a large party, up to Coire Grannda first, the secret loch in the heart of the Beinn Dearg desert. The spectacular twins of Cona Mheall and Beinn Dearg followed. A good day already, but, still miles away north lay the Eididh—and Seana Bhraigh. The more staid remained and the keener went on. We all met, several weary hours later, having 'done' Seana Bhraigh, and traversed the outlier Faochagach back to camp. Some skirted it down a flanking valley of four lochs but those who kept high over the gentle hill, which echoed with endless plaintive golden plovers, were back at camp first. 'The quick and the dead.' Half an hour later a thunderstorm raced the others home. The storm won.

The following June a similar round proved finer; some friends and I, with a dog, went over Faochagach in the evening and simply slept out right in the middle of this wilderness. We woke at four with deer about us and the palest dawn colours on Cona Mheall's rocky flanks.

Again, some went down the valley of the lochs with the bivouac gear while we went on, skirting in early day out to the far country, pilgrims almost to a promised land.

'Something lost behind the Ranges. Lost and waiting for you. Go! . . . Anybody might have found it, but—His Whisper came to Me!'

These odd words which I could not then trace (they are Kipling; *The Explorer*) kept going through my mind. Pictures of perfection that day—the dog dancing through blowing bog cotton puffs—a figure perched high above the precipices of the Luchd Choire, haloed with light above the blue depths—a lingering lunch by the cairn with the peaks right up to Sutherland in view—a tingling dip in a high pool with a plover calling its woes around—a thunder of hooves on dried peat bog as a hundred head of deer stormed past—the wheeling motion of a wing-set eagle. . . .

Is there anything to beat Scotland's soft and secret pageant? Alps? Andes? Antarctica? I doubt it. Subtle it is, the combination of all the senses, sharp in sun or snow, pulsing with life. It was good to be young on Seana Bhraigh.

A 'Mhaighdean, next. This might be the loneliest of all, unpronounceable to the ignorant—'Armageddon', we lazily used to call it. The traveller along the Diridh Mor looks into the sunset over the rugged crests of An Teallach. The road onto An Teallach is 'Destitution Road', built to give labour during one of the potato famines of last century. Between this road and the one which skirts the two-toned Torridon landscape by Loch Maree lies another great mountain fastness—perhaps the very greatest of our 'wilderness areas'.

'Deadly is the danger of destruction of all that makes dreaming possible.' It could be so easily lost, as has been so much of our irreplaceable highland scenery. For this is pre-eminently country to set one dreaming. In the north An Teallach is undisputedly one of the top ten peaks in the British Isles, while across from it is Beinn Dearg Mhor, hardly less spectacular. The south is hidden by Slioch and the gneiss ridges above Loch Maree. West lies a wilderness leading to the sea. East is the Coire Mhic Fhearchair group. In the centre stands A' Mhaighdean, *the Maiden*, crag-skirted and her back to the wild west.

Several visits into this maze of mountains have brought little familiarity. Lochs and peaks lie in a crazy pattern, a complex landscape of rock and water.

A' Mhaighdean gave me one of the longest solitary days I have ever experienced. A few of us were climbing in the Torridons over the Hogmanay holiday. One evening I was given a lift up the rough road to the now deserted Heights of Kinlochhewe where I managed to howff it in a stable for the cold winter night. A long time before day I had followed the path up to Loch Fada. Grey darkness changed for grey light.,

It is unhurrying landscape which never knew straight travelling—yet I romped along, for the loch was frozen into a grand highway. I saw no deer, no life at all, strangely. From the east the mountain presents no difficulty but arrival on the summit brings surprises: the other side falls sheer to the Fionn Loch, crag-girt and stupendous.

An empty landscape; for the last house now stands empty by its shores. No warm blood is left to drain from this dead world. Just the occasional fisherman or stalker or climber enters quietly, has his day and departs whence he came.

> Here have been only nights and days,
> Sun and clouds sailing,
> Moon and stars that went their ways
> And the dusk's soft veiling.
> Nothing has changed since time began
> But the slow ebb of the seasons.
> Go your ways, you questing men;
> Life has no need of reasons.
>
> (Douglas Fraser)

It was a long trek home down to Loch Maree and down the Glen Torridon road to the Ling Hut. Fitting to be among some of the oldest rocks in the world, chilled by the sneaking winter wind and humbled by a day that left tracks on more than just those pristine miles. I'm sure my memories are those of thousands of others: the memories that are all about us on our paths of days. It can be a sharp painful joy, this remembering. The land has been kind to us in storm and sun, comforting, aye restoring something lost in the bustle of life. It was good to be alone on A' Mhaighdean.

And now for Lurg Mhor. When Philip Tranter and his party were climbing in the Hindu Kush they named one of their new summits 'Sheasgaich' after one of our remote peaks. If any be hidden behind the ranges it is Bidein a' Choire Sheasgaich and her other half, Lurg Mhor. Many people who might know A' Mhaighdean or even Seana Bhraigh are at a loss to place this pair. A' Mhaighdean is centred in an area where walkers and climber are likely to camp and traverse for days on end, Seana Bhraigh is reached over singing heights, Bidein a' Choire Sheasgaich and Lurg Mhor have defences almost reminiscent of the Hindu Kush. There is no close accommodation, the way in is long and hard. The long shank of Lurg Mhor and the soaring cone of the other are apt to be late for one's visiting.

You set off from Strathcarron, an hour up through tall pine forests, delicious with dawn scents, you walk a further hour up the trench of glen above before crossing the pebbly burn to take a side valley with a stalkers' path up to a triple col, another hour of climbing steadily. Ahead lies a Corbett, Beinn Tarsuinn, 'twisted or cross peak'. (Any Tarsuinn is enough to make anyone cross, always getting in the way—have you noticed?) It is a hog's back which has to be climbed, traversed and descended on the other side, another couple of hours perhaps. Five hours out you are at the foot of Bidein a' Choire Sheasgaich—and *beyond it* is Lurg Mhor! Mercifully they are a splendid pair, even if a twelve-hour round is common enough, for you will linger often.

Again my memories are in triplicate; the first a solo winter visit hitching from Fife over a weekend—not planned but when lifts come, well, you take the chance. Best perhaps was a school trip: a gang of old friends, and enthusiastic youngsters.

> We ask no blessing of wealth nor any boon
>   save one—and one—
> The heart of the boy and health
>   with freedom to enjoy
> The precious things brought forth by the sun
> And the precious things thrust forth by the moon,
> Earth's fulness and the chill of snow-fed fountains
>   The rustling of wings
>   And our men's wills;
> The chief things of the ancient mountains
> And the precious things of the lasting hills.

Men's wills we were to need that long day.

It followed, by a day, the steps of a 'grand old master'. We were staying at Achnashellach Hostel and so were J H B Bell and his wife, Pat. The youngest of the party, a boy who had recently eyed Bell routes on Nevis commented, 'But he's History!'

We were three generations then, all with that freedom to enjoy. Precious indeed. It had been a long day for the doyen of Scottish climbing, it was a long day for all; but it could not have been long enough. . . . (Just out is a re-issue of the Scottish chapters of J H B Bell's classic book *A Progress in Mountaineering*.)

We were up at 5.30 to a big moon-cold clearness, tramped the miles through forest and strath and glen to the triple col with its multitude of frogs. Beinn Tarsuinn was clear, so Stuart and I, who had been before, could actually see the bulky symmetry of Bidein a' Choire Sheasgaich at last. We rock-scrambled up it, every man on his line of choosing. The dog romped among the scattering ptarmigan chicks while the mother flapped about his head. We ran to the col and up Lurg Mhor. Our shouts echoed along the craggy corrie, so the hot deer cantered away from the clinging snow patches. Here was a soft grassy summit with all the blue remembered hills about us. There are days lost behind the ranges like this where one feels tireless and timeless. Perhaps it was sunstroke!

We romped down off that furthest summit to Loch Morar to see the garrons. It was a long sticky pull up to the col so before the forest there was a great welcoming pool of yellow water for the end o' day dook. But the memory that lingers most is of young Alan, last down off Lurg Mhor, appearing with a dappled deer-calf at his heels. It would not leave us, that fragile thing thrust forth by the sun; Alan had to carry it off the crags to the grassy flanks. Still it held by us, in strange encounter with its chiefest predator.

The spell had to break, the meet scattered, but through all the fulness of that June day, every movement, every laugh, every song cried that it was good to be alive on Lurg Mhor, good to be behind the ranges on their sunny ways.

Jubilee Jaunt

I have lost count of how many times I have walked across Scotland but the Jubilee Juant coast-to-coast was one of the more unforgettable, both for its own incredible conditions (never matched since) and for being one of the major inspirations behind the annual coast-to-coast event, The Ultimate Challenge, soon to celebrate its first ten years of existence. A walk of this nature is quite extraordinarily rewarding. A whole variety of such treks are described in my previous book of collected articles, Travels (Scotsman/ G R F Sutherland) *and* The Great Outdoors *magazine each November carries accounts of that year's event and gives details of the next year's plans. Have a go sometime!*

As the walk was intended to finish the day before the Queen's Jubilee this code-name presented itself unimaginatively. I don't know what it did in your part of the world but from my Kinghorn home we looked over a rain-lashed Forth to the pathetic bonfire flicker on Arthur's Seat. Scotland's Jubilee was notoriously wet and there was much cheating to ensure the continuity of bonfires over bleak mountain tops. Our Jubilee Jaunt though was sunshine all the way—a real heatwave horror.

Ray wanted to do a coast-to-coast trip, I was very interested in a west-to-east Munro walk, so we combined forces to do both. Sgurr na Banachdich is Scotland's westmost Munro and Mount Keen is the most easterly. I had already tramped from Keen to Banachdich and also from Ben More of Mull to Keen, so this was a chance for further variety.

Ray lives in Cleethorpes on Humberside where a hundred-foot contour is called a hill. It is a resort of candyfloss and cars, donkey rides, pollution—and teeming people. Anything or anywhere more in contrast to the Rough Bounds of Knoydart would be hard to imagine. The dates of our hike, come to think of it, were determined by the days of sailings into Knoydart. No Humber Bridge there; just three boats a week.

Back-tracking from a sailing time gave us the starting date of 22 May in Glenbrittle. We took two days motoring up for we had to check various places for accommodation and leave parcels of food, fuel, film, maps and other necessities—or luxuries. The night before was spent at the Glenbrittle Camp Site where the friendly warden looked after my dormobile once we had left. There was still a great deal of snow filling the corrie headwalls and it was strange to sprawl in the sunny evening and see the returning climbers with ice axes on their rucksacks. As soon as we had set off north the barometer had shot up and, innocents that we were, that was the start of the grilling.

Scotland has a reputation for its somewhat erratic weather, which may or may not be justified, but is an endless topic for conversation among tourist victims. It averages out I suppose—otherwise we would have no tourists at all. As long as half go home saying 'Great weather' and half go home saying 'Rained the whole time' our economy will survive. Of course averages never happen, nor was our trip average. It was an extreme of heat such as I have seldom known.

We were off early, for the Cuillin in full heatwave conditions demand devious dodging. Not only is gabbro a very abrasive rock but it seems to absorb heat and radiate it out like an electric grill. Climbers in these conditions usually return to base 'well-done', their body-juices drained out of them and nose and ears like pork crackling.

We walked in our dreams till Ray realised he was ascending Sgurr Dearg instead of Coire na Banachdich. I sat in the corrie for an hour wondering if he had managed to break a leg. Once he had rejoined me it was a joy to wend up to the Cuillin Ridge at the Bealach na Banachdich. Ray's mind was working away at how to lighten his pack, and for days thereafter he was posting home this and that—or simply abandoning items. Ounces became debating topics. It is surprising what you can do without when you have to carry it, especially over Munros and high passes, and especially when the sun leans on you like a Bunyan's burden.

We outflanked much of the ridge to reach Sgurr na Banachdich, 3167 feet, the westmost Munro. The background was black Black Cuillin, striated with snow and girdled with shimmering heat. Photographically the trip was not a success, for as soon as the sun rose, at four o'clock, it veiled the landscape in stifling haze. By eight o'clock, when urban breakfasts happen, our grill was set at the top heat index—and stayed there till six in the evenings, when it switched off and we continued to bake gently till the night cold came and frosted our cake of contrast. On several occasions I was to wake with hoar frost on my beard.

We know cold all too well. It is much more difficult to describe heat adequately. Ray took five days of it—and then went home looking like an overcooked salmon. Twelve days out I could still go into Mar Lodge, on Deeside, in the afternoon, drink three cokes and seven cups of tea, and not need a pee till bedtime. Two days later, beyond Mount Keen, at five in the evening, the sun actually raised blisters on the back of my knees. Aye, it was 'warm walking,' as a Lochaber shepherd actually admitted.

Without ice axes we had to wriggle our way down off the Cuillin Ridge, keeping to the gaps between rocky walls and the big sweep of snow. After that it was screes and rough stuff and then a delightful dip in a blue pool before Loch Coruisk. The loch was benign, snoozing like an old man on a deckchair, not at all wild as Sir Walter Scott, Horatio McCulloch and others tell us. We walked its length and then round to the stark concrete box of the hut by Loch Scavaig. Day-trippers are apt to head for it in droves under the impression it is a public toilet.

It actually does have a flush toilet, running water, gas cooking, bunk beds and, last line in luxury, the resident English climbers had brought in a barrel of beer. Providence and profanity are close cousins. Such things in one of the most remote corners of Scotland could be regarded cynically but on that day beer on tap was not to be spurned on any grounds. Pity it was not Campbeltown Loch as well.

The next day we crossed 'the Bad Step' and followed the switchback path round to Camusunary Bay where Blaven sliced up into the blue. As it was a favourite hill I suggested doing it from the col to its south, up the Abhainn nan Leac, a stream full of sculptured pools. Ray, not being a peak-bagger, decided to go round so faced the rough track and then road miles. We made a rendezvous where the burn off Blaven reached Loch Slapin. Blaven was magnificent with a view of islands—and Highlands—hard to equal. I had taken a swim going up and dithered on top so ended having to romp down the miles to keep the appointment. I made it with several minutes in hand. An hour later there was still no Ray. I went on and sat at the head of the Loch. He could not pass me unnoticed. He came eventually, having tired of sitting by a burn flowing into Loch Slapin—two hundred yards along from the correct burn.

We walked on through sleepy Torrin and up the long glen to Broadford. A quick cup of tea with Bill Wallace, the welcoming Warden at the Youth Hostel, showers ('we are going soft' I thought) and then we went along to the hotel for dinner. Broadford Hotel is a friendly place and the food good. We made the most of it.

The next day was a killer. To avoid some of the tarred road we went over the hills and moors to the Sound of Sleat. I have a memory of us lying by a red, stone-lined pool in the middle of nowhere, Blaven a tooth in the blue, and not a murmur beyond the scurry of mice and the distant bleat of a lamb. Moment of bliss, followed by miles of dour road-bashing. Ben Sgriol, king of the little hills, hunched into the sky across the Sound. We took our thirsts down to Isle Ornsay and competed with the Navy in quenching them till the offshore frigate hooted and they departed. So did we. Those hot miles. Only once did we find a shop. As I left it I overhead Ray *beginning* his order with 'Three ice creams please, and . . . .'

The southern end of this peninsula is well wooded and lush. We saw the ferry come in from Mallaig and half thought to catch it there and then. Later, we were glad we had not done so for the Ardvarsar Hotel would have been missed. If the night before I had relished a shower, this time I lay in a deep bath, with a pot of tea beside me. A full-length mirror revealed a two-tone creature: very pale in the trunk and distinctly red at the extremities.

We sailed early to Mallaig, did a big shopping and at noon were off on the estate boat to Inverie of Knoydart where we had arranged to stay at the workers' hostel. Ray made the mistake of lying in the sun during the afternoon. The next morning, over breakfast at five, he admitted the sun was too much. Rather despairing we agreed to give it that day to cool, or he would go home. I took off for the tops but there was no breeze even there and a lochan at 2000 feet could only produce warm water. It was so obviously set fair that delay was pointless. Ray told me to go on so, after a big meal, I did so. He walked up the glen with me till I branched off for the Mam Meadail. It must have been disappointing for him but as the next few days led through wild, quite uninhabited country, the decision was a wise one. The heatwave continued.

I just made the pass in daylight but it hardly becomes really dark at the end of May and there was a moon to see me down the zig-zags to Carnoch and the curlew-crying sands of Loch Nevis. The Carnoch River can be desperate in spate (it and the Allt Coire na Ciche are now bridged) but this time it was just boulder-hopping. At midnight, still in shorts and shirt only, still dripping with sweat, I arrived at Sourlies.

A month before Sourlies had been some broken and overgrown walls. I'd pulled out rubbish from inside, then dug till I broke the spade handle, then collected stones and stripped moss off the interior walls—a very minor help to reconstruction. Now it was a neat, snug wee bothy, thanks to the Mountain Bothies Association, who had had a work-party there for a busy week not long after.

The estate landing craft helped take in materials for the head of the loch is too shallow for normal boats. There are so many pathetic piles of stones in the remote glens that it was almost cheering to tears to see one restored. I had a brew. The bed shelf smelt of freshly worked pinewood.

Hotels and hostels are fine but they are not conducive to early starts. I left Sourlies at five, for the path up to the Mam na Cloich Airde, 'as romantic a pass as the Kyber' as I heard one enthusiast call it. The made path twists and turns up to 1000 feet, there are lonely lochans and black crags—and suddenly the green sweep of Glen Dessarry beyond. It was the sort of place one might expect to meet Alan Breck Stewart and Davey Balfour.

I crossed over to another bothy, A' Chuil, where I met five Carn Dearg Club lads. Breakfast time. They had been wandering about, Munro-bagging, and were all 'weary o' the sun'—a rare complaint. Another pass took me over into Glen Kingie and I went up and down Sgurr Mor before collapsing into the river. The ochrous strath was a nightmare of heat so I lay up in Kinbreak bothy till after five, then ate, and went on down the glen. Even in the drought the river was not easy to cross but a herd of hinds showed me a ford. The empty strath fell behind. I wended up forestry roads through young plantings. Originally Tomdoun Hotel was my aim but it was off the direct line so I kept to the south of it and eventually just slept out in the heather, by Lochan an Staic. It was moon-bright and frosty cold. The hills of Glen Kingie looked remote, as they should, for I had covered 16 miles with 5000 feet of ascent. In the east the regular cone of the Corbett, Ben Tee, called the new day's walk ahead.

I rose amid the bubblings of blackcock at *lek* and descended to the River Garry which was smoking before the fiery sun. For years I had intended following along south of the River Garry—going west to east across the view one has from the hill road over to Glen Shiel—so today had the joys of new ground and an old longing. It was all forestry walking. I broke the back of it early, had a second breakfast, then followed a path up to the peaty col under Ben Tee. This hill is one of the finest Corbetts so just had to be climbed. What a view! From the top I could hear the noise of the repair work on the locks at South Laggan. The thought of the tea room there helped over the dusty miles of moor. A vast pot of tea and home baking was much appreciated. Even inside the building the sweat continued to run down my back. Coming out, I saw a herd of cattle all belly deep in Loch Lochy. I joined them.

The Frasers welcomed me at the Youth Hostel and between their store and the parcel we'd left I made a real pig of myself. Two female hitch-hikers sat goggle-eyed watching me eat. I only had tea; a tin of gooseberries, five fish fingers; a steak and kidney pudding with a tin of mixed vegetables, beans, fresh carrots and potatoes; peaches and cream; coffee; cheese and biscuits. When I looked at their egg and beans one of them actually put her arm round her plate. . . .

I had reached the Great Glen. The western wastes had gone easily enough apart from the heat. When I set out on the next part (to the A9 at Dalwhinnie), the sky was overcast but by afternoon had reverted to blazing sunshine again. I ran several planned days together to reach Dalwhinnie in two days. Leaving the Great Glen I headed up its wooded eastern slopes to cross bleak bogland and drop down to the head of Glen Roy of Parallel Roads fame. As it was only noon, instead of a bothy night there I traversed Beinn a' Chaorainn to Loch Laggan side. This Munro has been creating fun as the new surveys shifted the actual summit from one bump to another. Several new Munros and plenty of Corbetts have actually been created by the Ordnance Survey in the last few years; a comment on past mapping deficiencies rather then the actual growth of certain hills.

We had left a parcel hidden among the bracken so I soon had a good meal inside me. Again, I just slept out, and again had a clear, cold night, waking to the spraying of hoar frost onto my face as a curious coal tit swung on the birch scrub above me. I had only just set off when I ran into another blackcock *lek*. Curious coincidences of my bivouacs. The rewards of early starting.

I took the stalking path up to the col between Beinn a' Chlachair and Geal Charn. A solitary tent stood on it with a view over Laggan side to my snowy peak of yesterday. The burns were actually frosted or frozen as I cut round by the path skirting Geal Charn. Beyond I traversed slippery hillside to the col east of Geal Charn. Having virtually circumnavigated this hill I then went up and down it, carefully dodging snow flanks. When I crashed into Blackburn of Pattack bothy for a second breakfast (at nine o'clock) I roused a couple with two children who set about having their first.

A wandering stream took me up onto the southern end of the long ridge of the Fara whence I looked over to Ben Alder, Creag Meaghaidh, the Monadh Liaths and the hills of the A9. The hot miles of walking along the Fara almost overpowered me. It was stupefyingly hot. I found a burn, had a drink—and woke up an hour later!

I charged down from the massive cairn through a great herd of stags into Dalwhinnie. The Grampian Hotel gave a friendly reception, but with a name like Mrs Kettle for hostess, this was to be expected surely. In the morning I left a parcel of maps I'd walked-off, film, excess clothes and so on. I also abandoned sleeping bag, stove and heavy foods. That night I was aiming for a bothy and thereafter would be in proper accommodation. The bothy area could provide dry heather, Scots pine, or juniper for burning, each with its own distinctive scent, so the stove was a luxury. I decided I could survive one night without a sleeping bag. It was a case of survival too, for it froze hard and wearing clothes alone and inside the rucksack was hardly adequate. Besides, at the head of Glen Feshie I was over 1000 feet up. Nearby once stood a bothy made famous by Landseer who used it as a studio and left a painting of a stag on its wall. When I threw some paraffin on the wood to start cooking several stags outside the window reared up in fright at the sudden flames.

A devious route from Dalwhinnie over Meall Chuaich and the passes of Gaick and

Minigaig had led me through a slot of a pass to upper Glen Feshie, a delectable spot, despite being raped by an ill-placed bulldozed track. Beyond that however was all greens and browns of delight: the pines and young birch catching the dawn sun, brilliant, feathery greens against the rolling brown hills of heather. Barren Cuillin, the empty sweep out of Knoydart, the trees of Glen Garry, the grassy hills south of Laggan, now this—what a land of contrasts.

The Munro-bagger in me came out and from the Falls of Eidart I wended off into the Cairngorms over Beinn Bhrotain, Monadh Mor and Carn Cloich Mhuillin before descending to the River Dee. The last was a hill Munro himself was keeping to the end of *his* Munro-bagging but he was baulked by the Innaccessible Pinnacle and, ironically, Carn Cloich Mhuillin has been pruned from the Tables.

At the Chest of Dee I had a glorious swim in the large granite pools, then came out and dried in the sun while a fire of heather stalks produced the blessed brew. At White Bridge a foundered school party was lying on the grass—perhaps '*frying*' might be a better description. At the bothy I had picked up a copy of the biography of Richard Dimbleby and this book became my escape from the long, hard eleven miles to Braemar. I simply read all the way, delving into the book and cutting out the cruel hot world through which I walked. At the Linn o' Dee and certain other favourite spots I did surface again to enjoy the beauty. Reading of Auschwitz and Belsen, then looking along the glorious reaches of Mar had an unsettling effect. I was offered a lift and felt slightly crazy refusing—but it would have taken too many weary words to explain why I had to hoof it to Braemar. Twenty-five miles made this the longest leg.

Possibly due to the sun, or overeating, or both the next day felt a bit of a toil and was not enjoyed as it might have been—so I largely read the miles away again: through Glen Callater, along the loch and up Jock's Road. Instead of following this down to Glen Doll direct I took to the moors, as I had done a few years previously when doing all the Munros in a single trip, over Tolmount, Tom Buidhe Dreish and Mayar, an odd assortment of names. On the way I passed Finalty Hill and eventually descended into Glen Doll down the Shank of Drumfollow.

Dried-out peat bogs were teeming with deer. Their hoof-beating as they passed made just the same noise as herds of game on the plains of Africa. A dunlin sliced off from my feet and then stood watching anxiously. Very gingerly I moved about—and was lucky enough to spot its partner sitting tight on the nest. It is tiny incidetns like this that are never forgotten; they are the brush stroke kisses of children in the adult sweep of hills. I sang down into the green jungle of Glen Doll, leaving the empty heights, and the view, far off still, of Mount Keen. Perhaps there would be an ending after all.

After the Glen Feshie–Braemar crossing the next was to be my longest day—and a harder one as it had little in the way of beaten track. What there was came at the start; the brutal ascent of the Capel Mounth, the old drovers' route to Glen Muick and Ballater. As a youngster it had been one of my first hill crossings and Lochnagar one of my first hills. East of this pass lies one of the largest areas of peat bog landscape in Britain, as I knew from battling over it once before to Mount Keen. I started off from the same high corner but cut over to join the Water of Mark near its source. I nearly jumped onto a fox which was sleeping in the shadow of a peat bog. It fled and ran right into a herd of deer, which charged off, in turn setting up a great complaint of grouse. . . .

The winding Mark cuts deep into the hills—a whole area of peat domes, river-captures, meanders, waterfalls and quiet splendour. It deserves to be better known but then, there are no Munros in it—Mount Keen apart—and ninety-nine out of a hundred climb that hill by the same route. (Queen Victoria was one of the ninety-nine.) I followed the river, as bends or not, the going is quicker than the watershed above. After a swim and 'chittery bite' however I had to pull up on to the moors. Mount Keen's cone lay full ahead but my course was that of a ship tacking into the wind. The dry bogs made soft, if devious going. On one occasion I startled two hares; they exploded off round the bog in opposite directions and ran full pelt into each other with a crash that had me wincing.

Just before the final pull up the granite boulders to the trig point there are welcome springs by the old Mounth Road which crosses from Glenesk to Glen Tanar. Due to the proximity of path and hill, Mount Keen has one of the earliest recorded ascents of a British mountain: John Taylor, in 1618, wrote '. . . when I came to the top of it, my teeth began to dance in my head with cold, like virginal's jacks; and withall, a most familiar mist embraced me round . . . so that it did moysten throw all my clothes.'

Time was pressing as I had a bed and breakfast booked at Tarfside so I went on, this time on the watershed, over Braid Cairn and then miles of dried out, clawing, heather moors. The westering sun, far from cooling, seemed to burn like a magnifying glass. It raised blisters on the back of my well-tanned legs. The interminable heather at last died out as I lost height and descended into the lush tunnel of the North Esk Valley; in the no-man's land between fields and moor were the ruins of a considerable settlement: long lines of tumbled walls and guardian rowan trees over which the waups and pied pipers were crying a lament. Nobody I spoke to knew anything of its history, though it could not have been very old. History is what lies beyond grandfather's gossip it seems.

Weeks previously I had telephoned Tarfside Post Office to seek advice about accommodation—and landed lucky. It was all fixed up with the post mistress' sister at what was once the Parsonage, a large house, backing onto a farm, and with the front lawn running down to the 'English' Church. The smell of fields and trees was almost sickly sweet after the acrid moors. The village seemed *en fête*; an old man explained it was the kiddies' Jubilee Day so there was nobody likely to be in at the post office. While talking everyone seemed to come out from a hall and I was pounced on by a lady who turned out to be my hostess; 'Ach you looked like a walking person' no doubt politely covered my worn attire among all their Sunday best.

Mrs Guthrie knew how to look after a walking person anyway—a comment hundreds of Ultimate Challengers were to echo in the following decade. A cup of tea restored and after a bath I had a supper I will long remember: a fine salad and endless piles of home baking. The milk was yellow with cream. I thought of Ray and Cleethorpes, then revelled in the contrasts, the glorious contrasts—like the owl hooting while I stretched between clean sheets. How many nights ago had I shivered on the boards at Ruighaiteachain with the stags peering in at the window? The western seaboard seemed aeons of time and experience away. It was almost over now: Banachdich to Keen was done, all that remained was the walk to the eastern sea. The common denominator, all through, had been the beating of the sun. I put cream on my blisters, and slept.

It was tempting just to bomb down the road to Edzell and on to the sea but tarred roads make unfriendly feet and I was walking a mountain way after all. The Retreat, two miles down from Tarfside, is an outstanding folk museum but was shut when I passed so, having missed that, I crossed a swaying footbridge and wandered up onto the Hill of Wirren: a sort of ambulatory coda to my long symphony. It is only 2274 feet but being on the edge of the big hills had an extensive view: Clachnaben (to the north east) running west to Mount Battock, Mount Keen, Lochnagar and all the Grampian jumble. To the south I could see the Lomonds of Fife, my home hills, and Arthur's Seat where in two days the Jubilee bonfire would blaze. And I could see the sea.

Again it was tempting to hurry off. With exaggerated slowness, I threaded the last of peat moors to the summit. For the first time in the trip I actually used my compass. So dome-shaped is the top that I could not see the arm of the descending bump which was my way off—so I had to start on a bearing till it came in view. The dome is supported by many buttressing ridges so accuracy mattered—error would be measured in miles once down a wrong ridge.

I came down into a rich agricultural landscape which smelt of honey and was loud with bird song. Edzell Castle had to be explored: a proud, pink pile with a secret garden. Edzell itself was noisy too as a clay pigeon shoot seemed to be part of its celebrations. I chose an hotel and luxuriated lazily. (Tea in the lounge with a test match on the TV.) The overdressed manager asked me if I did not have anything to wear on my feet. I was padding about in stocking soles rather than my big boots. My brief 'No' rather ended the conversation. The place was all right, the food fine, but it lacked the feel of hills and the hospitality of hill folk.

The next morning I walked the 11 miles into Montrose, striding before a cloud-piling wind down to a near-empty beach. The Scurdie Ness lighthouse seemed a symbol of finality. I let the waves wash over my toes, then wended back, past kids flying kites, to the station—and caught a train home to Fife. There could hardly be a less dramatic ending.

The next night we sat before the TV as the bonfires spread out over the country. Taking our cue from the box we looked over the Forth to Edinburgh. The rain rattled on the glass, the roar of the sea came from below the house. It was then, suddenly, that I felt the Jubilee Jaunt was really over.

Sourlies Bothy

I need not go out to view the sweep
Of Nevis waters placid in the moon;
The glow of light comes through the roof,
Exploring through the room.
Wild pied-pipers call while dashing past
Beyond the thrift clumps in the tide-edged grass.
I lie awake—in eiderdown—
Contents to let time pass
For it is as real, awake, inside
The stoney, breathing, mousey bothy walls
As I were out upon the beach.
—Thus deep the mountain calls.

19   The head of Loch Nevis near Sourlies Bothy.

III   Western Wanderings

'Flirt with the West but marry the East' was advice I once heard, and have unconsciously followed, living as I do on the eastern seaboard. This is for bread and butter reasons (and an annual rainfall of under 30 inches) but 'the heart is Highland' and inclines westwards, 'west, where all dreams lie'. The words 'Beyond the Great Glen' can act like itching powder to my imagination, so let us wander awile in that western world, from the edge of Knoydart northwards to Sutherland.

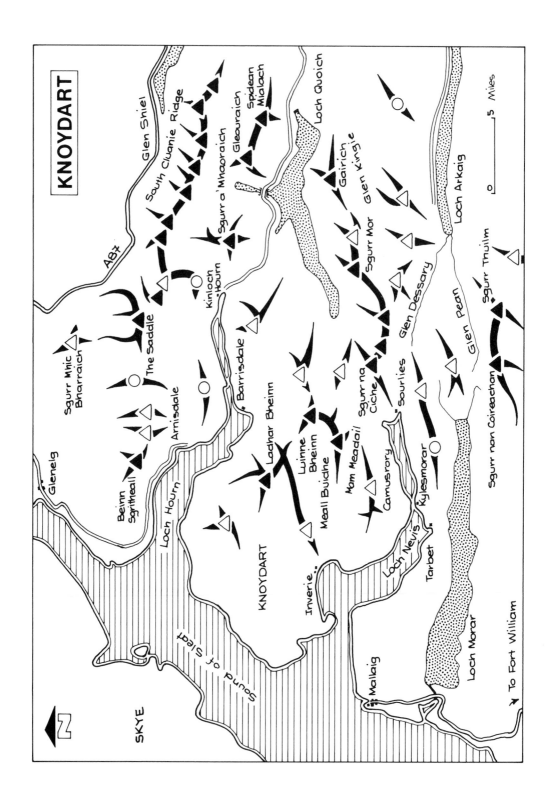

Knoydart: Just Passing Through

Knoydart, being almost an island, sets certain access problems to its own inimitable 'Rough Bounds'. The days of it being 'out-of-bounds' have gone. The estate has changed hands several times; there are now bothies and the dangerous rivers have been bridged. It has lost much in this process, but even though our welfare-state mentality demands things be made easy, safe, convenient, Knoydart's heart stonily disregards human weakness. It is a wild, rough, magnificent country, still yielding its best rewards to those who walk their miles to gain its smiles.

As there is no road in to the peninsula the sea becomes Knoydart's usual access. I have paddled my canoe to it across Loch Hourn several times and also up the far end of Loch Quoich (where a rain guage has the distinction of regularly recording Scotland's highest rainfall). I have landed at Inverie often enough, at Camusrory occasionally and both last year and this at Tarbet on Loch Nevis. Most exciting was a landing on the north shore of this loch when Bruce Watt edged *The Western Isles* towards a crag falling sheer into the sea and I simply stepped off the bow on to the rock before the boat drew back. A nice bit of seamanship.

I never tire of sailing in to Knoydart and then walking out over several days and several peaks and passes. The variations can be endless and can even incorporate a train journey back to Mallaig if a car has been left there. Last year we landed at Tarbet and took the north side of Loch Morar to Glen Pean, reaching the bothy there by moonlight, after midnight. That really is rough, steep country, and in a heatwave it was something of an endurance test. The only variant left seemed to be the south shore of Loch Nevis, and books gave it almost as grim a reputation. This, however, was quite misplaced. It was a grand way in to Knoydart's right ventricle!

There was a lively sea running in from the wrong direction so the boat, despite all the skipper's cunning, rolled violently. We chugged our way up the loch and in to the tight inlet of Tarbet Bay. Three or four buildings, tiny fields and a track wending over the hill—that is Tarbet.

Mr Macdonald, the only resident, greeted us and a flurry of dogs piled into the rowing boat as it grounded. One small mail bag was handed over. From Tarbet's empty church we joined a good path which pulled up to round Druim Chuilinn, the point of the bay. We watched our boat set off for Mallaig down a path of silver glitter. The path then corkscrewed down and along to the flats of Kylesmorar. Just as with

127

20   Hamish and his dog in the hills of Knoydart.

Loch Hourn, Loch Nevis has a very narrow waist. The tide was sweeping out from the inner loch at quite a speed and round the next headland we could look right up the loch to the 'pap' of Sgurr na Ciche (that is the apt Gaelic meaning). It was shrouded in black clouds shot with sun, and rainbows wandered about as brief showers came and went.

We had expected really rough going, but usually there were sheep tracks and obvious lines and it was never necessary to climb high up the hillside. Every small bay seemed to have a ruin overlooking it. Towards the end there seemed to be signs of a path again but the four miles in the middle took over two hours. A friend had walked over the Mam Meadail that morning from Inverie to stay at Sourlies bothy at the head of Loch Nevis so we agreed to join him there. The tide was out so we took to bare feet and walked straight across the sands and enjoyed the cool paddle of the river. I gave a 'yoo-hoo' which set the echoes ringing—but it ensured Ray had the tea ready when we paddled up.

I have mixed feelings about Sourlies. It makes Knoydart possible without a tent now and encourages more visitors. They in turn moaned at the difficult Carnoch river, so it was bridged—by the same people who fought against just such a bridge at Coruisk.

New this time was a sturdy estate bridge over the Allt na Ciche. Ray and I had an argument over that, for he said had it been there my friend Donald would not have drowned in the stream one Hogmanay. The last thing Donald would have wanted would have been a bridge. Knoydart *untamed* was the lure. Now it is demeaned, a lesser place in the scale of superlative landscapes. The safety argument is a fallacious one. Whatever you do there will be someone less able, someone still getting into trouble. The logical end is to bridge every river, blow up every bad step and level all the hills, which is absurd. Why can't we just leave alone? Or accept our limitations? Tread softly in the wild and lonely places?

Ray was just wandering through to Glen Kingie so we reciprocated the tea service and gave him tea in bed the next morning. We were up at 5 a.m. to be off at 6.30, for we planned to climb several hills as well as make it through to Glen Dessary for the night. Ray looked snug as we yawned through breakfast, but we had the last laugh for it was a brammer of a day and the sun shone with punishing power.

It was still quite cold when we set off, with the sky lemon-tinted and a whimper of wind from the pass. We saw a lamb being born into the raw morning.

The Mam na Cloich Airde (*the pass of the stony height*) is one of the finest passes in the west, even if the path on the map may not always be so distinctive on the ground. There is a lot of wending about before the waters of Lochan a' Mhaim appear. Not quite the watershed, but offering a tempting spot to snuggle down for a brew. Blue sky, the cackle of a passing red-throated diver, the first shy butterworts of the season, a refreshing paddle, and lying back with a mug of char—what could be better? Across the loch the whole hillside is a chaos of boulders where a huge cliff must have collapsed long ago in some cataclysmic event. The watershed is not far to the east and is marked by cairns and a gate which stands in solitude with no sign of fence or wall.

We left our rucksacks in a fast place and followed a stream up to the northwest under Garbh Chioch Mhor, from which an easy traverse across the head of Coire na Ciche led to the gully, the Feadan na Ciche (*Ciche's whistle* or *chanter*). The slabs and gravels had plenty of flowers: the last of the purple saxifrage and the first thyme, clubmosses and delicate ladies' alpine mantle. We had a pause at the gap of the col and through it, framed as a picture, was Sgurr Mor, one of the most distant of Munros thanks to Loch Quoich being dammed (at both ends!) and drowning the road and various buildings in its hydro-waters.

Ciche is craggy towards the col and the lie of the land leads to a natural left-flanking line. Lingering snow lay on some of the rakes and the rock gave some fun in the sun. It was a day of crystal sharpness so I kept my eyes down until reaching the summit cairn, then lifted them, fully to enjoy the shock of one of the grandest views in these isles. Sgurr na Ciche is the highest peak in Knoydart (as its several lightning-shattered OS pillars indicate) so the view is a 360° one. As the peak on which I finished my Munros, it has a special place in my affections anyway, and on this day it was at its stunning best.

Garbh Chioch Mhor (*the brig rough breast*) is a lively recent addition to Munro's Tables, having been, somehow, overlooked by Sir Hugh. A steady stream of letters over the years (provocative E W Hodge wrote *every* year) demanded its elevation and eventually it gained its rightful place. With its twin, Garbh Chioch Beag (*the wee rought tit*), this is one of the rockiest, most-contorted traverses outside Skye, a traverse line which is followed by a drystone wall, surely one of the most extraordinary walls ever built in Scotland. It can be a useful navigational aid in thick cloud.

From the summit we heard and then saw snow buntings. It is their sort of peak, but there is not much wildlife high up, for it is just too rough. The wet flanks can be a blaze of flowers though, with globeflower, kingcups, roseroot, asphodel and several saxifrages, while the trio of tormentil, bedstraw and milkwort appreciate the drier turf and thrift keeps to the rockier parts. Thrift is Virgin Mary's Pillow, *Cluasag Mhuire,* in Gaelic.

The northern flanks are exceptionally slabby and bare and the crest is a jagged edge of strata. There was no water till down on the Bealach nan Gall where a tiny trickle announced itself in sweet sound. We traversed across the brutal slopes of Sgurr nan Coireachan (peak of the corries) and only found one miserable water source. We actually ended on the opposite ridge, having traversed the corrie headwall looking for water. Even without rucksacks it was a sizzle-and-melt day. I once wrote of a gang of us climbing Ladhar Bheinn in Knoydart on just such a day and described how we 'collapsed by the cairn and drank our bars of chocolate'. The editor was obviously no hillman. He changed it to 'ate our bars of chocolate'. Every year the May Ultimate Challenge coast-to-coast event sees people falling out due to heat exhaustion or sunstroke. I was not long back from seven sun-smiting weeks in Morocco's mountains yet found this heat far more exhausting. Scotland the hot!

We trundled back down to the col and up on to the first spur of Garbh Chioch Beag to cut over a spur before the long descending traverse back to the hidden rucksacks. The heat had generated a breeze so the tramp down Glen Dessary was pleasant, and even dry underfoot, for the path (originally made by the redcoats) has been swallowed by bog in places. We skirted above the new plantings and then dipped down and up to the bothy. The rest of the club were soon in. As they had motored to the west end of Loch Arkaig (the nearest car access to Loch Nevis), they had only an hour's walk in, so certain luxuries had been carried. We had a bottle of wine with dinner and a bedtime dram as we watched the shadows sweep up the flanks of the Garbh-Ciochs, a toast was drunk to a grand day and the successful passage through Knoydart. *Slainte!*

Glenelg

One of the rain-bound tent games we used to play as youngsters was compiling lists of words which were spelt the same backwards as forwards. Glenelg always topped my list—far more interesting than the usual mum, toot, tit, and tat . . .

Recently I revisited Glenelg and it struck me again that it is a delightful place which is strangely ignored or undiscovered by visitors. While this is no doubt a joy to some it does not help the Glenelg economy. As our local mountaineering club maintains a bothy beyond Mam Ratagan we have a certain interest in Glenelg, with liberal contributions to the Telford Inn.

21   A quiet bay at Glenelg.

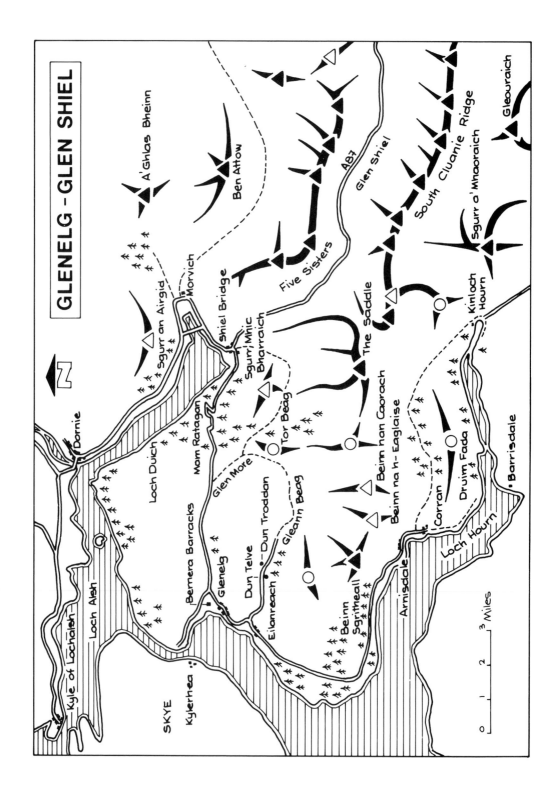

GLENELG - GLEN SHIEL

N

SKYE

Kyle of Lochalsh
Loch Alsh
Dornie
Loch Duich

A'Ghlas Bheinn
Ben Attow

Sgurr an Airgid
Morvich
Shiel Bridge

Five Sisters
A87
Glen Shiel

Bernera Barracks
Mam Ratagan
Glenelg
Dun Telve
Dun Troddan
Eilanreach
Gleann Beag

Glen More
Sgurr Mhic Bharraich
Tor Beag

The Saddle
South Cluanie Ridge
Sgurr a' Mhaoraich
Gleouraich

Beinn nan Caorach
Beinn na h-Eaglaise

Beinn Sgritheall
Arnisdale
Corran
Druim Fada
Loch Hourn
Kinloch Hourn

Barrisdale

0   1   2   3 Miles

It is the Mam Ratagan pass which makes Glenelg different and difficult, particularly just now when you run the gauntlet of meeting huge timber lorries. Along with the Bealach nam Bo to Applecross it is the most spectacular hill route to any seaside hamlet in Scotland; not quite as tough as Hardknott or Wrynose in the Lake District but with grander settings.

With the Forestry Commission busy felling and replanting Ratagan Forest this is actually a good time to visit Glenelg. For long stretches the view, which disappeared half a lifetime ago, is suddenly clear again.

Loch Duich and the Five Sisters of Kintail form no mean view. Near the top of the pass there is a car park so you can have a rest from first or second gear progression and actually look at the view. It is quite a pleasing walk up too—or walk down depending on whither you are an uppy or a doonie when it comes to raxing the knees.

Glenelg only got its road access in the eighteenth century and that was because of military necessity as part of the pacification of the Highlands. A road was built from Kingussie to Glenelg where the Bernera Barracks were built to an almost identical plan of the Ruthven Barracks.

Pacfication meant an increase in commerce and the narrows of Kyle Rhea soon had an identical inn on each side. The one on the Glenelg side was a youth hostel for some years and a much regretted closure.

Cattle were swum across the kyle—which can zip through at eight knots—and in summer now a car ferry operates, making it an alternative approach to Skye. Dr Samuel Johnson came this way. With his portly figure he had to take turn about with two ponies for the crossing of Mam Ratagan.

Seeing-in Hogmanay near Glenelg has given us a sound respect for the pass, however much horse power we may command. Glenelg should produce rally drivers of competence from the practice its drivers receive. A post bus allows the car-less to cross the pass and this can link with the train at Kyle of Lochalsh or the Kyle-Glasgow bus through Glen Shiel.

The road up the pass starts from the foot of Glen Shiel and rounds the end of Loch Duich before suddenly rearing upwards. If the tide is out there are acres of ochrous seaweed. It is worth a branching-off along the lochside road (a dead end) to admire the reflections. You can have Ten Sisters instead of Five when you turn round.

After the compulsory camera stop just before the top you will probably want to stop again just as you begin the descent into Glenmore. With the trees felled there is a view to Ben Sgriol and other rugged hills. The Cairnwell (ex-Devil's Elbow) may be higher but is league tables lower. This is premier division road scenery.

Two parallel glens: Glenmore (*the big glen*) and Gleann Beag (*the small glen*) run into the Sound of Sleat (which is pronounced 'slate', not 'sleet'). Glenelg lies along the bay linking them and round to the Kyle Rhea narrows. Glenelg folk still ken how to use their feet. It may be a wee village but they've made it go a long way—at least three miles from ferry to Eileanreach at the mouth of Gleann Beag.

Glenmore is a long valley with several crofts which can give vivid patchwork colours against the steep hills above. What impressed me last time was how rich the place was in trees. Perhaps it was because I'd been in Sutherland for a month or perhaps it was autumn placing her match to the fading colours of summer—but Glenelg has

22 The Eas Mor Falls in Glen Beag near Glenelg.

avenues of trees: sycamore, beech, ash, oak, Scots pine, chestnut. At the entrance to Glenelg a rowan in brilliant berry-colours was like a tapestry against a wall of patterned chestnuts.

Where ferry and village roads split stands 'Schima Craft' where they design and make up-market jewellery and also run a popular restaurant and tea room. You don't just have a cup of tea. You choose one of seven types of tea. Down the avenue you pass the shinty pitch and the primary school. Shinty I once heard described as a cross between hockey and mayhem. Most of Glenelg's young men are forestry workers with powerful arm muscles.

The barracks sit on an open meadow—no way of sneaking up unobserved—but are now just roofless ruins. The village, briefly, has something like a street. It runs from post office to petrol pumps. The latter happen to be at the Telford Inn where optimistically there are outside seats so that you can sup the appropriate beverage and look over the sea to Skye.

The road jinks round the church: a typical white-washed building of simple design with a 'lantern' belfry on top of one gable. As there are three windows down the side it is not a Telford church. Telford churches (he built about thirty) all have this simplicity and belfry but invariably there are four doors and/or windows on the side.

Beyond the church you are on the sound with its shingles and tidal inlets, its beached ferry and a bead-bright scattering of rowing boats. Then you meet the improbable war memorial.

This is a big bronze group with a winged victory holding aloft a victor's wreath while a naked female figure reaches up to her. Below the wreath stands a kilted Jock, leaning wearily on his rifle, too much in a dream to notice the enticing forms beside him. It's a monstrosity of a memorial (even if designed by a famous architect) but it was to a monstrous war; for a small place there's a sad length of names listed. The year 1914 changed things in the Highlands almost as much as the coming of the Cheviots.

There are plenty of Bed and Breakfasts here, some strung along a stone's throw from the sea, so it is a great place for a lazy holiday, or to fish, or to walk and climb the hills. Glenelg is nine miles from the A87 Shiel Bridge rat-race but the road meanders on past the big house of Eileanreach and away round to Loch Hourn (the *Loch of Hell* hints at its wild setting) to finish beyond Arnisdale village, nine miles on. There's much to do and see in that brief span.

If you turn up Gleann Beag from Eileanreach you come on Dun Telve and Dun Troddan which are brochs: Pictish forts which are as mysterious as they are impressive. 'Like dry-stone cooling towers' was one apt description. These are the best mainland examples of this type of building—which are only found in Scotland.

The best walk, up Gleann Beag and back by Glenmore (it can feel more and more!), passes several other sites. Torr Beag has little to show of its prehistoric defences but it gives my favourite view of Sgriol—Glenelg's solitary Munro and the king of the little mountains. Its summit view takes in half of Scotland, including Skye and the hills of Rhum, and gives the bonus of the dazzling 'Ring of Bright Water'. A great wee place is Glenelg, however you spell it.

23 Storm in his glory—looking to Ben Sgriol.

Ben Attow

From the main road at the head of Loch Duich Ben Attow appears to be all lumps and bumps. It is, but there is more to this hill than the map cares to tell. I would go so far as to place it among the top thirty hills in Scotland. I knew Ben Attow well but like all such hills every ascent, far from exhausting the hill, merely showed further attractions and possibilities for future visits. No hill should be climbed once only. Familiarity comes best with actually staying on it—sleeping on it. So I have often preached.

Attow presents a frightening wall to Gleann Lichd: those mathematically inclined can work out the gradient but in one inch of map it rises at least 2500 feet. That is steep. This intimidating flank is also moated by the River Croe. There is no sane reason for peching up it. However there is one feature which had long intrigued me.

One of the rushing torrents that run down this flank is shown rising in a diminutive lochan at 2000 feet. It was the most unlikely sort of creation. Worth visiting some day. I had failed to see it looking down from the ground above. I had failed to see it from the Five Sisters across Gleann Lichd. It had taken on a sort of 'lost-world' attraction. So heading north this winter I decided, suddenly, to visit the lost lochan.

I had travelled up on a superb day but a poisoned toe had kept me off the hills. That night it thawed and the snow line rolled up the hillside like a carpet. I had a disgusting flounder over the Conbharein hills and was back at the car with half the day left. The madness hit me then.

24   The view south from the summit of Ben Attow.

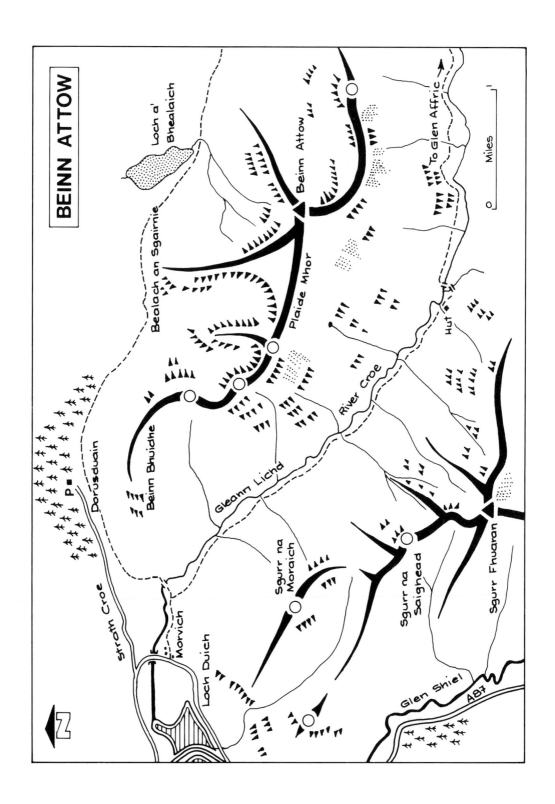

BEINN ATTOW

I raced down to Loch Duich and up to the Morvich road-end, then had an hour of chaotic packing, cooking and eating, all at once. I nearly grilled a stocking and picked up a hot instead of a cold dixie, so, of course, dropped it and had to chase my peas and spuds all over the floor. I had cooked haggis which was the biggest mistake of all. Though early, by eating then I would not have to carry and cook an evening meal on the hill. The theory was good.

With less than two hours of daylight left I went tramping off up Gleann Lichd. The track was booby-trapped with sheets of ice. A shepherd was yelling what sounded very rude things up the hill at his dogs. Another shepherd was sound asleep in his Land-Rover in the middle of the track. I had a great temptation to slap its metal roof right beside his lug—but he was an awful-big-looking lad. Where the glen opens out I crossed the river; wide but slow-moving. Midwinter paddling is a chilly sort of pastime. I had a good look at my poor toe. A pinprick of a hole marked where some germ had entered and the whole foot went up like a balloon, the very day of a party for the local climbing club committee. I sat through it watching the dancing. Injury was added to insult when a girl saw my foot on the only available stool and came up and kicked my foot off it. She looked surprised when I went whimpering into the corner. So with five Munros that day already, here was I paddling icebound rivers and setting off for 2500 feet of scrambling under a camping pack. Kill or cure!

It was now I regretted my haggis supper. It weighed far more heavily on my stomach than it would have done on my back. I zig-zagged up and across to hit my burn half way up in the last of the light. The northern corries of the Five Sisters across the way looked like something out of the Himalayas.

In the gloaming the deer stood watching me go by. They obviously could not work out what this strange silhouette could be. They had probably never seen a human there before.

The new metric map showed quite a circular pool and contour, which is what made me decide to camp. It looked quite spacious. In reality it was not and I almost climbed past the site, for the loch was a mere navel among the bellyfolds of rock at this point. Far from being spacious it was hemmed in in a 'V' slot, the wall of which was too narrow for a tent. I had to pitch in the bottom of the 'V', tramping and digging out a level platform in the snow.

As soon as the tent was standing, wobbly though it was, the stove went on for a brew. I then covered the flaps with snow and guyed the tent with boulders, fetched water from the lochan (it was not frozen though even the sea was at the head of Loch Duich), had a last look at the starry landscape—and crawled in to the tent. By the time my frozen fingers had the boots off, the tea was ready. Into bed. A book. A cup of tea. Sounds great, doesn't it? But it was only five thirty. Daylight would be at eight thirty. Midwinter sleep is apt to be lengthy, in fact it is one of the major occupations of climbing—something wives and mothers are apt to forget when they say, 'Don't overdo things now!'

Contrary to what you think, snow is not soft to life on. I stayed in the tent till full day. A candle burning all night had kept the temperature just on the freezing but the inside skin of the tent glittered with frost so that it snowed when I shook it out to pack it.

The Plaide Mor, the wide saddle of Attow, was all breakable crust, the most ill-natured of all snow conditions for walking on and gave a right old sweat up to the cairn. Attow has several fine northern corries, the western pair being especially fine. If they lay in the Cairngorms they would be full of climbs. The Bealach an Sgairne, the gateway to Glen Affric, has a path up from Morvich and off it another twists up the Sgairne corrie arm—the "tourist route" so to speak for Ben Attow. The ridge along to the western peaks, all those lumps and bumps you see from Loch Duich, is one of the best.

Once over the main peak on this ridge people tend to relax, until faced with an unavoidable slab up another bump. Quite a few walkers find this just too much though only a short scramble. Today it was banked up in good snow and took five minutes, tiptoeing. I followed every lump and bump, revelling in the hard snow, then slid down to Beinn Bhuidhe, scattering deer, then chuntered down, scattering sheep, back to the vehicle, back to clean the cold haggis pot. If there is a moral hidden anywhere it is something to do with haggis I'm sure!

25   On the ridges of The Saddle, Kintail.

By the Crags

A good brew
for the two
linked for hours
by the powers
of a rope
to their hope.

After?

Rest
the next best:
a wind, kind
to tired mind,
a pool, deep,
grassy sleep . . .

Tomorrow
we'll borrow
one more climb
of tight time.
We'll belay
one more day
that yields this
borrowed bliss.

Bagging Benula

The summers of 1984 and 1985 were rather different in precipitation levels and it was during the former that I made several Munro-bagging forays by canoe. A canoe, like a pony or a bike or skis, I regard primarily as an aid to exploration, a means to various ends, rather than an end in itself. Thus it was the remoter corners that I was seeking out in the dry days of blessed 1984. The drought had some odd results.

I remember reading once how a walker threatened his friends (jokingly, I trust, rather than in dead earnest) with a stipulation in his will that his ashes were to be scattered on top of Beinn Fhionnlaidh. You probably have to be pretty far gone in Munro brokerage to either pronounce that name or know where it is. Shares in Beinn Fhionnlaidh (Benula) are not traded too frequently. The price is too high.

Tom Weir in *Highland Days*, tells of a wet and wild penetration west from Cannich which led to this and other peaks and fine hospitality from the folk at Benula Lodge. You will look in vain for Benula Lodge now for it is drowned by 'the Atlantic' as the locals call the massive reservoir of Loch Mullardoch. Few tourists ever see it for the secretive wee road leaves Cannich by a steep brae and a 'no-through-road' sign is an added deterrent. (I've had some very cross reactions at the head of Glen Nevis from visitors who have asked me if there was not a through-road to Inverness!)

Come to think of it my first meeting with Tom was when I had a gang of kids camping near the dam. A stocky figure in a toorie bunnet came up and was chatting away to them. Just as I arrived there was a *screetch* from a bird up-by and the visitor cried: 'Hear that? The hunting cry of a kestrel.' It could only be one person, even if his accent was not the well-kent one it is now.

Tom was lucky to get in to the area before the dam flooded it. I first came on it over the hills, in a south–north expedition, and was furious to find the valley shown on my map had changed into one of the longest man-made lochs in Scotland: a ten-mile diversion of trackless wastes to regain a path less than a mile of water away. Because of this severe moating of Beinn Fhionnlaidh most people now approach it from Glen Affric: a none too easy takeover bid by Messrs Munro & Co. Those who have invested in it can usually be told by their smug smirks whenever the hill is mentioned.

A couple of winter ascents like that made me determined on new and livelier approaches so the next time we traversed all the Munros north of Loch Mullardoch, camped at the west end of the loch, and traversed back to the dam along all the

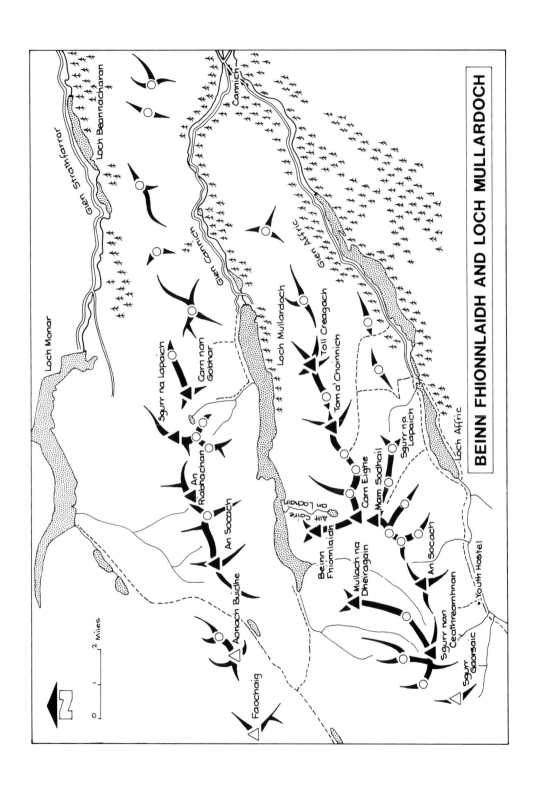

BEINN FHIONNLAIDH AND LOCH MULLARDOCH

southern Munros—a marathon winter weekend. Most ascents since have been from the Mullardoch side, the remoteness and approach problems being an irresistible attraction. Going with the canoe from Inverness camp site to its far shores in the height of summer was a startling contrast.

The sight that met my eyes on topping the dam was almost unbelievable. The tide was out! We had last been there on 1 January with the waves crashing over the dam like TV pictures of American hurricanes and the streams were all rumbling down in uncrossable ferocity.

The sunny summer had followed and the waters were away down, leaving unsightly tide-lines. Mullardoch's water flows through a tunnel to Loch Benevian in Glen Affric and as it is kept topped-up and beautiful, poor Mullardoch often looks a bit derelict. I drove down on to a huge beach under the Chisholm Cairn.

My plan was to canoe to the far end and camp for the hills there, then visit the middle reaches on both sides—returning with all the area's Munros. The plan lasted about two hours, though it nearly didn't even start. Dog and I happily went down towards the water and sank, without warning, up to out thighs in black peat mud which lay in ambush under a film of gravel. It was not the best launching I've had.

The wind blew from the west of course. The navigation proved peculiar as well, for the shape of the loch on the map and in reality were quite different. Many burns, 'obvious features', had dried up and vanished then, horror of horrors, it seemed the loch ended at the narrows about two-thirds of the way along.

A wee channel however twisted on and just when I thought it was going to be all right it went all wrong. I could *hear* the sound of rushing water to the west and round another bend the loch became a rocky river that should not be there. The perversity of the situation struck me at once. On that first visit, half a lifetime before, I cursed finding my north–south route barred by the raised level. Now that I wanted to utilise the loch it had reverted to being two lochs and I was baulked by a river—across which north–south access could be made dry shod.

There was only about 200 yards of river to the original Loch Lungard so I decided to camp there and canoe to the west as a day-sortie on the morrow.

It took an hour after tea to line the canoe up the 200 yards of river. In the morning it was so windy from the west I decided I'd have to walk rather than canoe. There was only a mile of Loch Lungard anyway, the west end being vast acres of exposed peat.

Storm and I had a good day on the Ceathreamhnan hills (wind and sun) and as we had gone out along the south shore we returned by the north of Loch Lungard.

The wind changed so we had to turn the tent round for comfort. The fire went like a blast furnace. Any midges had either gone to ground or they'd be blowing on the way to St Kilda and Newfoundland. There were a few spare millions to make breakfast early and quick. I set off for Beinn Fhionnlaidh, pleased that I had lined the canoe down to Loch Mullardoch (original) again before going to sleep.

From the loch the hill gives a brutally regular and steep slope. A gang of us once discovered this by going up direct from the now-vanished bothy on Loch Lungard, so that was not repeated. This time dog and I followed the Allt Coire an Lochain up to its remote birth spot—sure enough, in a lochan, in a corrie, and then had little more effort to gain the ridge to Fhionnlaidh.

We traversed to Mam Sodhail and back again as I grudged losing height on a day of such brilliance. These are the highest summits north of the Great Glen so half of Scotland seemed to be in sight and, for once, we had the time (being local residents) to look at everything from Sutherland to Skye and Cairngorms to Outer Hebrides. It was hot enough that, had we lingered, I think we would have left *our* ashes on Benula.

We followed down a northeast spur to regain the river of our ascent and we drank one half of it and swam in the other. Nearing camp Storm's nose was twitching and we came on two lads (with mud to their knees) who had landed from an inflatable. I wonder if they made it back for it was hard work in the canoe, battling (perversity again) into the evening's east wind.

Beinn Fhionnlaidh is never easy. What a pity there isn't some form of trading in Munros. I've several Benulas in hand and the Munro market is definitely bullish.

The Coulin Pass

We discovered the Coulin Pass on the first long walk I ever made in the remoter west Highlands.

We were just three laddies on a stravaig which led us from Ullapool to Skye and if I smile now at how we tingled with the sense of excitement it gave us, the memory is still sharp, clear—and exciting. There is a certain (modern) daftness about climbing up mountains but to travel through them touches on our origins. Our earliest ancestors did that.

Though we did not know it at the time, the natural lie of the land led our novice route-finding along ways which had known centuries of passage: packmen, drovers, clansmen, redcoats, the dispossessed, the gangrels, the hikers—all these had passed before.

To discover this, afterwards, rather than before, was no bad thing. We had the thrill of exploratory originality and then the fascination of historical discovery. In our empty hills and glens the very stones cry out.

On that early trek we came out from the big country between Dundonnell and Loch Maree down to Kinlochewe and then pushed on down Torridon to camp near Loch Clair on a night of dark and wet. The rhododendrons gave good shelter but they also secreted most of Scotland's midges we found over breakfast. It was a quick breakfast!

We fled for the Coulin Pass but before pulling up to it we hid our packs and set off to climb Beinn Laith Mhor. The path up, by a succession of waterfalls in the fine Scots pine woodland, was irresistible. The roughness of heather, rock, bog, and tree when the path ended was something else.

So was Beinn Liath Mhor. The *big grey hill* is a long bastion of ridge, rising into three tops of quartzite, this rock, like devil's cube sugar, tumbling down the flanks in grey acres of scree.

We toiled up in a rising storm and actually made the crest but the half mile to the true summit might as well have been miles to the moon. We were blasted off. Donkey jackets and home-knitted balaclavas were no match for screaming rain and wind.

We raced down the screes in a frenzy, trying in physical activity to regain the warmth that had been sucked from us on the heights.

In a hut at the path-end we wrung out our clothes (and put them on again), crammed our mouths with glucose sweets, and hurried on to retrieve rucksacks and

26 Ardessie Falls near Dundonnell, with Sail Mhor behind.

cross the Coulin Pass before conditions deteriorated any further. It was a long fight up and the wind contested our every step. We will not forget our first meeting with the Coulin Pass.

We will not forget the day's end either. We descended to Achnashellach Station and the A890—and there was a youth hostel we did not know existed. It was a collection of old forestry huts, long gone now of course, hardly posh enough for modern youth, but it was haven to us. A black-visaged warden took in the strays. A black kettle sang on the old cast iron range.

Later on we read something of the Coulin. It was an old route, leading to the north west, and from Strath Carron two branches gathered together (for strength perhaps) before tackling the thousand foot ascent.

From the south people travelled via Strome Ferry (which now has the odd road sign declaring 'Strome Ferry—No ferry'), and up to Achnashellach. From the east people travelled via Glen Conon, the River Meig, to reach Craig in Strathcarron, a couple of miles up from Achnashellach.

A remarkably straight line over the Coulin northwards leads to Kinlochewe, and by Loch Maree's north shore another score of miles led to Gairloch and sea routes to the Isles. James Hogg was one famous traveller to cross the Coulin and he was gey glad to reach Kinlochewe.

The Coulin is still popular with walkers and with an independent hostel at Craig can well be woven into the larger tapestry of a cross-country journey.

All that north side of the glen is forestry-planted and to walk all the way down to Achnashellach and back up to Craig is tedious, but descending through trees can be trying; yet there must have been a path, once. By pure chance, on one such short-cut down through the trees, I found it.

I meant to return to study it properly but only on last Christmas Day did two of us finally pin down the route of the old pony path.

It was another of those Achnashellach wet days when Gerry's fire tempted but restlessness won over lethargy. We hit the path deep in the forest so followed it up. We lost it in the pass but descending from there it is easy to pick up, and we tidied it a bit (removing fallen trees and clearing drains) as we dropped down to the A890.

The Coulin Pass road makes a sharp 'elbow' bend not far down from the top (map ref. 024496) and if you cross the burn to a cairn there are others beyond which turn down to the top edge of big, mature trees.

The path runs along this and then goes down in continuous zig zags to the main road (031490) half a mile west of Craig and the hostel.

Trees were carefully not planted on the path, and branches only obstruct it in a couple of places. Still, it had almost been forgotten and lost and its survival probably depends on it being used. How about walking it this summer sometime—add your footnote to history?

The Anvil of the Forge

One of Scotland's boldest-and-best hills is An Teallach, *the forge* as it translates, and if you are caught on its jagged crests or cauldron corries in bad weather the name seems most appropriate. It is an anvil on which experience is hammered hard.

I once did a magazine survey to find a 'Top Twenty Scottish Peaks' and the readers placed Liathach and An Teallach in a joint lead—far beyond all others. In C S Lewis' language, An Teallach is not a tame mountain. Its front row position (playing against the mauling Minch), combined with its tough physique, means it is a redoubtable personality. Anthropomorphism renders An Teallach as masculine.

Like many notable mountains it has an odd dual physical character. The motoring tourists may pass and hardly notice it, the mere Munro-bagger may dander up over pebbly domes but the side away from the sea and the Braemore–Gairloch road is different: cliffs and corries on a spectacular scale, a chaos of red rock and grey rock, of emerald turf and enamelled waters. It is an unforgettable side whether approached by the easy flanks, which leave a startling surprise when the ground suddenly vanishes in the big cliffs, or by the long haul up into the corries, which engenders awe as the scale grows and grows till you seem to be swallowed by the mountain.

There are two big corries that look east over Destitution Road to the Fannichs: A' Ghlas Thuill *the green hollow* and Toll an Lochan *the hollow of the loch*. It is the latter that is best known, the former, quite unfairly, is seldom visited. It may lack the magic mirror under the cliffs but the crags rise tier on tier, the screes are neatly frost-combed and the grass has that sort of bright green which, in clothes, would indicate bad taste. It is a corrie of deer and the mountain blackbirds sing in its heart. It is a corrie of summer gaiety.

Toll an Lochan is different. It has the cosiness of a dinosaur. You enter the cirque as you would the tiger house in a zoo. The scratch marks of creation are still clear on its walls. There is no music in the doomword *toll* (hollow, hole, cauldron) and the weird *lochan* has a grue of ice in its moonstone waters. It is a corrie of winter impotence.

My first visit to An Teallach was made during a trek with friends down the west coast. We first spied it, like some Promised Land, from afar off, while wandering in the crazy clutch of Coigach hills. Such a jagged crest on the skyline was irresistible to strong youth. We walked to Ullapool, sailed out of Loch Broom into a golden sunset and returned to the youth hostel to cook a supper of fresh mackerel. Next day we

27   From the slopes of An Teallach looking over to Beinn Dearg Mor.

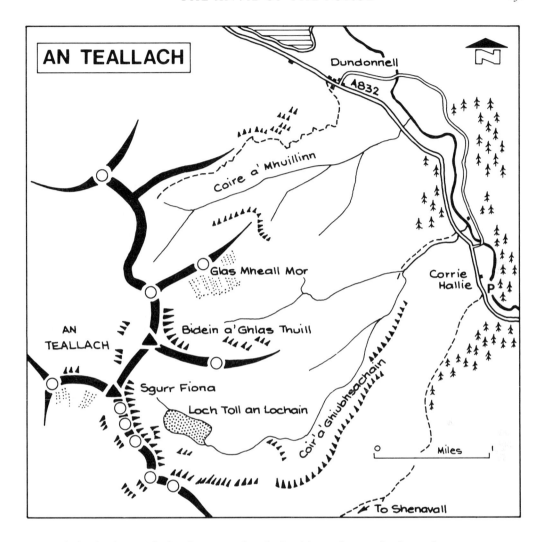

crossed the loch to Clachnaharrie and toiled with packs up the brae that acts as outer baillie to An Teallach. The Promised Land was revealed as a mighty fortress.

Respectfully we crept up the road from Corriehallie (what unforgettable journeys have started there over the years) and on the scoured, bare, plover-pleading moor we pitched our tent, door to the east, for we dared not look into that hungry corrie. A lot of nonsense is talked about rash ventures in the hills. Youth is timid and the hills are approached with all the apprehension of a first romance. A sneeze from An Teallach would have sent us packing.

The sun rose over the Fannichs and roused us in our eyrie. An hour later, clad in donkey jackets and ex-army vibrams, a precious rope on shoulder—and 'pieces' in pockets—we set off for the final fray.

We had to wriggle down a quartz-sharp line of crags before we could turn up into the corrie on the gritty sandstone. The early sun made the crags a cascade of red, but it was the crest that held the eye. Never had we seen such a ragged crest. And we sought to climb it!

The loch lay hidden for a long time. The glaciers had gouged deep and left a convex bar of bedrock. On it were perched the stones left when the carrying ice retreated. The loch itself was polished steel in which the mountain stood on its head. The silence of an ambush held the place. A stream tumbling off a crag into the water was much the loudest sound. The wind whispered. Not for a second could we have shouted out to set the echoes ringing. We had magically crept in through an open door while the defenders slept.

An hour of sweat and toil took us up to lie gasping on the crest and if some romance had evaporated the triumph loosed our tongues. An Teallach was ours. We set the echoes ringing then all right.

I have climbed mountains in many ranges in many lands since and the lure abides. This country of the heart's desire is there for all who put legs to their dreams. I am so glad to have found it as a youngster, so glad to have An Teallach as an abiding memory. Joe, Mike and I traversed the whole crest of that peak of many peaks that day and we then went stravaiging southwards to Skye, to a lifetime of wanderings since.

I have not seen them for some years but I see An Teallach regularly, An Teallach of which, when I once explained its Gaelic name was *the forge* to a school party, heard the retort, 'Forge! You canna forge yon. That's the real thing.'

It is indeed.

Familiarity Breeds Content

With some regularity I am asked a question which, to me, is surprising: 'Do you not get tired of climbing some of the same hills again and again?'

Diplomacy usually has me give a gentle answer, rather than a snort, for the question I feel indicates a lack in the questioner's emotive or imaginative faculties—which you can hardly say in public!

The same thing crops up when comments are made such as 'don't believe in this Munro-climbing business. I go to the hills for pleasure.' This really puts my birse up. It implies other motives and no one has shouted longer or louder than I have that fun is the only justification for the self-indulgent pastime of enjoying mountains. Of course you cannot get tired of any hill.

This is not to deny that some hills are more spectacular or exciting than others. A great number of Geal Charns still do not equal one An Teallach and I could produce, from close encounters of the best kind, a long list of fabulous bens which do not even rise to the magical antique Munro altitude of 3000 feet or even the Corbett 2500 feet mark.

Ben Klibreck is often dismissed as a pretty dull hill in the league table of Munro appreciation, which is largely due to its being unceremoniously grabbed by Munro-baggers, by the quickest route, in a frantic Sutherland foray, even doing Klibreck and Ben Hope the same day.

Ben Klibreck is so typical of how appreciation grows *only* with coming again and again. At a bothy near Glenelg recently I heard a discussion about a man who had climbed Ben Lomond several hundred times and I have a friend with many hundreds of ascents of Meall na Teanga behind him. It can only be an enthusiastic devotion that impels that sort of activity. Klibreck, then, I consider a Loyal hill and have every Hope of returning to it!

We first climbed it by accident. Brother and I had borrowed our father's car and while motoring round to Ben Hope it had been giving trouble, so, after climbing Ben Hope, brother nobly took it to a garage at Lairg and rather than hang about there the rest of us were dropped off in Strath Vagastie and made a quick raid across the moors to 'do' Klibreck. A 4 p.m. start in October probably indicated more zeal than discretion. May we never run out of zeal!

The side facing the Altnaharra–Lairg road has only one feature on its long hogs-back: an area of crags split by a big gully. We climbed a buttress beside this. We did not linger on top but just had to stop on the descent to watch the golden disc of sun vanish behind the array of western mountains.

The stags were bellowing and the lochs glowed then turned mother-of-pearl. We topped a rise and saw the winking of car lights.

A bellow from us was answered and, two minutes before the estimated time, we reached the (repaired) car where a hot apple concoction and coffee was waiting for us. There was nothing dull about our introduction to Ben Klibreck. The peak is either *the mountain of the speckled stone* or *the mountain of the fish* and is pronounced *Clib-ree.*

A visit was made in similar fashion the following summer as the lady of the party was set on her 100th Munro in passing. Sometime, between the visits, a bolt of lightning had shattered the trig point. Kent suffers far more thunderstorms than Klibreck but is is always much more frightening on the hills. Isolated summits are best fled from when one's hair stands on end or ice axes sing!

Perhaps I should gloss over the next visit. It was entirely discreditable, but they do say experience is the sum of near-misses. Two of us set off, two days before Christmas, for those alluring crags. Well over the soggy moor we realised we had left our ice axes in the car yet somehow our errant feet headed us up into the big gully.

We were just going to have a look of course, then we were just going to plod up it as the snow was soft enough to kick safe steps. But it steepened (steep enough for knees to dent the snow as we kicked) and eventually became a worn water channel up which we climbed.

It became harder above and jabbing frozen fingers into the hard snow was agony. A long slope led to a dripping corner which was impassable in our state.

We inched out rightwards on foul snow on ice or slippery grass—really setting the adrenalin going—for we would have first fallen 100 feet and then slid a long way before reaching the foot. Our tenseness must have communicated itself to the dog for he co-operated perfectly with every move.

The feeling had gone from our fingers and we went through that peculiar agony of thawing them out. We could not see over the step so shoved the dog up first. Silence. Then from well beyond, his 'come on!' bark. On steps cut by penknife we forced the bulge—and an easy snow tunnel led us out to safety.

'Excellent fun' we wrote, afterwards, even if the fear was not forgotten.

On the way down one end of a lochan was heaped with thousands of ice balls, ranging from golf ball to football in size, a new oddity then, but seen since on Loch Pattack. (This was simply spray/waves crashing onto the beach and freezing.)

A few years later we had a rather dreich day with a school party and then, at last, managed a traverse of the whole ridge on the penultimate day of the mountain walk that had taken in all the Munros in a single trip. For a month the weather had been wild and wet but Klibreck relented. I set off with the black west held back by a rainbow.

I went up by the path from the Crask Inn, with the ground covered in big, hairy caterpillars. I collected a score and eventually they were crawling all over my hairy pullover. The game palled when one adventured down my neck.

The miles of whaleback ridge gave a sun-splattered windy highway and the circle of stones round the trig point was sheltered enough that I fell asleep.

Another mile and a bitty and a descent was made by a stalking path to Loch Naver and Altnaharra Inn. This is undoubtedly the asthetic day but sets problems if car-based. A round from either inn is pleasant in itself and such a route we did later while preparing for the *Groats End Walk*. Perhaps the finest view I have had of Klibreck occurred a week into that jaunt.

Though it was May I had fought blizzards most of the way from John o' Groats to Tongue but for a high camp on Ben Hope it cleared—and Klibreck sprawled like a dream of Ahab on the stands of the south.

This summer the new dog had his introduction to the hill and we did a round from the head of Strath Vagastie, setting off a six to try to avoid the devastating heat. We went up by the outlying Cnoc Sgriodain and back by the lochs. Their waters felt tepid. Blaeberries were ready to eat five weeks earlier than usual. We watched a buzzard and a peregrine have an argument.

Near the sumit is a ruin and a series of level platforms which were a puzzle. Despite reading since they remain a puzzle. Does anybody know about them? Or even notice them? (It was my seventh visit before I did.) We found them because Storm, the dog, was fascinated by a golden plover doing a broken-wing act.

Being cooler on top we lingered by the cairn, eyes squinting east into wild Caithness, a golden glare of sun which glittered a hundred lochs and surrounded the cones of Beinn Griam in fire. Next time, it must be these remote eastern slopes.

Peanmeanach

The grey stones fall outward,
Pockmarking the dead green
That corrugates to the sea
In tired lazy beds.
The grey stones fall inward
And are swallowed quickly
In a rash of nettles
And the rusty pain of decay.

An orange bus stopped on the hill
While the noisy youngsters
Swung down, transistors over-riding
A lone peewit's plea.
A week later the same songs crash
In an orange bus down the M6.

In time the green will cover the scars
Of burnt turf, soured grass
And a ruin full of baked-bean tins.
Even the bothy book
(Full of obscenities)
Cannot stop the tide and the wind.

How many centuries have we sinned?

IV   Islands, Islands, Islands

Before the last section I quoted 'the heart is Highland' but that was only a partial quotation. The whole stanza (from the anonymous Canadian Boat Song*) really sums up all one can say about an absentee's feelings for the Islands.*

> *From the lone shieling of the misty island*
> *Mountains divide us, and the waste of seas—*
> *Yet still the blood is strong, the heart is Highland,*
> *And we in dreams behold the Hebrides.*

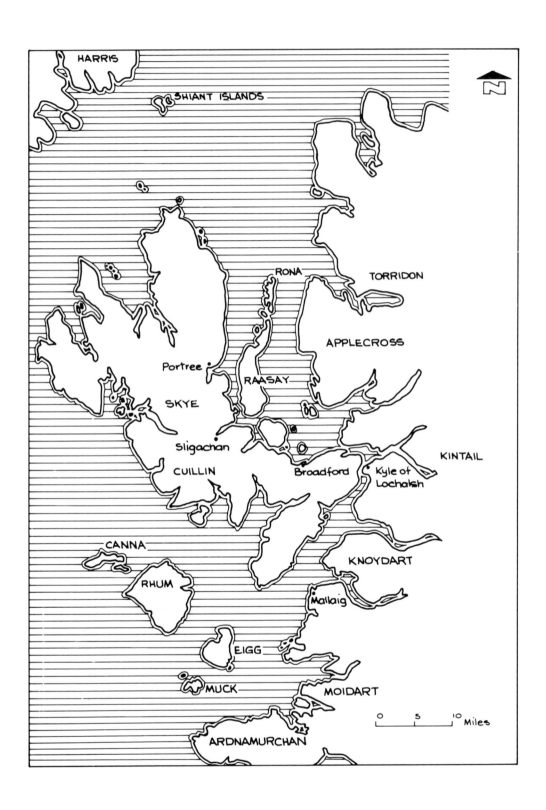

On Jura's Empty Quarter

We might have the chance to see it, the Corrievreckan, between Jura and Scarba—racing waters and legendary whirlpool.

The wind blew gently, but enough to keep the sweat from our sundrenched toil. Rucksacks seemed to have grown heavier and lead rather than water seemed to have seeped into our boots. The western coast of Jura is one of the roughest of Scotland's rough landscapes. Cave-ridden rock prows stand grimly against the Atlantic storms.

Man, a generation ago, deserted the last dwelling that faces west. The deer and the goats alone remain to fight for a living; deer carcases littered the hillsides of *Deer Island* as the Norse named Jura; innumerable skeletons of goats lay among the soft, sweet-smelling droppings that carpeted the caves.

The gap was boggy, for impervious quartzite is amongst the most unprofitable bases nature has tried to build on. It ran like a square-cut funnel behind the headland whose indented circumference we were only too glad to avoid, even at the cost of uphill work. We were rewarded.

At the end of the gap we found ourselves looking down the russet slopes of a glen to a silver-sanded bay on which the waves were chattering. Beyond a cove lay another tidy bay, the twin circles of shining water hugged by black buttresses with their deep sockets of caves and hollows.

The boys stood puzzling a minute, eyes screwed up in the magic light, ears straining for comprehension. The little splashing of the bay was clear, for there was barely wind enough to ruffle tousled hair. There was no burn of any strength. A glance showed no silver dart trailing vapour trails across the sky. Yet the whole world seemed dominated by a deep-set, throbbing roar—like wind waves in a forest, or a great river in spate, or bombers pulsing through the air.

Then, one by one, through the shimmer of sun they saw the waters of Corrievreckan, and stood silent.

We had reached Jura through the Dorus Mor (*the great door*). In a small Loch Fyne boat it had been exciting enough; as bad a sea as I have ever known in a small craft. In the tide races it had felt like riding a bucking horse or trying to float a thimble in a boiling kettle. The skipper was glad to land his teenage cargo and the teenage cargo was glad enough to be landed.

Having witnessed those lesser tide races afar off—and then crashed and spun through

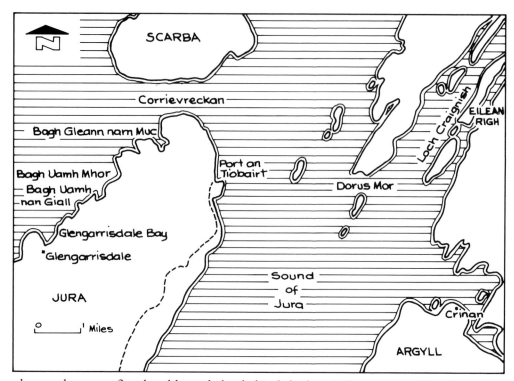

them—there was first-hand knowledge behind the boys' silent staring. The Dorus Mor had been a murmur—and frightening—the Corrievreckan, two miles off, growled and pushed and tossed up great surges, while white, washing waves still danced at its disturbing power miles further out. There is something overwhelming in a display of natural power—Krakatau is more amazing than Hiroshima, the Victoria Falls than the Kariba Dam. The Corrievreckan, on its headlong surge westwards, is of this large impressiveness.

We streamed down to the twin bays (Bagh nam Muc), left our rucksacks above the plastic-littered tidemark, and went out to the furthest rocks opposite the tide race. Some of its vehemence had passed, but its sheer pushing, rushing bulk sweeping along made the imagination shudder. Even on our sheltered side the water swirled creamily. Shags and black guillemot sat on the undulating flow. A seal eyed us from offshore. The boys decided closer investigation would be safest from a helicopter.

The maelstrom occurs in the two-mile-long gulf between Jura and Scarba. It is a mile wide, and the cause of the troubled waters can be seen in the strata on the Scarba side, where vertical runs of rock sweep down like ribs. Under the Sound, where the water rushes through at nine knots, this forms walls and hollows (soundings vary from forty to a hundred and twenty fathoms). At one place a jagged cone comes up to a mere fifteen fathoms and this creates an upsurge which crashes through the top hundred feet of speeding water to form the frightful, smashing waves and whirlpool which could be the end of any small craft.

Drunk with the sight and sound, we returned to Bagh nam Muc. Some boys gathered wood for the fire, some bracken for bedding, Brian and John cooked—soup, black pudding, cheese, toast, and gallons of tea.

The gloaming came, the wind died away, the tide lapped high up the sands. Surely there could be few more deserted spots, and few so romantic or satisfying.

Like a black shadow against the setting sun, a fishing boat came into the bay. I wonder what they thought—this utterly remote anchorage, noisy, not only with oystercatchers and ringed plovers, but the laughs and shouts of youngsters; in one bay stags munching the seaweed, in the next schoolboys roasting their sausages.

Corrievreckan comes from *Coire Bhreacain.* Legend, spinning many yarns, has given the derivation from Breacan, son of a Norse king. To win an island bride this hero had to anchor his boat between Jura and Scarba for three days and nights.

He had three ropes made—one of wool, one of hemp, and one of virgins' hair. On the first night the wool rope failed, on the second the hemp, and in a rising tempest during the third night the last rope parted, the galley plunged into the maw and Breacan's body was washed ashore to be buried in a cave now named Uamh Bhreacain.

The boys were sceptical of the third rope. "There could not be that number of virgins in all Scotland," Ronnie pronounced! And Breacan should have used No. 3 nylon, as any climber could have told him.

Scepticism about the cave was fortunately lifted when the fishermen gave George directions. It lies well out on the southern arm of the double bay, past an obvious dark hollow in the hillside. It is large enough to hold a cottage and the entrance is circled by walls. Fort or shrine, legend has given place to musty modernity. The boys left a note under a cairn to be sent back by the next visitor. (By a surprising coincidence it was found and returned later by the sister of a climbing friend of mine.)

There is no bonfire quite like that built of crackling driftwood. It rose eight feet and blazed merrily. David's wet socks scorched through and no bare flesh could come near the heat. Long after sleeping boys lay snug on top of the pile of bracken and the frost had come down on the polythene sheet I had picked up from the shore), it glowed and pulsed or sent showers of sparks up among the stars. A solitary kid bleating for its mother was the only noise above the soft whimper of the waves.

I lay and wondered at our being there. Many said it was mad to take a party of young teenagers to Jura in February. Yet we ran bare-foot over the grass and sand before our bothy in Glengarrisdale Bay, played 'crocker' and 'wide games' stripped to our pants. There were no midges, just an occasional smir of drizzle, and in the whole week no human walked our way.

I let my mind wander back over the journey. We had motored from Buckhaven, in Fife, to Crinan, in our school bus. There was no sign of the boat that was to ferry us to Jura. An hour later a white dot was seen bouncing over the incredibly blue water and soon we were loading rucksacks, paraffin, boxes of foods, sleeping-bags and tents on board.

But there was no chance of reaching Jura that day. It was blowing hard and cold enough for us to pull on cagouls. We went up Loch Craignish instead and camped for the night on a fine grassy stretch by Loch Craignish, opposite Eilean Righ, hoping to try for Jura on the morrow.

It was possible—just. So it was off for the Dorus Mor and the tide race beyond. The noisy yells barely hid the fright and excitement as the huge rollers surged under or passed us by. It was good to land at the old slipway at Port an Tiobairt, a sheltered inlet on the northeast corner of Jura.

The skipper then took the gear round through the Sound while we walked across and down the west coast. There were blackcock in the woods and a heron slowly flapped away like a grey duster. The moors were desolate apart from deer. They stood on the bluffs as we wended through the gaps. We climbed steeply down the coast at Bagh Uamh Mhor, then over the sneck to Bagh Uamh nan Giall, goats everywhere, and deer, caves, and rock arches, windbuilt cones of grass on the headlands, and west, the restless Atlantic 'with only America beyond'.

So we came to Glengarrisdale, our base. The skip had a fire on in the bothy and before leaving, some of the boys went out to help lay lobster pots. From the door a wide 'football pitch' of grass stretched to the fine sands. The dinghy lay high and dry while the boat bobbed beyond Maclaine's Skull, one of the rocky islets. The scene glittered in sun and shadow, blue seas flecked white to Mull of clouds and rainbows. The orange tents were pitched to dry out, and from beach and glen and the brown hills around came the sounds of occupation. This was ours awhile with all the glory of it. We slept under the rafters, and my last memory was looking up to a pane of stars.

How the days sped at Glengarrisdale! We would rise after listening to the weather forecast at seven, and only dusk would drive us indoors again, to cook a vast meal with, perhaps, pancakes and drinking chocolate after log books had been written up, and some nights a game of 'Pit'.

The list of birds rose to over thirty; there were long hours at low tide among rocks and weeds looking for gunnels, butterfish, blennies, rockling, and thousands of tiny, transparent elvers.

There were plenty of good walls and pinnacles for rock-climbing. Nabby managed a spectacular 'peel' from a stance and now *knows* the reassuring strength of nylon rope; those of us spectating below were still shaking when Nabby was happily aloft again.

Days were all too few. We *had* to see the Corrievreckan, so in the early greyness we set off, imprinting our Vibram boot marks on top of hinds' hoof marks along the sand, stumbling over the rounded rubble of the raised beach, on to the first headland—where adventure befell us. There was a small herd of goats, and by dropping our rucksacks and forming a line we managed to drive them out where there was no escape. My camera clicked away, one longing being fulfilled.

A kid slipped into a pool and yelled when helped out. Feet back on firm rock, it scampered off with enviable grace.

Human yells brought us racing to one end of the line, where an adult goat, in panic, had jumped into the sea to try and bypass the enemy, but it was a wild Atlantic sea which came roaring up the rifts in the rocks. In a couple of minutes the beast ceased its struggle for life; that awful cessation which man refuses but which comes so easily to wild creatures (were there not half a dozen deer lying in the 'peaceful' sleep—of death—within stone's throw of the bothy?). I passed my camera and watch to Ian and scrambled down.

Knee-deep, I just reached those curving horns, but the next swelling wave caught us both and we bowled over in the foam. I held on, and between surges inched the hapless animal up the near-vertical rocks. It had cut a leg. When reporting the incident later one boy said, 'We rescued a goat from the sea,' but Ian added the rider—'Aye, and it was us that drove it there.' I lay a while on the rocks, then forced the goat to stand, taking away my support bit by bit, while the humans slowly filed out of sight. We then left it alone. It began picking its way skilfully once more over the rocks and tufts of thrift.

We were cosy in our bivouacs above the twin bays on that northern tip of Jura. The fire smouldered. The fishing boat had vanished in the dark shadow of the hill. There was only one crying kid—nature crying out its feebleness in the dark. A goat is rescued. A goat is lost. The caves are full of their bones. Perhaps it *was* foolish to be there. It was a treacherous place, desolate and cruel. Men had long given up any desire to try and live on its inhospitable shoreline.

Let those who romantically wish the drift from the Highlands to stop go and live there. Let them grow potatoes on the old lazy beds, let them carry the driftwood over the rocks on their backs, let them ferry their groceries through the Corrievreckan—the vanished descendants of Glengarrisdale are happier buying their potatoes at the supermarket, filling the car with petrol on the way home to a house lit and heated at the touch of a switch.

What if one of the boys went down with an appendix? What if one broke his spine on the vicious rocks? Reality is always double-faced. There was only a few boxes of groceries, a good first-aid kit, some paraffin and stores between us and the hardest, cruellest coast imaginable in Britain.

But that was enough to let us exult in being there. I have seldom seen a gang of youngsters so happy. They were well aware of the dangers, and perhaps because of this were doubly aware of the basic blessings of life—sun, wind and water, health and strength, food, friendship and sleep. Such freedom is perhaps worth some risk; they may never taste it again.

When I woke at dawn the bay was empty, a smir hung on the hills, the kid was silent, the tide far out again. We roused ourselves. Bread wrappers flared up on the hot ashes of the fire and breakfast over and ourselves on that pass for 'home' again, we could still see the rebuilt bonfire flaring a farewell.

Back at Glengarrisdale we were marooned for two days while gales lashed the island. We had to walk out again, meeting the skipper in the hills coming to meet us; but for all of us the climax of our visit was that trek to the uttermost tip of Jura and our twenty-four hours within the roar of the Corrievreckan.

For Nabby, David, Brian, Charlie, John, Sid, George, Ronnie, Ian—and Hamish—it was a memory to last a lifetime.

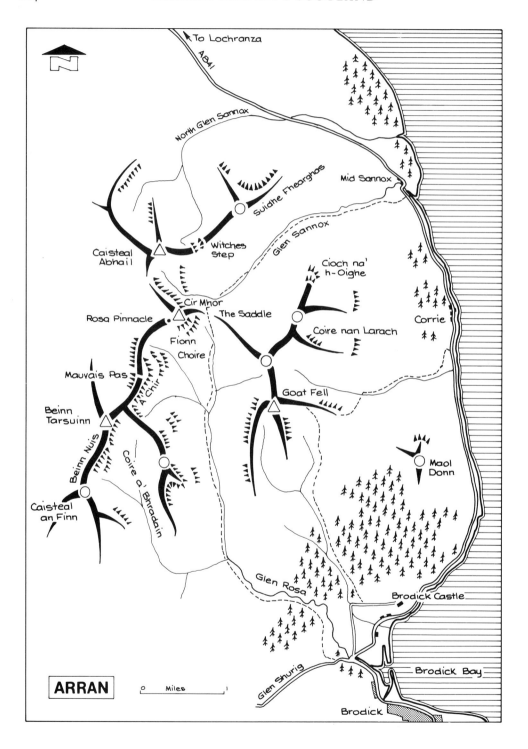

To Lochranza

ABNI

North Glen Sannox

Suidhe Fhearghas

Mid Sannox

Witches
Step

Glen Sannox

Caisteal
Abhail

Cioch na'
h-Oighe

Cir Mhor

The Saddle

Corrie

Rosa Pinnacle

Coire nan Larach

Fionn
Choire

Mauvais Pas

A'Chir

Goat Fell

Beinn
Tarsuinn

Beinn Nuis

Maol
Donn

Coire a' Bhradain

Caisteal
an Finn

Glen Rosa

Brodick Castle

Brodick Bay

Glen Shurig

Brodick

ARRAN

0   Miles   1

Arran is Magic

'Arran is magic' was the reaction of a lad I spoke to recently. He had taken his cycle over and explored the island thoroughly by road, by tramping and camping its glens and ridges and enjoying several rock climbs.

Few places can crowd in such a variety of good things and my list would add prehistoric monuments, wildlife, seashore, and garden interests. That lad had actually, unprompted, commented on the 'bonny bright bushes' at Brodick Castle—having been there at rhododendron time.

The moment one lands on the pier at Brodick, Goat Fell catches the eye. It rises behind the castle across the bay as gracefully as Fuji Yama. Most people fall for Arran instantly.

Glen Rosa and Glen Sannox reach into the big granite hills as if they were trying to remove Goat Fell from the rest of the peaks. Goat Fell is really a solitary summit and, being the highest, dominates the island. I can still remember the thrill of reaching it the first time, as a boy, and seeing the Clyde glittering in the sun and Tarsuinn, Cir Mhor, and Caisteal Abhail ranged raggedly against the sunset colours.

I'd reached Arran by cycling from home in Dollar and staying in Brodick youth hostel (a bad gap now without a hostel) and, like the youth I was speaking to thirty years on, I explored thoroughly, beside traversing all the ridges and getting gripped on the granite crags. It was magic all right. Some things don't change.

There is a well-marked path for Goat Fell from Brodick, starting from the lushness of the castle grounds. On the moors the map shows a burn splitting into two (a very unusual natural phenomenon) and I remember going to inspect this only to find it was caused by an old mill dam. I've only found perhaps four genuine stream bifurcations in Scotland.

The path curves up from the corrie to reach the summit via the east ridge. There is something special about mountains which rise so steeply from expansive seascapes. I had a gull's view of the Clyde.

One of the few mountain books I read over and over again is Janet Adam Smith's Mountain Holidays. It opens with a chapter on Arran, where she climbed Goat Fell at the age of nine, having been blasted off the east ridge the year before. Those were family holiday visits, under the care of the poet and mountaineer W P Ker and they led to many of the participants going on to climb and explore in many parts of the world.

28   Cir Mhor, Arran—a poem in granite.

The book goes on to describe Alpine holidays and I found it infectious. Even the
Alps can be fun, as Goat Fell was fun. A fun based on acquired skills, but still fun.
Where grim-faced Wymper had left me gasping, this book beguiled me to the Alps—
and beyond.

I'd already read about Arran's ridges, for Dollar was the home of W K Holmes and
his sister who were kind to the maverick youth who already ran wild on the Ochils.

W K H's modest book *Tramping Scottish Hills* has a chapter on the Goat Fell
Horseshoe. That book I knew almost by heart. I suspect W K H and W P K were very
alike in many ways. Their quiet, solid, yet visionary approach to the hills, I feel, is sadly
lacking today when big egos seems to want instant trips.

I've no idea how I came down again on that first visit, so it was probably by the
'tourist path' I'd ascended, but I can recall the next descent, to Sannox, and this, with
the ascent from Brodick, is the classic traverse.

The descent edges down along the cliffs of Coire nam Fuaran (in 1889 a young man was murdered and his body found below these cliffs). The ridge levels off, then becomes a rocky crest, sheer on the east side and super-steep above Glen Sannox, over Cioch na h-Oighe, the Maiden's Breast.

For a young lad on his own it was exciting: a first taste of exposure and the friendly adhesiveness of granite scrambling.

In the seventies I was to see plenty of young men react to Arran's hills, for we came there several time with trainees from the topsail schooner Captain Scott. We had a survival camp in Glen Rosa on one occasion and when climbing Goat Fell the wind periodically knocked whole groups to the ground at once. Some of the townies found it quite frightening.

On another occasion we carried everything over Goat Fell to camp on The Saddle with a view down Glen Rosa and the wind and cloud racing harmlessly up Cir Mhor from Glen Sannox.

The first recorded crossing of the Saddle to link Brodick and Sannox was in 1822 when two Kilmarnock ladies living in Brodick did this, their feat 'exciting no small wonder'. Even twenty years later it was a walk for which one would normally take a guide.

The lateness of the Saddle becoming a regular pass is strange as (early as 1800) a route is marked up Glen Rosa, round Cir Mhor and Caisteal Abhail to Lochranza—a much more demanding walk. These hills behind Goat Fell give a splendid long day over their crests.

Walkers are sometimes put off the Arran hills by reports of difficulties, of unavoidable climbing, of 'Bad Steps', of 'cyclopean' rocks and boiler-plate slabs, which is a pity for Arran is a great place for walkers and for backpacking.

The young *Captain Scott* trainees happily carried their gear over Goat Fell to that camp on The Saddle and the next day traversed Cir Mhor and Caisteal Abhail to camp before climbing Beinn Bharran above the west coast and rejoining ship off Lochranza Castle.

The walk begins from Glen Rosa and follows up the Garbh Allt (*rough burn*) to gain Beinn Nuis. The walk north to Beinn Tarsuinn presents no difficulty though the east face is an amazing world of granite slabs and pinnacles. Exposed but easy scrambling leads along to the summit of A' Chir (the comb), the top being a large, undercut boulder which is a minor challenge in itself.

Beyond the summit, on the descent, lies the *mauvais pass*, which is basically unavoidable so has to be faced. The exposure rather than any technical difficulty gives the Bad Step its reputation. A cairn shows where the ridge has to be left to descend a 12-foot wall on the east face to the ledge angling along to easier ground.

Some people claim this is not the actual 'Bad Step' but just a difficult section of ridge. That name they would keep for a feature met not long before, at the foot of the initial descent off A' Chir, where a foot-wide col (the narrowest part of the whole ridge) has a cleft cutting it so you have to make a step across space so to speak. You can allocate the name as you choose!

Easy grass slopes lead up to Cir Mhor, which is best remembered by the Rosa Pinnacle, a soaring, curving buttress of granite on the right. (The best view of the pinnacle is from the Fionn Choire, having walked up Glen Rosa).

There is a welcome spring on the shoulder of Caisteal Abhail as one pulls up the *Ptarmigan's Castles*—a good resting place. The castles are a collection of summital boulders and tors, as is the route's continuation eastwards and then there is the *Witches' Step*, the *Carlin's Leap*, Ceum na Caillich.

This is the deep gash in the ridge caused by the weathering away of a whin dyke with a tricky exit up the far side, which looks intimidating but goes with just one awkward sloping slab. It can all be avoided by contouring away round under the crags.

The ridge runs out to Suidhe Fhearghas, *Fergus's Seat*, from which the descent can be made to the nineteenth hole of the Sannox Golf Course. Fergus was the bard of the Fiana, who often hunted in Arran according to Irish legends, or Fergus was the king who came up here to survey his domains.

When I had the dog on Arran his exuberance was alarming. On the Bad Step wall I tied clothes together to make a rope to lower Storm in the rucksack, but he decided to jump out halfway down. As often as not when I was struggling he'd be peering down at me, mocking my incompetence. He's very hard to live up to. But so is Arran.

The Cocktail Islands: Eigg

Rhum, Eigg, Muck, and Canna. What a cocktail of names for any group of islands but these Inner Hebridean islands are as cheerfully individualistic as their names.

Having to rewrite my old guidebook to Rhum was a good excuse for renewing acquaintance with them—not that any excuse is needed. I am an incorrigible island-goer and as these all have superb scenery, interesting wildlife, good walking, and friendly folk, they should be much more popular with visitors.

The mere fact of having to catch a ferry (and dealing with leaving the dictator-car and organising food for the visit) is obviously too much for most. Rhum remains that jagged crest in the sunset, and Eigg that improbably broken-backed shape with a spike at the end. Canna and Muck are too close to the horizon even at that distance. They are 'out of sight out of mind' places.

29   The Sgurr of Eigg.

All are linked by the redoubtable *Lochmor*, which looks like a pile of seaborne scaffolding and gives accommodation the equivalent of roadworkers' huts—but we love her dearly for all her sins. Her predecessor, the *Loch Arkaig*, sank in Mallaig Harbour! Walk up the Mallaig train and you will spot quiet passengers, well-garbed for wild weather, with holdalls and well tied cartons on the rack. They are the old island-goers.

You will also see the noisy, scantily-clad who are nascent island-goers. Later on you will see them on the *Lochmor*, with blue legs and chattering teeth, as you climb down into one of the bobbing launches which will finally take you onto Rhum, Eigg, or Muck.

Just to be different last time we went to Eigg it was on the *Shearwater* which operates out of Arisaig. She operates only from Easter to autumn but, taking an octogenarian mother with me, there was the advantage of being able to go alongside the pier at Eigg. We had rented a chalet for a week on the island. Most of the island seemed to be at the pier to welcome newcomers, only it was *Shearwater* rather than her passengers that had them licking their lips. The boat is licensed and when you live on an island without a pub there is nothing quite like having the pub motor into your backyard so to speak!

The Sgurr of Eigg is remarkable from the mainland. At the pier it hangs over one like a blunt instrument and, wherever you wander, it has a certain threatening presence. Rhum was a centre of volcanic activity (many safe millions of years ago) and all these islands are basically lavas of one kind or another, with only some of the original standstone breaking through from underneath, like the north part of Rhum or the 'skirts' of Eigg. The Sgurr is columnar pitchstone (like Fingal's Cave), its harder rock left stark when the softer rock surrounding it was eroded away.

Climbers have climbed that bulging prow that faces the pier. Mother was happy just to look, while the dog and I took it by the flank and an easy way up.

The last bastion has a wall across it, the defence line of some prehistoric people. It is quite as spectacular a place to look *from* as to look *at* with Rhum ranged craggily to the north, Muck plattered in the sea (with Ardnamurchan and Mull beyond), a whole dappling of mainland hills to test one's geographical knowledge, and a western rim of mysterious Outer Isles.

A scattering of lochans (full of nasty legends) dots the moor, contrasting with the greener farmlands. The gap (*eige*) in the middle of the island may be the origin of its name.

The earliest historical event was the landing of St Donan in the early seventh century. There is still a hamlet and its bay called Kildonan (*the church of Donan*) but Saint Donan and his monks were all massacred in the year 617, perhaps the work of pirates for the Vikings were still two centuries away then. Was there perhaps a holy site on Rhum too for the Norse named one spot Papadil (*priest's valley*), about which nothing is known?

St Donan's Day in April was an Eigg holiday till last century. Names like Cleadale and Galmisdale on Eigg show the Viking influence here and grave mounds have yielded a rich haul of artefacts which would have belonged to the affluent. The Battle of Largs in 1263 was the Vikings' 1066. Until last century Eigg was largely in Clan Ranald possession. It was not always a peaceful history.

In 1577, a vengeance-seeking MacLeod party descended on Eigg and the people hid in a cave. A scout, sent out the next day, was seen by the departing MacLeods who landed once more and tracked him in the snow back to the refuge. They fired the cave, smothering 395 people. Eleven years later MacLean of Duart, helped by the Spaniards off the Armada ship *Florencia* (now at the bottom of Tobermory Bay), raided Eigg and wiped out most of the population.

I visited the cave which, unlike so many, was big and deep once the narrow entrance was penetrated. Last century vast quantities of human bones were reportedly brought out and reburied. One never quite knows what to believe of these stories but enough was enough anyway.

Eigg also suffered after the '45 when the cruel Captain Ferguson landed and captured a leading Jacobite who had a roll of 'supporters' names. These were rounded up by trickery and after a year in prison most ended, innocent or guilty, in the slave fields of the West Indies. The Clearances hit Eigg, too, though from 1893 until the First World War the island was helped by landowners who invested heavily in the island.

Pre-war, ten steamers a week called. Now there is just the *Lochmor* and the occasional *Shearwater*.

Like so many peripheral places, Eigg is facing economic difficulties. Cattle have gone and with them another part of the population. Most of the vital jobs are done by 'incomers', yet there is no island bakery or dairy. All imports are costly.

We were staying in a small wooden chalet but most of the houses in this south-east corner are let to holiday visitors while the dwindling crofting population lives at the other end of the island, often in poor housing. A shop sits, unhandily, half-way between. There are plenty of problems.

Ours was a fairly lazy holiday but I did hire a bike to cross the island to Cleadale and Camus Sciotaig with its 'singing sands'. They did not sing that day and my main interest was seeing my first sea-eagle—no doubt one of those released on Rhum as part of the effort at re-introducing this once common enough Western Isles bird.

We climbed the Sgurr from the south after a breezy walk along the green slopes of Gruline. A lonely whitewashed cottage lay in a fold of hill looking out to Muck and the isles of the silver sea. It was my dream of a holiday spot: utterly remote and peaceful. There would be no guilt in hiring it either for in these days nobody wants to live beyond electricity and tarred roads—and who could blame them?

These are actually benefits which have come in my lifetime. Some of my early memories are of gutting mackerel by candlelight in a tiny scullery or playing Monopoly in the comfortable, hissing light of a Tilley lamp, and cycling the rough untarred roads to the isles.

The midges haven't changed and they were bad on windless evenings in our wooded, sheltered part of Eigg. Just up the road was the Lodge, the owner's house, with its luxuriant gardens—which even had eucalyptus trees, Dragon's Blood palms, and other exotics to tesity to the relative benevolence of the climate. Fortunately a wind blew most days, which is another reason for island-bagging in the summer months.

As a learned journal once informed me, 'midges do not like strong sun, wind, and will not be found above 10,000 feet.' On the first two counts islands have a great deal to recommend them.

The rain is usually less persistent, even if vigorous at times, and there is always a busy restfulness which has been lost on the mainland of life. We actually need islands.

Information on Eigg can be obtained from the Estate Tourist Officer, Isle of Eigg, by Mallaig (telephone 0687 82413), and there is a useful booklet, A Guide to Eigg and Muck, *written by Lawrence MacEwen of Muck, to which we go next.*

The Cocktail Islands: Muck

It was a snap-decision that took me to Muck. I'd left a rucksack packed in the car (parked at the friendly West Highland Hotel) ready to go off somewhere else but, in the boat, returning from island wanderings I just did not want to leave the West and decided I could maybe fit in a couple of nights on Muck.

So as soon as we landed at Mallaig I phoned Muck and came out grinning at the confirmation. I had a cup of tea in the Fisherman's Mission to work out logistics—IN with MacBraynes on Saturday, OUT to Arisaig on Monday and train back to Mallaig for the car. I had to be home on Tuesday.

At 5 a.m. sharp the *Lochmor* wiggled her way out from the weekend fishing boats and set off for the Small Isles. There were six passengers (in a midsummer week) so the early start seems crazy economics if nothing else. It was a grey, cloudy day so I retreated to the saloon and slept the miles to Canna and Rhum. The weather was furling its clouds when I came on deck off Eigg.

We circled a couple of times off Muck before the launch came out to meet us. Big boats give Muck plenty of room. Even the launch steered off towards Ardnamurchan lighthouse before doubling back inside invisible reefs for the quiet creek of Port Mor.

The port is the only hamlet on the island and most of its score of people dwell there. There is a school, a craft workshop, and assorted farm buildings. A hayfield beside the loch was being turned over by a dragonfly red tractor—grabbing this advent of sun from the 'flaws of fine weather we call summer'. The telephone box was red too and the grassy knoll up to it bore no trace of frantic feet.

Walls and fences kept cows and sheep separated from the corduroy rows of potato fields: brown where already lifted and green for the rest. The green gladdened the eye after weeks of wandering among isles of vanished people and barren slopes still traced by the lines of lazy beds. By a geological gift, and by man's work, Muck is the green garden of the weary Hebrides.

Mr McEwan met a couple and their dogs, staying at the guest house, while my remit was 'Camp anywhere except on the hayfields.' Pressed for a near site I was pointed up the hill where grey stones showed the site of the old village of Keil. 'If you are not afraid of ghosts, you could try up there.'

I wandered up through a circle of graveyard with old stones studding its interior and one Victorian oddity of a monument to lads drowned while boating over on Horse

30 Port Muck—the view from the tent door.

Island in 1895. There are some graves of German sailors—washed ashore during the war. Wood is still beachcombed as the main fuel is puffer-delivered coal.

Anciently the people brought peat in from Rhum or Ardnamurchan and heather, for kindling, from Eigg. Foxgloves grew on the ruin walls and the insides were nettle-furnished. My site belonged to the reeling larks, the drumming snipe, and a restless wheatear family.

We pitched the tent with its door open to the blue sea and Ardnamurchan's lumpy skyline. Sitting by the door I looked to the long, bold flank of Eigg. After a brew I threw lunch into the rucker and set off westwards, on a surface kind as a golf course, which led by gentle switchbacks across long glens which still held old walls and braken-swamped cottages in their secret, sheltered corners.

Sheep and cows roam it now in sensible combination, so it is still green and fertile. Sheep alone create a desert with their destructive grazing—as most of the Highlands testify.

Above the west side of the bay lay Beinn Airein, 137 metres, the highest point of Muck. The lure of the highest won. We swung up for its breezy top, rewarded with a rich view, which could not be excelled by any view from a mere Munro. Quality and height are not synonymous.

The narrow waist of the island, between Camus Mor and Bagh a' Ghallanaich had already been cut for hay, leaving yellowy swathes in the deeper growths of green. Because knobbles of rock had been avoided the effect was of oddly geometrical arcs and curves.

The clean-gleaming farm buildings, the white sands, the dark seaweed strands, the snaking road ($1\frac{1}{4}$ miles of it), all blended into a neat, perfection of form. Muck could be looked at from a seat in the gods while, as backcloth to the play, the bigger islands were painted in theatrical brilliance: Canna's western end with its cut-off prow, Rhum with mountains clear and stark, the Skye Cuillin hull-down and blue with distance, and Eigg with the long Gibraltar of the Sgurr hiding its real shape.

West lay the Catholic Outer Isles, south lay Coll, the Dutchman's Cap and other islands off Mull. Ben More peered over ranging Ardnamurchan. Up the mainland eyes followed endless hills: the peaks of Morven and Moidart, the Rough Bounds of Knoydart and Kintail. It is a mere list of names now but its beauty cut like a pain. It was lovely beyond the telling.

I cut down to the farm. Rhode Island pullets made an unusual foreground to the Cuillin Hills of Rhum. Gallanach Farm looked as tidy as everything else on Muck.

There are several small plantings of trees in the sheltered corners of Muck with some oak and sycamore mixed in with the conifers. Along from the guest house at Port Mor there are several more ornamental plots and some thriving fruit and vegetable gardens. From the top of the road we cut over to the tent and sat outside, midge-free.

Later I explored the south end of the island, being curious at the 'fort' shown on the map. This was a Bronze Age site, a natural knoll, reinforced where not naturally sheer-sided. Out to sea were the reefs that make Port Mor too risky for all but small boats.

Muck is a somewhat unfortunate name but it doubtless comes from *muc,* meaning pig, which is by no means an uncommon name. (There's Eilean nam Muc, *island of the pig,* north of Loch Eatharna in Coll, after all.) Being pig-shaped is less likely; mapmakers took long enough to see shapes of islands. 'Sea-pigs' in Gaelic are porpoises and they are plentiful enough round these islands. Boswell records the then owner objecting to just being called Muck. 'Isle of Muck' he insisted.

Dean Munro in the sixteenth century called it 'Swynes ile, and verey fertill and fruitful of cornes and grassing for all store, and very guid for fishing, inhabit, and manurit, a good falcon nest in it, it perteynis to the Bishope of the Isles, with ane guid heighland haven in it, the entrey quherof is at the west cheik.'

Before I realised what had happened, the day began to ebb. It was mid-summer and hardly became completely dark but reading became impossible. It was the first time in months that I had had a day of untrammelled freedom and the evening passed very easily 'doing nothing and resting afterwards'.

There were children playing down below and their yells and laughter were one of my last memories, along with the drumming of the snipe in the gloaming.

> O, for the gilded age of seven
> When a yard of sand, and a puddle,
> Reflected heaven!

I suppose there is a richer satisfaction in our more concentrated adult approach, even if we might long for the simple joys of childhood. Perhaps this is why we so gleefully escape to havens like Muck. We can roll up our trouser years and plash white feet once again in innocent seas. Social history and economics evaporate in summer suns.

I haven't actually said much about Muck, having just given the feel of a solitary day, but I hope I have hinted at its main charms for the visitor—quite and beauty—and its rich productivity. It is lived in and farmed, it is tidy, diversifying and expanding its work opportunities, seeing new houses built, altogether not a common picture in the Hebrides.

Lawrence MacEwen has written a booklet guide to Eigg and Muck (regularly updated) which is worth writing for to find out about accommodation and services as well as the history of the island. One entry I liked. Under 'Land Transport' it had 'Muck: none—walk!' I did. Next day, on the *Shearwater* to Arisaig, I dropped off a brief card. It summarised, as briefly, 'Muck: small—one of the best!'

For information on Muck contact the estate office or telephone Mallaig (0687) 2362 or 2365.

The Cocktail Islands: Canna

As soon as we tied up at the pier on Canna we staggered ashore, thankful that the bouncy journey was over. Fishing boats (even the converted *Ocean Bounty*) have a propensity for bouncing. Supper could wait.

I went along past the Presbyterian church with its pseudo Round Tower (modelled on Glendalough) and through to the castle, known as The Prison, a tiny ruin atop a stumpy crag looking over the eastern sea. The doorway looked precarious and if the scramble up was made casually enough the down-climb was made more cannily.

I put off the descent until hunger won over travel wobbles, so was able to have a good look at Canna from my perch. Thomas Pennant, when he visited Canna, described this perch as 'a lofty, slender rock that juts into the sea: on one side is a little tower, at a vast height above us, accessible by a narrow and horrible path . . . Tradition says it was built by some jealous *regulus* to confine a handsome wife in,' which is about all that is known of a persisting story.

Canna is almost five miles long by about one mile wide and apart from the southeast corner with the harbour and its 1½-mile long sheltering island of Sanday is usually cliff-girt. There is a great deal of pudding stone—conglomerates of basalt, sandstones, and schists, pointing to a fine old baker's dough as volcanic rivers flowed over this part of the world a mere 40 million years ago. Compass Hill (458 feet) above us at the east end, contains such highly-magnetised basalt that it upsets compass readings—not a useful navigation mark. (Martin Martin mentions this.)

Carn a' Ghall, along a bit at 690 feet, is the highest point of Canna. Sanday doesn't make 200 feet, but some of that is sheer cliff, pinnacles, and caves, which I saw better from Guirdil bothy on Rhum than from trying to peer over their edges. A new navigation light on the end of Sandy winked over those miles, a friendly gesture in a lonely howff.

A frigate, F18, passed through the Sound when I was studying Canna from Rhum. It set the scale nicely. What I'd never noticed before was a solitary rock several miles off Canna, called Umaolo (how do you pronounce that, it looks like Swahili?). This must be a real hazard to sailors. Heiskeir, even farther out, at least has a tall lighthouse on its jigsaw of black reefs.

This island is only 34 feet at the highest yet ships have been known to shelter from gales in its heart with the spray flying overhead. Last century Canna cattle were grazed

177

on its 10 acres. There is a spring. And now it is quite deserted, lighthouse apart, and ships give it a wide berth. It is still owned by John Lorne Campbell though he gave Canna/Sanday to the National Trust for Scotland in 1981, after forty-three years of ownership.

Canna has had far fewer landowners than some of the other islands. The Thom family was there from 1881 till 1938 when it was sold to John Lorne Campbell. He is a Gaelic scholar of international repute with a unique Highland/Gaelic library on Canna. His wife, Margaret Fay Shaw (from Pennsylvania) is a scholar in her own right, her *Folk Songs and Folk Lore of South Uist* being the work of two decades. Both have been tied up with Canna life in every way.

'I measure my success here by the happiness of the people of Canna,' he has said, which must make advancing years and current economics something of a heartbreak though some continuity is assured under the NTS. Dr Campbell still lives at Canna House and one of his memorials must be his thorough and fascinating definitive history published in 1984—the 'inside story' so to speak and not always a pleasant tale. Central government propaganda is nothing new, and if Edinburgh suffers London, the isles have had to thole both. And still do.

There was some pleasant mixed woodland (always an enriching habitat for birds) and shrubs like escallonia, senecio, and fuschia pointed to the mildness of its western climate (last winter cut down all our outdoor fuschias on the east coast). A child's outrigger made of beer cans lay marooned on the shore and farther along was a dead dogfish. Several eider families were dooking among the swaying seaweeds as I reached the pier.

Canna is the only one of the small isles to have a pier which is usable by boats the size of MacBrayne's *Lochmor.* Built at the end of last century it was rebuilt in concrete just before the Second World War. On the rocks near it are painted the names of generations of fishing boats, yachts, and other craft. I remember crawling along to touch up the name 'Captain Scott' (she now sails the Gulf of Oman because Scotland couldn't support even one training schooner). I presumed *Ocean Bounty* had her name somewhere.

One of the few advantages of Canna is that it does not have a public road so vehicles are not registered or taxed. The island though, hardly buzzes with traffic, one of its charms. After supper I went off to see the standing stone and the cross. The former is thought to be an old pillory, the latter is broken and badly weathered but has some fascinating features.

St Columba may well have founded a monastery on Canna (the Hinba of Adamnan?) and ruins of that date occupy a site three miles along to the west. The current map oddly marks it 'Cashel', an Irish world for a fortified site but then Dr Campbell's book shows a score of place names minced by the OS machine.

Dun Channa (Channa's Fort) at the extreme west end of Canna may have given the island its name from a person unknown. Some suggest the Gaelic for porpoise (Cana) is a possible derivation but so is Kanin, isle of rabbits. Old maps have Cannay. Take your pick. There are rabbits and porpoises. There are also seals and otters and feral goats, eagles, shearwater, and puffins for the lucky observer. The island has been treated as a bird sanctuary since 1938, and Dr Campbell was a noted lepidopterist.

Like Muck, it is so green compared to neighbouring Rhum, and sheep and cows are still part of its economy. The NTS are experimenting with oyster farming and have both self-catering and bothy accommodation for visitors, who can also camp.

The NTS would like to see more people permanently settling on the island, but they would have to bring work with them. The island operates as a single farm. Like Muck, it is very much a place for a restful holiday. Electricity is home-made and goes off at 11 p.m.

The next day we ranged farther afield but having to sail at midday left so much unexplored. Across on Sanday a solitary church in eye-catching stone demanded a visit. Canna has been a Catholic place throughout history and this church was completed in 1890, its site chosen so it would be a landmark to shipping.

With the decline in Sanday's population, services have reverted to Canna and we found this building stark, damp, and derelict. The kelp industry was responsible for the many houses on Sanday, and its collapse was just one island disaster in the west. Crofting on Sanday has now run down entirely.

To reach Sanday we crossed a long footbridge which was originally built to allow children safe access to school rather than depending on low tides for their education. Typically the authorities (who have done nothing for Canna in the way of pier-building, road works, hydro, or other accepted works) only maintain it with great reluctace.

The children, of course, are packed off to boarding school in Fort William after the age of 11—an insidious drain on the population and a detraction to incomers with young children—who are especially needed to maintain a primary school for a balanced community.

Corroghon Bay, where the Prizon is sited, saw a German ship run ashore in an autumn storm. Five crew were taken off by breeches buoy, the captain and mate stayed on board and the lifeboat later towed the *Widder* to Rhum and then collected the crew. It took an emergency like this to see the local telephone services were improved.

Living on islands is not so romantic really. When we sailed off I took out Dr Campbell's book, *Canna* (just out then), to read in my bunk.

Truth lies best in the book's coloured illustrations and the truth is better than the romancing. The picture of Corroghon Bay shows its curve of silver sands running to a tidal islet, the Prison boldly in the centre, and MacBrayne's *Lochmo*r heading off for Rhum in the background, and it is to Rhum we must go next, the biggest of these Small Isles.

For current information on Canna, contact the NTS representative on the islands—ring Mallaig (0687) 2466—or (for accommodation) the NTS in Edinburgh (031 226 5922). As I have mentioned the book several times and highly recommend it, not only for Canna, but for island-understanding generally, here are its bibliographical details—J L Campbell: Canna, The Story of a Hebridean Island. *NTS/OUP. 1984.*

The Cocktail Islands: Rhum

Most of what I wrote about Eigg, Muck, and Canna was scribbled while staying on Rhum. This I begin as the *Lochmor* bears us off to the mainland. It is really an attempt to overcome the sadness of leaving. I have only been on Rhum for one week but islands instantly become timeless places and leaving them is always something of a pang.

We are heading over a gloss-grey sea with the shearwaters swanking their powers of flight round us. Rhum is green-grey, rising to blue-grey and the peaks of Hallival and Askival are buried in clouds nearer black than grey. Askival's Prow and Beinn nan Stac jut out below the murk. Was it only yesterday I perched up there in the timelessness of wind and sun and watched the sunset colours sink Eigg into night?

I had spent two nights alone at the bothy at Dibidil and one splendid day on Askival via Beinn nan Stac where I was checking out some route descriptions noted in the bothy book. I was beguiled onto the rocks myself and once again had that tingling fun-fright feel of working up an unknown crag. With a wobbly ankle and an unbalancing wind there was a deal more fright than fun in it! Still, the revision of the guidebook had to be done.

Most of it was accomplished more sociably in the NCC office with its fascinating collection of books and papers on many topics. One of my calls was on Kate Johnson, who has spent three years studying the shearwaters for her thesis.

Rhum has about a third of the world's population of Manx shearwaters, extraordinary birds which get a few paragraphs in the guide (which I refused to do as a catalogue of climbs, Rhum being much more than just the ego-fun of climbing) and Kate has some interesting new comments.

She had found one bird ringed by the first chief warden 25 years ago—before she was born! Last year their arrival in March coincided with heavy snow lying and their tracks were very useful in yielding information. The poor birds had to dig down to find their burrows. They are now beginning to colonise Newfoundland. They will quite happily nip down to the Bay of Biscay to feed and return with food for their burrow-safe chicks.

Guirdil bothy on the north coast has a setting even finer than Dibidil but, not being in the climbing area, receives fewer visitors. It sits on the edge of a boulder beach in the lee of Bloodstone Hill and looks out to Canna the way Dibidil looks to Eigg. Deer,

31   The Cuillin of Rhum from the Island of Eigg.

goats, and Highland cattle were always visible from the bothy, grazing the lush green grass of these northern glens. Man's past is seen in the acres and acres of lazy bed stripes and the sad shells of abandoned dwellings.

The cows came down overnight and one bellowed non-stop outside the door from 4 a.m. until 6 a.m. when I got up in self-defence. When I opened the door to give her a piece of my mind three stags in velvet clattered off along the beach, setting all the oystercatchers into loud complaint.

The cows are normally at Harris, where they help keep the grass in good order. Grass, grazed right down by sheep, suffers while grass, grazed by cows, thrives. The whole of Highland history is one of figurative (and literal) overgrazing. The good of the land itself is seldom considered, nor the long-term effects. The fast buck still wins even if the future loses thereby. Rhum is one of the few places where the future is considered.

As it is an island National Nature Reserve, the Nature Conservancy Council have a superbly 'fenced' research area. Deer cannot wander off from the control area, for instance. I was at Guirdil on a Saturday night so that I could see Kilmory on the Sunday, which is the only day it is 'open' to visitors.

Being a sunny Sunday it lured most of the visitors and residents: a Norfolk school group on a field studies project, the voluntary workers on one of their off-days (forestry lads who were weeding the beds of seedling trees), and all the children of the NCC workers. The NCC only employs staff with young children so as to keep the school and community viable. (It plays havoc with the average age of the Rhum population figures!)

Kilmory is normally closed because it has been set aside as a unique deer research area. Here the deer are allowed to live 'naturally': they are not culled and everything about them is studied, from birth to death, in a way never undertaken before. I met Fiona Guiness, the main researcher, who spends most of her life with these deer and knows them all as well as we ken our neighbours.

Earlier studies on Rhum produced information which is used throughout the country in culling and maintaining healthy stocks of deer.

Walking back from Kilmory I passed several fenced-off areas where another long-term study is in progress. These are plots in which have been planted a blend of the natural woodland tree types in an effort to try and recreate this now largely extinct asset in Scotland. These early plots have thrived and birches rise 30 feet high with primroses and wood sorrel dotting the ground.

Hazel, alder, aspen, hawthorn, Scots pine, and holly are some of the other trees used, and both to north and south of Loch Scresort big areas have been and are being planted with these species. They are then left to sort themselves out in an experiment that will see a couple of generations of man come and go. Again, only a place like Rhum could undertake such a long-term study. If only we hadn't—and didn't—wreck our environment in the first place.

Because of the NCC ownership and commitment Rhum probably has a more assured future than the other islands but it shares with all of them the problem of schooling. They may keep the primary school but secondary school means the children being packaged off to Fort William and only seen for the holidays. For many it is too high a price to pay for living on Rhum, Eigg, Canna, or Muck. They move and traditions are broken and replacements not always possible.

This year should see the new guidebook to Rhum published. (Cicerone Press). Information on the island can be updated by contacting The Chief Warden, The White House, Kinloch, Isle of Rhum, Mallaig (tel: 0687 2026).

Skye High

The other night I listened to a young lad bemoaning that Skye would be a difficult area to deal with in his Munro-bagging plans. 'It's all rock-climbing,' he complained, 'and I'm only a walker.' I hope I managed to change his mind, for his fears were quite groundless, and perhaps a reiteration of some facts here can also help to deal with the myths.

There are, of course, people who 'have done all the Munros, except one or two on Skye'. I know several and have actually, physically, helped some of them to rectify their lack. Certainly one or two, or even four, Munros on Skye, are of a standard beyond anything else in the Tables. But that is only a third of the Cuillin Munros—and Skye is far more than just the Black Cuillin. Remove the Cuillin completely and Skye is still a rewarding place for the walker to visit.

Reaching Skye from the mainland is easy enough with an all-year ferry shuttling across the narrows at Kyle of Lochalsh, but the more adventurous motorist might enjoy taking the spectacular mountain pass of Mam Ratagan to Glenelg for the historic ferry to Kylerhea. There is also a ferry (five a day) from Mallaig to Armadale on the Point of Sleat.

Broadford is the main shopping place available if only going in to the Cuillin ranges, as Portree lies north of the big hills. Portree is, however, a tidy, attractive town and worth visiting for its own sake. Like the whole of Skye, it is rich in historical interest, and if it seems Bonnie Prince Charlie went everywhere—he did! Much of the history of Skye and the Isles can be discovered at the Clan Donald Centre at Armadale Castle.

From Elgol you can see why the *Black* Cuillin are so called, for the dark gabbro rock makes them just that, in contrast to the weathered red domes of hills at the head of Loch Slapin and behind Broadford which are, not surprisingly, called the Red Cuillin.

For practical detail of Black Cuillin walking ascents, consult either *Scrambles in Skye*, by J Wilson Parker (Cicerone Press), or *Black Cuillin Ridge; Scramblers' Guide*, by S P Bull (SMC); while *Magic of Skye*, by W A Poucher (Constable), though a pocket-size reprint of this classic collection of photographs, does give visual assistance, and not just to the Black Cuillin. There is also the rather dated SMC General Guide, *Island of Skye*, by Slesser— but, of course, the hills described do not change and this is the best guide for all the other hill walking areas. For more general interest, Derek Cooper's *Skye* (Routledge & Kegan Paul) is worth borrowing from the library. *Skye, The Island and its Legends*, by Otta F Swire, is the best on older lore. You can't go to Skye without a load of books and, if it rains for two weeks, with midges thrown in, you'll be glad of them!

Maps are a problem and you'll probably end up with a collection of them as well. Bartholomew, at 1:100,000, conveniently has the whole island on one sheet (54)—very useful for general planning and for motoring. For walking other than on the Cuillin ranges, the Ordnance Survey 1:50,000 is adequate, but this series is inadequate when it comes to the complexities of the Black Cuillin, a situation exacerbated by the fact that on most of the crest of the ridge the compass is magnetically affected and cannot be relied on. The OS, however, have an invaluable 1:25,000 Outdoor Leisure Map, *The Cuillin and Torridon Hills* (Skye on one side, Torridon on the other), and the SMC have a simplified *kamkarte* style map which picks out the most useful features very clearly: The Black Cuillin, 1:15,000. There is also a 1:20,000 map, The Black Cuillin, by J Wilson Parker. Take you pick—I've been lost with all of them.

Blaven is the only Black Cuillin Munro not on the main ridge. The walker climbs it from the east or via the SSW ridge. The former is kindlier, the latter long and exhausting and less accessible for it leads down to Camasunary Bay (bothy) which can only be reached by a rough coast path from Elgol or over the Strathaid *mam* (pass), three miles before Elgol.

Blaven is linked to Clach Glas (a climber's peak) then the black gives way to red for Marsco, the Beinn Deargs and Glamaig; peaks worth doing on a clear day, for views to

32   Skye. Looking to Blaven from the Marsco-Glamaig ridges.

33   The view from Blaven, looking towards Sgurr nan Gillean.

the other side of the glen are of the massed array of the main Black Cuillin hills. The Red Hills are covered with bad screes so careful route-picking is essential.

Sligachan has a famous old climbers' inn, but this gets rather swamped by tourists in summer and outdoor folk tend to camp wild nearby. The Bealach a' Mhaim is a famous path/pass (eight miles) linking Sligachan and the climbers' valhalla of Glenbrittle. Bruach na Frithe, perhaps the easiest Skye Munro, can be added en route. It is the only summit with a trig point. From Glenbrittle a rough coast walk leads round to Loch Scavaig and Loch Coruisk (JMCS hut) and a couple of miles on (over 'The Bad Step') to Camusunary.

Walkers should not miss Beinn na Caillich (the old woman's hill) above Broadford (it will change your ideas about the capabilities of elderly females!); while the glens walk from Luib to Loch Slapin to Strollamus to Luib is a classic. I've also had a wild and lonely hill day going into the peaks of Belig and the Corbett Garb-bheinn from the head of Loch Ainort—an area that does not merit a green path line on the big OS map! But the poet Sorley Maclean wrote exultantly of the Loch Ainort side of the peaks.

The road now goes steeply up and over to swing round past Sconser to Sligachan. Sconser is the pier for the small vehicle ferry to Raasay, *The Jewel of Skye*. There is both hotel and youth hostel accommodation and camping presents no problems. Allow time for Raasay. A circuit walk to take in Dun Caan, the lopped-off summit of the island, is a must, and so is a day spent walking to the northern extremity beyond Castle Brochel.

The charms of Glenbrittle are not strikingly obvious but in no time at all it becomes a special place. When you have bathed in a pool under the Eas Mor waterfall, marvelled at the Inaccessible Pinnacle and seen sunsets from the silver sands of the bay, it becomes very special indeed. Just about all the great names in British climbing seem to have stayed at Glenbrittle, but it is equally a good base to be enjoyed by ordinary walkers. There are several places now doing Bed and Breakfast or guest house accommodation. Probably the best base is the Memorial Hut, built with money raised in memory to hill-goers who died in the Second World War. It is well laid out and equipped and runs for the benefit of its clients. The warden is often an experienced climber able to help with advice. The hut tends to be busiest at Easter, which makes it doubly attractive as a summer base. The booking secretary is J W Simpson, 15 Branks Avenue, Chapelton, Strathaven, Lanarkshire.

The hut looks up to the spur of Sgurr nan Gobhar, and by outflanking this to the north a path leads up to Sgurr na Banachdich which really is the easiest Munro on Skye. Banachdich, Bruach na Freithe and Blaven will present easier ascents than many mainland Munros but the next few are the equivalent of coping with the Aonach Eagach or Torridon or An Teallach ridges. Navigation is not easy so good weather is advisable.

Sgurr nan Eag has an easy flank of considerable toil and monotony and I'd advise the path up into Coir a' Ghrunnda and reaching it by the north ridge: a good adventure for the walker. From the same dramatic corrie, Sgurr Dubh na Da Bheinn can be reached, and its offshoot Munro, Sgurr Dubh Mor—a steep, twisting, scramble that needs a head for heights. Sgurr Alasdair is usually climbed by the Great Stone Shoot (a vile scree gully) but from the head of this to the top there is a short, exposed, scramble. (Sgurr Mhic Choinnich and the Inaccessible Pinnacle are in the top grade.) Sgurr a'

34 Skye. Bruach na Freithe, one of the easier Cuillin peaks.

Ghreadaidh and Sgurr a' Mhadaidh can be climbed with fewest complications from the col of An Dorus but a few awkward bits, exposure and route-finding problems puts them a grade above peaks mentioned already. At the Sligachan end Am Basteir and Sgurr nan Gillean are harder ascents.

Don't be fooled by the title 'Tourist Route' for Gillean. It no more deserves that title than does the Aonach Eagach. Nevertheless, the southeast ridge is the easiest way up. There is a long moorland walk, much loose hillside and then a ridge which sets some problems before the final narrow crest. Am Basteir requires careful approach as the gorge draining Coire a' Bhasteir is virtually impassable and the path west of it is exposed in places. Once onto the Bealach a' Bhasteir, there is a thin hog's back to work along with some nasty, loose stones on slabby reaches and one decidedly unsettling ten-foot wall to lower down, with big drops all too visible beyond. My dog goes in the rucksack at that stage! Sgurr Mhic Choinnich's problems are something similar only more so, as there is plenty of scrambling, while the summit approach is a sloping rooftop which can be very slippery in wet conditions. It is not to be under-rated.

The 'Inn Pinn' never is, though in reality its bark is worse than its bite. People tend to get thoroughly worked up abouind it almost an anticlimax. It is a climb; it is exposed; but it is a technically easy climb and the climbing thrilling enough to overcome all other emotions. It is worth learning to abseil so as to descend by the steep, short side rather than having to climb down the longer, but easier, ascent ridge. Because it is what it is, problems don't really arise. You will automatically cope or enrol help for this special case. Make it a goal for early, rather than late, in the Munro game.

There are two undeservedly neglected Glenbrittle walks which I'd recommend—and not as bad-weather alternatives. One is the walk out to Rubh' an Dunain along the south shore of Loch Brittle. A bivouac on a knoll there is a fond memory of my last visit to Skye: the divers flew overhead in the sunset and offshore lay Rhum and Canna. There is also a fine prehistoric fort. The other walk is a traverse of the gentle hills west of Glen Brittle. Arrange a morning lift to the head of the glen and go up one of the fire breaks. You walk between sea and Cuillin.

You really should pity those who just go to Skye to climb. They sit moping because one bit of rock is wet. The walker has the whole island to relish, rain or sun, from sea-level, to Inn Pinn, to Alasdair. Beware though, Skye is one of the more dangerous drugs in use today. There are thousands of us high on Skye. It's well worth the trip.

35 The classic view of Sgurr nan Gillean across the Sligachan moors.

Bonxies on the Shiants

We went to the Shiant Islands because storms prevented us going to St Kilda. We had spent one hopeful day in Tarbet on a tour ranging from Callanish and Dun Carloway to the Butt of Lewis.

The gannets, Concordes of the avian world, were turning west into the gale—homing in to St Kilda. Seeing those seas we were content not to be heading west. One boat did and it ended on the boulders of Village Bay.

A grey calm lured us out early the next morning. There was just time for one day somewhere. 'Ever been to the Shiants?' the skipper asked. I didn't even know where they were, though I'd seen them several times when battling seas and seasickness in The Minch. 'They lie sort of off Lewis, pretty well due east from Tarbet if only Scalpay didn't get in the way.'

Our first contact was with the Galtacheans, a set of smashed teeth scattered for a mile westwards from the main islands: Galta Mor, Galta Beag and Damhag. We wended past them right round Garbh Eilean to the secret heart of the group. There are really three main islands: Garbh Eilean (*Rough Island,* sure enough), Eilean an Tighe (*House Island,* correct enough), these two joined by a mere ridge of storm beach and, facing them, Eilean Mhuire (*Mary's Island,* riddled with caves, girdled with cliffs, and mined with reefs). 'We'll no gang there,' the skipper puffed. We took the inflatable in to the storm beach and made a splashy landfall on their slippery thousand-footballs surface.

Sailing round Garbh Eilean it had appeared to be an impregnable bastion of basalt columns, hundreds of feet high—500 feet compared to Fingal's Cave's mere 20! The east side below which we'd anchored looked much the same, the great columns skirted at the foot by a jumble of fallen rock, brilliant yellow in colour from its lichen covering.

Perhaps, if we could not climp up, we could force a way along the Screes, as this yellow skirt is called but, once ashore, we found there was a tortuous route up from the neck. We still went along the Screes for they are the home of shags and puffins in great numbers and there is nothing so alluring as puffins.

Half a mile of scrambling took us to the far end where I managed to scramble up rather than return by the rocky route we'd come. The others preferred to keep closer to sea level so struggled back along the Screes. The Screes ended at a jutting headland which was completely cut through by the sea so it formed a natural arch. The sea sucked noisily through and shiny wrack swung to and fro. Some big whale bones lay on the rocks.

It was an eerie sort of place. Yet a ruin lay tucked in the corner and unlikely lazy beds striped the slope. People once lived there. The Shiants were occupied back in Martin Martin's day (late seventeenth century) when hay grew and cows climbed to the rolling top of Garbh Eilean.

I was met on top by a dive-bombing bonxie (great skua) which only gave up its attack when I cringed by some ruins of what looked like beehive huts to eat my lunch sandwiches. A bonxie is considerably bigger than any gull so if its legs do hit your head it can be sore! Usually the rush of wings gives you a split second's warning.

I'd known bonxies from St Kilda and the Northern Isles: these were the first I'd met inside the Minch. Perhaps they were expanding as the puffins did, for they like puffin suppers. They are also piratical in that they harry other gulls in the air until they are forced to disgorge whatever they have eaten, which the bonxie will catch and devour.

A noisy wren shared my ruin. Just an ordinary wren for the Shiants are too close to Lewis for a sub-species to have developed.

T S Muir, a mid-nineteenth-century visitor, seemed to find a sense of release and freedom on the wind-fresh, springy surfaced plateau. 'You ramble and skip about like an antic, full of your deliverance from the qualms of the seafaring and tricksy cliff-work,' he wrote. The tricksy cliff-work I was having to tackle without an uphill preview and it took a couple of casts to hit off the correct route down.

It was a corkscrew of gritty, loose path down the crumbling prow facing Eilean an Tighe and it was astonishing to think of cows once tackling it. Having more recently seen the Rhum Highlanders in action on its sea cliffs I would not be surprised by anything bovine. They are not just milk machines, they're athletic milk machines!

Martin Martin mentioned these athletic cows and he also mentioned Eilean Mhuire's having a chapel dedicated to the Virgin. Other records also point to it having been a Catholic refuge. As the island looks impregnable its devotees must have been pretty athletic too.

By Muir's time (1859) all three islands were uninhabited but at least one shepherd was then installed and lived in the house (new then) on Eilean an Tighe.

Harvie-Brown in 1879 was entertained by the family. By the turn of the century just an old man and a girl were left. The girl went courting to Lewis by rowing the seven miles of dangerous sound, but when the old man died she was marooned for ten days before storms let her row off for help.

Compton Mackenzie, owned the islands, pre-war, and stayed in the house, along with several cats to ward off its encroaching rats. The turn of the century saw the last of the Shiant sea-eagles which had first been mentioned in print 200 years earlier. Who knows, perhaps a pair of Rhum's re-introduced *ernes* will recolonise these great cliffs. They deserve each other.

We regrouped on the boulder beach before walking along to the house, sited on a grass-green and silverweed corner on the west side of Eilean an Tighe, for the east side is a continuation of the cliffs of basalt pillars. The door was a bit stiff so I gave it a good shove and more or less fell into the inside—scaring the wits out of a couple who were sitting before a driftwood fire. The man proved to be the owner of the islands! There can't be many landowners who are dropped off by boat to live in a bothy in order to populate their property!

Our time was about up, but we walked along to a well before turning back. It was a flowery corner with each expected species in place; the cliffs a mass of thrift, campion, rose root, honeysuckle and primroses; the tighter sward a tapestry of tormentil, bedstraw, scabious and milkwort, the damp bits were bright with spearwort, lousewort, mint and meadowsweet.

It was with a thought of gales that we re-embarked and fled across The Minch to put Skye between us and any westerly wickedness. We chugged on into the evening to finish the day snug in Portree Harbour. The Shiants are no friendlier than St Kilda when it comes to storm. Eilean Mhuire must wait till next time.

A Day in the Life of Handa

I had been out once in the night to find a shock of stars, so I set the alarm for six and went back to my warm bed in the old shepherd's bothy.

In the stolen moments of peace after the alarm shattered my dreams I could hear a robin *tchicking* outside the door, a redshank's sad voice from the shore and the racket of calling arctic skuas overhead. Midges, or not, the outside called. I opened the door and two wrens, perching on the fish boxes (for firewood), bobbed and called their pleasure of the day.

I walked steadily uphill, at the angle of the red sandstone strata, passing the sheepfold and ruined croft houses. Great skuas eyed me malevolently or swooshed down to brush my hair. It was their island!

After a mile there was a sighing, as of distant seas breaking, then, at a step, I was on the edge of a cliff with the waves sucking at the slabby rocks 300 feet below. Half a mile on the cliffs and the Great Stack rise to 400 feet: uncompromisingly vertical and with the tilt of the rock banded with ledges on which thousands and thousands of birds breed, the 100,000 'seafowl' of the old wandering travellers' tales. Birds in numbers are certainly impressive.

The ledges were rather empty now, however. Summer was really over. The fulmars swung along the cliff edge and their chicks had a scruffy near-adult look to them. It was really the time for waders and sure enough a skulking 'little brown bird' teased my identification powers as I went up to the trig point, at 406 feet the highest point of the island. Another 'bloody *widget*' I muttered. (It proved to be a reeve in winter plumage.)

The island lay map-like below me, a ragged oval two miles long by one across, rising from white shell beaches, dunes and machair through coarse, boggy grasslands to the cake layer, outward-facing cliffs. Handa forms a natural shelter for Tarbet on the mainland opposite. Once it must surely have been the home of happy people. It was—but they were cleared off to make way for sheep (this is Sutherland!), an emigration finally completed by the potato famines in mid-nineteenth century.

There were about seven crofting families before that, working the land and fishing the sea. It was a very close community, ruled by the oldest widow as 'Queen'. It was entirely Gaelic-speaking but no doubt the eviction orders came in Queen's English!

In 1962 the island became a bird reserve managed by the RSPB. Mainland crofters still graze sheep on it but numbers have declined and the vegetation is now recovering

36 The sea cliffs on the island of Handa in Sutherland.

from a past of overgrazing and moor-burning. Beside the bothy a small plantation of lodgepole pine has been established to form a wind break and in the lee of it alder, rowan, birch and other native trees have been planted. The top end of the wood is burnt brown by the blasting of winds—just like the pines in our garden that juts out into the Forth.

From the summit of the island there is a grand view to the mainland with hills ranging from Fionaven and Arkle down to Suilven and Coigach. West over sea lies the Butt of Lewis, south the Old Man of Stoer sets an exclamation mark to this extravagance of wild scenery. It is almost restful to bring one's eyes back to the bonxie-controlled moors of the island. There is a silver scatter of lochans and from one I could hear the weird laughing call of a diver. They often commute overhead between mountain home and their fishing work and their calling echoes the air of desolate places.

My early morning walk had not just been self-indulgence. I had gone round a circular trail to see its state after hundreds of feet had trampled it through the summer. From April to mid-September the island is wardened and open to visitors who are ferried out by small boats from Tarbet. The ferrymen are crofter-fishermen in an old tradition but Tarbet now has several B & B's and a good restaurant to which people come out from Scourie, seven miles off and the nearest 'town'. The bank calls once a month!

It is surprising how people do find their way to Tarbet and cross to the island. There is a small charge for non-RSPB members but the warden or one of his assistants usually meets parties and there is a shelter with information and a display.

Being moorland the visitors' walking route has become boggy and, alas, duckboards have to go down. Unlike many marked walks, however, this one loses nothing of its birdlife or scenic interest by such concentration. It is vital that people don't just stray anywhere for if a nesting bird is driven off for even a few minutes the robber skuas will pillage vulnerable eggs or young. This is not a site for rarities bringing the worst enemy of all—the species-listing 'twitcher'—it simply gives a huge presence of puffins, guillemots, razorbills, fulmars and the like.

Between welcoming visitors (it was a sunny day) I spent the morning hammering duckboards together. John Ridgeway's School of Adventure lies just up the coast and two days hence he is bringing a party who will help to carry them up to the site. Mike, the warden, is working on the roof of the Day Shelter, Fiona, the other assistant, is busy painting doors, window, hands, hair, etc. There is a foolscap page listing work to be done. Just what is done when depends on wind and midges and 'the gentle rain from Heaven'. A craze of midges on Handa is no joke.

The visitors are all away by six and so often the wind dies then and the midges come out. We retreat to the bothy for supper and a dram and good crack round the peat and driftwood fire. A warden's lot is quite a happy one.

The most dramatic feature of the island is the Great Stack: a monolithic rock pillar with half a football pitch of grass capping it and with sea-worn tunnels through its base. Set in the mouth of a *geo* (a deep cut bay or inlet) it has countless birds nesting on its ledges. It is a physical challenge to the daring of man and (three or four times) the bold have stood on its top.

The first arrival is reported only at second hand and sounds dubious in detail. A line was supposedly thrown over and caught (!) and a lad sent across to secure a heavier rope. Certainly about 100 years ago a party from Lewis reached the top. They walked a rope out both arms of the bay and anchored it while the middle lay across the stack. The gap was crossed arm over arm with no security at all. Their motive was collecting birds to eat. Tom Patey repeated this performance in the 1960s and even with modern climbing aids it was no easy crossing. A couple of years later the Stack's outside face was climbed from sea level by a party led by Hamish MacInnes.

The skuas are still screaming over the bothy as I turn in. I listen to a Sibelius symphony, then blow out the candle: the end of another good day on Handa Island.

Hurryings

The sea seemed in a hurry today,
Scaling along under the flensing sun.
Why should it scurry, hurry? It is governed—
Must return.

The sky seemed in a hurry today,
Bustling cumulus crowds off to the game.
Why should they churn and turn? They will come again—
Much the same.

The boy seemed in a hurry today
Running a damp sand band on the edge of time.
Why should he race and pace? His creel of years waits—
Unlike mine.

Orkney's Italian Connection

In the First World War, Scapa Flow was the scene of an end-of-war gesture when the Germans scuttled their surrendered fleet in its waters.

A Sunday School outing watched from its boat in amazement as the warships all round them sank into the sea. Scapa Flow was also to produce early action in the Second World War.

The sinking of the battleship *Royal Oak* with the loss of 800 lives in October 1939 was one unhappy early action in that war. It was an embarrassment, too, as this island-sheltered anchorage was thought safe. The Navy departed till they thought again.

Four channels led into Scapa Flow from the east and these had been blockaded with sunken ships to make them impassable. One brilliant U-boat commander, however, found a gap and made his way in, sank the *Royal Oak* and then escaped. The 'Think Tank' came up with what was to be called the Churchill Barrier: the passages between the islands were filled in with a wall of massive concrete blocks: 66,000 of them!

A road was laid along the top which was, and is, a great convenience to residents—and visitors. I motored south from island to island but one connection with the Churchill Barrier made a halt on Lamb Holm memorable.

The work on the barrier made use of Italian prisoners of war and several hundred of them were based on Lamb Holm. It must have been a contrast to North Africa where they were captured. Camp 60 has gone but one monument remains.

The Italian Chapel is one of Orkney's most famous landmarks, young in the sweep of time since Skara Brae or Maes Howe or the Ring of Brodgar, but very much in the best questing spirit of man.

The Italian camp was an uninspiring collection of Nissen huts but the prisoners laid paths and planted flowers and one artist created a figure of St George and the Dragon to decorate the main 'Piazza'. It was made of cement over a framework of bared wire. The artist was Domenico Chiocchetti and in 1943 he began working on a much more ambitious project—a camp chapel.

Two Nissen huts were joined, end to end, to form a church and school. Chiocchetti started work on a sanctuary at one end and, out of nothing almost, an ambitious, imaginative development began which went on right to the close of the war.

Chiocchetti even stayed on in 1945 to finish working on the font. It was a team effort, of course, with cement workers, electricians, and smiths, as well as painters, playing a part.

37   The Italian Chapel, Orkney.

The Nissen hut shape caught my eye as soon as we drove up (I'd slept in them for years after all) but at the end the full façade of a chapel had been constructed, all in the unfriendly medium of concrete—a *tour de force* in itself. A rondel with the head of Christ stands above the pillared doorway, mellowed by the scouring winds of the north. A belfry surmounts the gable.

The interior was astonishing. There is no other word to describe the combination of craft and artistry which could turn corrugated iron into a vaulted chapel which could have been quite at home in the friendly Dolomites.

The chancel was separated by a superb wrought-iron rood-screen (the work of one Palumbo who had worked in this medium in America) while all the furniture and fittings were either concrete or simply a marvellous *coup d'oeil* impression achieved by painting.

The ceiling over the whole body of the kirk appears to be ribbed and tiled but is really just plasterboard painted to give that impression. The magnitude of painting thousands of tiles left me full of admiration for Chiocchetti and his helpers.

Candelabras were made from scrap metal, the wood for the tabernacle came from a wrecked ship, and the curtains were ordered from Devon with money from the prisoners' welfare fund. When the prisoners departed the then Lord Lieutenant of Orkney (who also owned Lamb Holm) promised that the Orkney people would look after the chapel. The promise has been kept.

Everything has gone now—except the chapel and the statue. The chapel has been cherished, maintained, and restored over the years, a symbol reaching between differing nations and faiths, an example which certain other places of strife and bigotry could study. On the ceiling above the alter there is a fresco of a dove.

Domenico Chiocchetti has made return visits to Orkney and even repainted some of his frescos which had suffered the effects of time. His home town, Moena (near Trento), presented the wayside shrine that stands at the entrace gate. The figure came from Italy. The cross and canopy were made in Kirkwall.

There have been happy visits between the two communities over the years and I find the continuing story rather moving, especially in these harsh times of little faith or goodwill among men. As we drove off across the Churchill Barrier, I noticed how its being there has altered winds and tides so that a vast area of sand has piled up, creating new land.

Renewal was the warm feeling we bore away from a place which had its origins in the fates of war.

Shetland, a Summer Sojourn

As a fanatic for brochs I knew a visit to Shetland was inevitable. After all the broch of Mousa (on an island off the main island—which is the Mainland) is the best-preserved and most complete species we have of this rare specimen.

Brochs look like nothing so much as dry-stane cooling towers and one is left wondering just how much of what we build today will be surviving a thousand years hence, assuming man has not wiped out his old world meantime. The Mousa broch was having some work done on it—and the modern experts were using *cement* on it! Tut. Tut.

Shetland is all islands, and every island seems to have cairns, brochs, standing stones, and other prehistoric remains. I had my Dormobile with me and soon became used to nipping on and off ferries as we ranged the islands from Herma Ness with the lighthouse of Muckle Flugga (our UK's farthest north) to Jarlshof in the south (a prehistoric village just down the road from Sumburgh Airport, which oil-development boosts into the most profitable in Scotland). Sullom Voe lit up the sky at night wherever I stopped to camp. I asked a farmer what difference it had made to life. 'Now I lock my door at nights,' he replied.

Remote islands are another of my gangrel's delights and after the frantic rushing about looking at things we retired to a caravan on Papa Stour, off the west mainland, and probably the remotest island in Scotland without electricity, though it is only a short channel away from the mainland.

Foula, much farther off on the horizon, does have electricity. St Kilda, remotest of remote, has electricity. Why Papa is penalised I do not know. But going to bed when it became too dark to read and rising early gave us unusually long days anyway. In early summer there is only a pretence at darkness—the 'simmer dim' as they call it.

Papa Stour is only three miles long at the most and about two at its widest, yet so indented is the coastline that it took several days of nosey, exploratory walking to circumambulate the island. Unlike Gaul, Papa Stour is divided into two. You could not really call these the desert and the sown, though part is barren heath grazing but some is walled-off for fields.

It is a bit like St Kilda in this respect: the population strung along one road (we lived at its end, 1½ miles from the landing slip), with a school and simple church, and behind the wall, the wilderness of lochs, moors, cliffs, and the ever-attacking bonxies.

38 The broch of Mousa, Shetland—the best preserved in Scotland.

Like St Kilda Papa nearly died, as the population had drifted dangerously low, but an influx of newcomers has helped it hang on. Life is hard. Self-sufficiency is a reality not a dream, but it gives a lifestyle, a community unity, which all city-dwellers have long lost.

The school was next to the caravan and our hosts, Kevin and Vicki Coleman, provided a third of its nine pupils. Just beyond the dyke is the rough airstrip. In the byre Kevin had the windsock stored, ready for use in an emergency. There is no doctor resident.

It was the coastline which made the walking memorable (the highest hill, Verda Field, is only 87 metres high) as, all along, it is shot through with natural arches, *geos*, stacks, and a wealth of bird life. The hinterland largely belonged to the bonxies and their attacks would drive the dog into a frenzy of frustration.

He was useful for finding their chicks however. Along Hamna Voe, the largest of the bays or fiods, there was a string of *planti crubs* which were room-size walled enclosures for growing potatoes and vegetables. A few were still in use.

The old mills were all ruinous and a score of them were sited wherever a run of water could be found to set a wheel in motion. One stone wheel was studded with garnets. These mills were of Norse origin and Shetland as a whole has very close ties with Norway. The names all seem to be Scandinavian, what with *geos* and *voes* and *bonxies* and *tysties.* The redshank goes by the charming name of *watery pleeps*. Papa Stour is Norse for *Large Priest Island*.

There must be about fifty islands or sea-pinnacles on the coast. Some of these are remarkable fingers of rock— a challenge to the climber. Others, like the Maiden Stack, bear legends. The island has a fascinating history and folklore and even its own sword dance.

It is not a popular holiday island but the post-office-cum-shop offers self-catering accommodation and there are a few caravans for hiring. For a really different holiday I'd return like a shot. Economically we also give back something on a place like Papa. They like their apartness, however much the outside calls.

Some years back an edict went out from London that all exam papers were to be collected locally, taken to the nearest railway station, and sent to London. A bus duly made a score of ferry crossings to collect them and Lerwick (with true Shetland spirit) took them to the nearest station for sending on—which was Bergen, in Norway. You will certainly find Shetland different.

St Kilda, a World of its Own

When the forces were trying to establish themselves on St Kilda they requisitioned cold, wet-weather protective clothing only to have the War Office turn down the request. It was commented that such items were not needed in the Pacific: Outer Hebrides had been confused with New Hebrides.

St Kilda, lying out in the Atlantic beyond the Hebrides is well defended against easy visiting. From London one could probably reach Cuzco as quickly. Last summer the normal 24-hour journey (by sturdy fishing boat) took 56 hours thanks to the weather. The time before we did not manage beyond Lochmaddy and another boat that did was wrecked in Village Bay.

Hirta, the main island, has had an army establishment for twenty-seven years. Before that the island lay deserted for twenty-seven years, its evacuation in 1930 bringing to an end a decline which was partly a result of a self-sufficient, poor society coming in contact with visitors from the wealthier world outside. It is a fate more familiar in Tierra del Fuego or Amazonia.

St Kilda was bequeathed to the National Trust for Scotland in 1956 and they leased it to the Nature Conservancy Council to manage as a nature reserve—surely one of the most dramatic reserves anywhere in the world. Part is sub-leased to the army who operate a rocket-tracking station in conjunction with the base on Benbecula.

In the summer the NTS run work parties which seek to restore the old village. It is visited by hardy yachtsmen and vessels chartered by divers. The base is stocked by huge landing craft which come in every two weeks in the summer. Once summer is over winter storms and isolation give it an arctic atmosphere.

These many difficulties and challenges do not deter the determined traveller or those suffering from island-fever. They add to the lure of St Kilda, the wildest and loveliest corner of the British Isles. The scenery is dramatic for on Handa lies the highest seacliff in Britain, just part of a cliff-and-cave shattered coastline, while the stacks of Boreray are as weird as Macbeth's witches.

A quarter of the total number of gannets in Britain (150,000) nest on these stacks. There are tens of thousands of puffins on Dun (half the United Kingdom total). The Soay sheep are the oldest domestic breed in Europe, and Hirta has its own sub-species of mouse and wren. There is something of the Galapagos about the wildlife.

The original inhabitants came long before history and their souterains and horn-structured dwellings are there to puzzle us still. How did they reach the islands—3–4000 years ago?

St Kilda for most of history belonged to the Dunvegan Macleods and the annual visit of the factor was often the only contact with the outside world. He brought in some commodities (like tea) and took off rent in kind: tweed, feathers and oil. One autumn a party were fowling on Boreray when their boat was lost and there they stayed till June when the factor sailed to St Kilda.

The people took young gannets, fulmars and puffins for food and oil, and feathers to export. They were expert climbers long before climbing became a sport for urban gentlemen in Victorian times. Their bare feet grew broad, nearly prehensile. There is almost no flat ground and no trees exist.

The village, one street of 16 houses, circles Village Bay, with fields running down from houses to shore. The bay is exposed to the southeast and boats had to be kept out of the water, even in sumer, so fishing was only a minor activity. A small population could not afford the loss of adult males. It was a tough life.

To preserve the carcases of thousands of birds culled in the summer the St Kildans evolved the *cleit*: a dry stone structure like a miniature cottage which was capped with turf. This allowed the wind to pass through but kept out the rain. The *cleits* stored perishable goods like corn and seabirds, peat and ropes.

39   St Kilda. Stac Lee, speckled with gannets with Stac an Armin (left) and Boreray (right) behind.

There are about 1000 of them on Hirta, giving the village surroundings a speckled appearance. The whole bay area has a big boundary wall and there are walled fields elsewhere. Some of the stonework is almost cyclopean, and most of it still stands.

Much of my time during this summer's visit on a NTS work party was spent rebuilding the end of a black house gable which had collapsed. It had been poorly constructed in the first place—and so fell down. Black houses had walls up to 10 feet thick, with tiny windows and a thatched roof set well back from the walls edge. Smoke escaped as best it could and one half of the building belonged to their livestock. The floor was beaten earth. It was primitive and in 1861–62 the new cottages replaced these old *tigh dubh* structures.

Two things sapped the community's will to survive. One was a constrictive ultra-religious church rule which killed the lively character of the people, the other was the fearsome mortality-rate among new-born babies, the dread 'eight-day sickness'. A woman might bear ten children and only one would survive. So people left, the young men especially.

Once numbers drop to about thirty a community cannot long survive. The St Kilda 'parliament' decided to accept the solution of evacuation. The government shipped them to Morven and the men were enrolled to work in forestry—most of them having never seen a tree in their lives!

The village now is the haunt of wrens and field mice (the house mouse died out, being dependent on the presence of people) and even rare birds like Leach's forktailed petrels nest in wall cavities. Petrels and shearwaters fly only at night and three of us spent a night on the cliffs to experience their nocturnal activity. We watched the sun down, observed the lights of Norwegian fishing boats (the Vikings again), sipped tea from flasks and waited.

As it grew to the darkest hours there was a sudden flurry and birds flew into our laps. We were sitting on their burrows. In a few minutes the night was loud with the caterwauling of petrels and shearwaters. How these could navigate in the blackness was a puzzle but they whirred in and out in a way which scared us.

In early 1912 the islanders were desperately short of food and relief expeditions were sent. The *Daily Mirror* opened a fund to establish a radio station and this was operational in July 1913. It broke down in October. A German, Gustaf Flick, repaired it and ran it for some months but as the government would not assist with expenses it closed just as the First World War began. The navy then re-opened it.

A U-boat came in to the bay and shelled the installations. No human beings suffered. Another U-boat commander was able to tell a Norwegian ship's crew to take their lifeboats to St Kilda 'where they would be well looked after'. They even gave them the name of the postmaster. Herr Flick had obviously been useful to German Intelligence. When the War was over the postmaster received a postcard from Gustaf Flick posted in St Kilda, Melbourne.

There was nothing exciting during the Second World War, the island being uninhabited by then, but three aircraft (a Wellington, a Beaufighter and a Sunderland) crashed on it.

There is no public transport as such. NTS work parties or safari parties, diving groups and others all charter converted fishing boats for travel and perhaps for accommodation. The only shore accommodation is used by the NTS. Other visitors ashore need permission to camp. (The recently restored feather store now offers bothy accommodation.)

What would the old St Kildans make of it today I wonder with radar scanners on top of their hills, a girl in number 2 using a hair dryer and a merry crowd watching a film in the pub, *The Puff Inn*? Much has changed but the attractions remain. St Kilda has been described as being 'out of this world', and so it is—in the best of senses.

The Strange Case of Lord and Lady Grange

St Kilda, our remotest inhabited island, is probably seeing more visitors now than at any time in its past history; however it is still a challenging place to reach and being marooned on Hirta or cast on the rocks by gales still can happen, while seasickness is commonplace on any voyage out to these shark's teeth islands on the edge of nowhere. A good place to end our wandering, it could not have been such fun for Lady Grange.

The early to mid-eighteenth century was a fairly unsettled period in Scottish history: the enervating years of the Stewarts, of religious intolerance, strife, and poverty were at last being overcome. The explosion of real talent lay not so far ahead.

In this limbo-period some extraordinary events happened and none was more strange than the story of Lord and Lady Grange.

The most cursory reading on St Kilda mentions the latter's unhappy incarceration on Hirta. 'Lady Grange's House' is one of the places lucky visitors make for, and from which they return with some sympathy for the prisoner and thankfulness to be living in a later century.

The popular belief is that she was brutally abducted at her husband's word, to shut her mouth in case she betrayed his Jacobite sympathies. It very much makes him out to be 'the baddy'. He was an unattractive person certainly, but no worse than many of his contemporaries, and Lady Grange, far from being the poor innocent, received no more than she deserved. In couthy terms, they were 'a right pair'.

Looking at that tomb-like dwelling on St Kilda aroused my curiosity sufficiently that I dug into old histories to find out more. After blowing off dust and cobwebs and cutting pages on books that had not been read in their century of existence I began to piece together something of her story, but I wonder just how much we can find out about old truth, overlaid as it is with variants.

James Erskine was the brother of the Earl of Mar who led the 1715 Jacobite rebellion, not out of any deep attachment to that cause, but basically for political expediency. The Earl was not nicknamed 'Bobing John' without good reason. James, his brother, could perhaps surpass him in hypocrisy and double-dealings and double standards. He was outwardly a staunch and bigoted Presbyterian but his private life was riddled with self-indulgent dabblings and his only interests were his own.

He returned to Scotland from foreign law studies in 1705 and was admitted a member of the Faculty of Advocates. Being a lad o' pairts and with big brother Principal Secretary of State his advancement was ensured. In the year of the union he was made first a Lord of Session and then a Lord of Justiciary, taking the title of Grange. His beautiful newlywed wife, Rachel Chiesley, was styled Lady Grange.

James Erskine had no intentions of marrying this lady but she, being made pregnant, confronted the culprit with marriage lines in one hand and a loaded pistol in the other.

Rachel Chiesley's father had deserted his wife and family and took such a dim view of the Lord President's order that he pay them alimony that he followed the judge after service one Sunday and shot him dead in his close. Chiesley was tortured, had his hand struck off, and was hanged with the pistol dangling from his neck.

Grange was promoted Lord Justice-Clerk when the Tories came to power in 1710 but fell when Queen Anne died and Walpole regained power. Grange had kept well clear of the '15 Rising that saw his brother's ruin, surely an indication of how unimportant any dabbling of his could be considered by the government. He kept to his house and spacious gardens, built a pavilion to house his library of books on demonology, whored, drank, prayed, and argued on the minutiae of Calvinism.

Grange was 'thick' with Simon Frazer, Lord Lovat of the '45, and hated Walpole, the most powerful man in Britain. Somehow he survived and thrived. In the early 1730s he was involved in a strange way with his brother's deranged wife who was in the care of a lady close to Walpole, while Mar was in exile in France. Maybe he was trying to save or gain the Mar estates.

In 1734 he proposed entering politics fully but Walpole inserted a clause in a bill which rendered the election of a Scottish judge illegal. Grange resigned his offices and in due course became MP for Stirling Burghs. His career however fell flat from the start.

The Act repealing the statute of James I against witchcraft was his chance. He rose and gave a grand discourse on witchcraft (of which he was an authority) but Parliament was not a General Assembly and he was simply laughed at and failed ever to gain authority.

He drifted back to Edinburgh and practised as an advocate before the court where he had been a judge for twenty-seven years. To crown his misfortunes in 1740 a letter from his supposedly long-dead wife turned up—which caused quite a stir.

The beautiful young Lady Grange had turned out to be unpredictable, violent, drank too much, and became physically dangerous so, after twenty years, there was a separation when her behaviour became unbearable. She had borne eight children. She was sent to live in the country but loathed it.

Lady Grange soon returned to a house near Grange's house in Niddry's Wynd where she paraded in noisy demonstration or followed him through the streets. As a private woe had become a public scandal something had to be done, especially as she now loudly proclaimed she had 'evidence enough to hang him' of his involvement with Jacobite plotting, and was off to London with this.

We will probably never know the truth of this claim. Maybe she had evidence which could endanger him or some of his friends. Grange himself could even have used this threat as the means of ensuring her removal by those who were Jacobite sympathisers.

It seems clear that Lovat was approached and certainly a Lovat gang broke into her home (January 1732) where, after a fierce fight, she was gagged and bound and carried off in a sedan chair. As she had been about to depart to London her disappearance caused little stir (her absence was no doubt preferable to her presence) and eventually Grange declared she was dead.

Gossip however was telling the truth and her lawyer Mr Hope of Rankeillor, who had power of attorney, took the matter up. Lovet denied all involvement and warned Rankeillor off. The matter rested.

Eight years later came the bombshell of her letter (or letters—the sources differ, but one letter certainly still exists, a pathetic plea from St Kilda) and Hope again took things up, but Grange had more power with the Lord Advocate and nothing happened.

Hope then chartered a brig and sailed to St Kilda but Lady Grange had been moved on. Soon more important issues were afoot: 1745 saw rebellion and in its aftermath Lovat lost his head on Tower Hill. Grange fell on evil days, eeking out life on a pension in London having married a long-time 'friend' with whom he had lived over many debauched London visits. He died in 1754, aged 75.

Lady Grange, after being seized from Edinburgh, was carried to Polmaise and sequestrated in a small room at the top of a tower for 13 weeks, without any light and with minimal comforts. Lovat's men then bore her to the Highlands and, via ruinous Castle Tioram in Moidart (or Loch Hourn) she finally reached Heskeir in September.

Some of the books declare this to be Heskeir 'near Skye' (west of Canna) but it is undoubtedly in the Monach Islands off North Uist for it is declared to be the property of Sir Alexander MacDonald of Sleat. After two years she was handed over to MacLeod (a nephew of Lovat) and for greater security (she had tried to escape) was taken to St Kilda.

She spoke no Gaelic (on arrival anyway: some accounts say she learnt it on St Kilda), was lodged in what was basically a cell with minimal comforts, no books, no interests, in the remotest island of Britain, with a harsh climate to match its austere landscape.

Perhaps her character saved her for the first years, for there is a touch of the heroic in her desperate efforts to try to send word out, but slowly she grew more violent, she drank, she slept all day and at night would wander on that tiny, lonely strand in broken spirit, madness finally almost complete.

Hers are the first recorded attempts at sending messages by sea from St Kilda. 'St Kilda mailboats' were later used in emergencies and helped avoid starvation crises.

Dr Johnson, when travelling with Boswell, heard of this story and said of MacLeod of MacLeod that he could have been on a good thing had he let it be known he had such a convenient island for holding unwanted females! Oddly, in 1715 Robertson of Struan had his sister abducted and she was on her way to St Kilda when she escaped in Uist, so perhaps Grange or Lovat knew of this incident and applied it more effectively.

Some accounts even state Lady Grange died on Hirta and there are many variants as to how a letter eventually did reach Edinburgh but the likeliest one is that it was hidden in a roll of cloth (or a skein of yarn) which was collected on the factor's annual visit. It still exists. Dated January 1738 it did not reach Hope's hands till the winter of 1740.

By the time he had worked through the 'proper channels', to no effect, and mounted his own voyage to St Kilda, there had been plenty of time for the removal of Lady Grange from the island where she had been held for seven or eight years. She was shuttled about between Harris and Skye and, in some sources, Assynt, till she finally died in Skye, completely insane.

They must have given her a grand funeral for the bill, for £30, is still preserved. Nearly all the accounts say she was buried secretly at Trumpan Church in Waternish while a public funeral, with a coffin filled with soil and stones, was held at Duirinish.

There is a bit of confusion over Lady Grange's House on St Kilda. Most older sources say it fell down or was pulled down. A visitor in 1838 'inspected the ruins', accompanied by a grandson of her warder, but the site itself is most likely accurate. In the 1928 volume of the *Proceedings of the Society of Antiquaries of Scotland* a survey of St Kilda sites says, 'The original house was roofed with timber, and when it fell in it was rebuilt as a cleit.' What we see today is a restoration.

Lady Grange caused quite a stir one way or another. She died in May 1745 and in July 1745 Prince Charles Edward Stuart landed on Eriskay. A bigger tragic legend would largely replace her sad story in the annals of time.

Hodden Solitude

There is an island of pine trees
Buttoned on a silk-sheen loch
Under a shawl of cloud.

Rocked in a boat in the gloaming
When the grey is trimmed with red
A heartbeat knits too loud.

Clothe me with hodden solitude,
Step me, peace-shod, to the west.
The world can wear the rest.

V   Stories of Places

These stories have very definite settings in my mind's eye. THE ORNITHOLOGISTS *is set in the Trossachs to which I used to cycle fairly often in my own youth. The caterpillar episode is true but it was the sanest among us, Davy Glen, who showed me what was happening.* TAIT'S TOMB *still stands in a circling arm of the road west from Dollar to Tillicoultry and, certainly, we boys often had to walk back from 'the pictures' at Tilly. We never gave Tait's Tomb a thought. The story came years later, to satisfy school kids in the bothy in the Black Wood of Rannoch, who demanded 'a spooky story' before going off to bed.* THE CROSS *also has a Dollar setting but the only veracity in it was the banning of the dog from the practice runs. It obviously rankled! The rest is fiction—or wishful thinking.* THE FISHERMAN'S RELEASE *might be recognised as Inverey and the Dee. I can hardly claim this to be autobiographical—beyond once fishing in the Linn o' Dee with the ineffectual bent pin. The brushstrokes of the personal are incidental, at heart is the feeling for a place. Scotland hardly needs to be fictionalized; but it can be fun.*

40 An abstract on the frozen surface of a loch.

The Ornithologists

Wee Davie Sproul and Jock Tamson lay on the grass beside the tent with the deep content of youth. They had hardly said a word that morning. It would have been a kind of sacrilege if they had done so.

They had woken at four to the silvery, secretive, first light of spring. It was the dawn chorus that woke them. They lay thrilled while bird after bird joined in: blackbirds, a missel thrush, a robin, these they could pick out, but there were so many others still unknown. Neither spoke. The tickly blankets kept off the raw edge of dawn and the aches of the day before had gone during the night.

They were ordinary boys but no less interesting for that. Over the winter a new teacher had come to the school and inspired in many of the boys an interest in birdwatching. They were ornithologists in fact—not young nest-robbers or those who used gutties on the speugs. They were proud of the big word and what it meant for them. They were proud of being Paisley boys too (better than Glasgow any day) and they were proud of their bikes, earned by delivering rolls all through the bitter winter. Their fathers had given them a bird book and a pair of binoculars (second-hand from the 'barras') as reward for their hard saving.

Their joy was complete when allowed to plan a camping trip to the Trossachs. The BB had lent the small tent and Friday seemed to take years to come. They hardly heard their mothers' 'Min an no get yir shoen wet!' as they pedalled off. The Duke's Pass had almost puggled them and they were glad to lift their bikes over the dyke and put up the tent among the trees near the road skirting Loch Achray. Tea and 'pieces' and they were soon asleep.

The Saturday morning soon passed. The weather was balmy as it had been all week. When they had risen at six o'clock they had breakfast and then a swim and then another breakfast. This all took time because they kept seeing new birds. A snipe shot its wild way across their clearing, leaving them scrambling for their glasses—far too late as the bird had gone. A sandpiper had gone off, too, by the burn; that one took a bit of finding in the book.

A bullfinch had really thrilled them. And all through the morning there was the cuckoo's call, an incessant, echoing mystery. Nobody every seemed to have seen a cuckoo. That was their plan for the afternoon.

They left the burnt frying pan in the burn in disgust (Davie's mother had something to say about that!) and walked along to the hotel. It was full of posh cars and people coming out from lunch. The road was crowded with cars so they turned back.

At once they saw a path rising up into the trees. They looked at each other.

'Cuckoo' came the call from the hills.

Ten minutes later and some hundreds of feet higher they collapsed by the path.

'Whit a pech!' gasped wee Davie.

'Dinnae move,' whispered Jock. 'There's a blue tit ahint yir left lug.'

'Well, hoo can ah see it then?' hissed back Davie.

The tit flew to the next tree and they watched it dangle upside down on the end of the swaying birch branch.

'Cuckoo,' came the call from higher up the brae.

'Cuckoo,' came a call again at no distance at all.

'Come on,' they whispered and scrambled off. The tit flitted to the next branch.

The boys inched forward, carefully placing feet between twigs and scarce daring to breathe.

'Cuckoo,' came the distant call.

'Cuckoo,' came the nearer answer.

'Jist roond they rocks.'

They crept round and then stopped dead. Two blazing eyes glowered at them. The face surrounding those eyes seemed all hair—great blacks locks and matted growth of beard. The man held his hands cupped in front of his thick lips.

The boys stood awkwardly. Wee Davie's lugs had a tinge of red about them.

'Well,' said the stranger. It was neither question nor statement.

'We wis tryin tae see a cuckoo,' explained Jock uncertainly.

The man lowered his hands quickly and he in turn flushed red.

'It wis you that wis cawin cuckoo!' blurted out Davie.

There was an awkward silence again.

'Are you interested in birds?' asked the man.

'Aye,' they replied together.

'Are you sure?'

'Aye. Sure we're sure.'

'You don't steal eggs?' he demanded, and the fierce light danced in his eyes again.

'Jings, naw. We're ornithologists. We ken better.'

There was another silence as they stood before those piercing eyes; youth on one side, man on the other, and a great gulf between.

'Would you like to see a cuckoo?'

The gulf contracted to a span.

'Could ye show us yin? Are ye a bird man? Dae ye ken a nest?' The questions poured out.

'Aye,' he said softly, and smiled.

Being boys they did not notice the weirdness of the man: his wild face and agitated hands, his dirty clothes and boots. The span had gone. They were all ornithologists. They could trust each other.

They told him of their camp and all they had done and seen. He apparently had seen their camp and watched them eating. This rather upset them as they had tried to be well hidden in case anybody should see them and tell them they couldn't camp there. But this man missed nothing.

'Do you see that ant?'

'Aye.'

'Well, it's drunk.'

'How dae ye mean?'

'It attacked a caterpillar a few minutes ago. The caterpillar rolled up tight and oozed out little drops of liquid which the ant licked up as it walked over it. Then it began to stagger and fell over. The caterpillar then went off. I lost sight of it when I started answering the cuckoo.'

The boys, gasped in amazement.

'Cuckoo,' came the call.

They moved into cover.

'Cuckoo,' called out the beared naturalist.

Davie spotted a movement first. A bird flew down from a tree. He got his glasses on it. 'Sparrowhawk maybe?' he suggested. The man had his eye to a small telescope he had pulled out from some inner pocket. He gave it to Jock.

'What do you say?'

'It's no a hawk. It's no— is it—a cuckoo?'

'Yes.'

They sucked in their breath. It flew up again and then glided down to a tree stump twenty yards away.

'Cuckoo!'

'Wait till we tell teacher!'

All afternoon the knowledgeable stranger led them about the woods above Loch Achray. They wended towards Ben A'n but the crags were full of noisy climbers so they turned and went down into Glen Finglas.

Their list of new birds grew: a mallard, tree-creeper, a peewit, woodpecker, sparrowhawk, curlew, blackheaded gull, dunnock, dipper, chaffinch, heron, willow-warbler—these were some. On the moor they found seven larks' nests—at least *he* did—for they could never find them even when they saw the bird fly up.

'That is why,' he explained. 'They always move several yards away before flying up.'

They cut back over the hill in the cool of the evening to avoid the busy road. They were slightly dizzy with the joy of it all.

The strange man left them before they came back to the top of the path. They had shared their pieces, but he would go no further with them.

'I watch here.' he said, and somehow his words left a momentary and unreasonable fear. He shook their hands in his massive grip and wished them well. He also gave them a list of all the birds they had seen—put, as he informed them, in the Wetmore order of classification.

The boys took the steep downward path, chatting merrily and already planning further ornithological expeditions 'doon the water', and up to the whaup-loud moors near Eaglesham. ('Wi a name like yon!') They were slightly startled to meet a small party toiling up the path. The first two figures were plainly policemen.

'It wisnae me, officer, honest!' grinned wee Davie.

'Hello, lads?' greeted the placid officer in return—between puffs while the party collected at his back on the narrow track—'You haven't seen a man who looks a bit like a tramp anywhere in the wood, now have you?'

'The bird man?' queried Davie.

'Aye, that'll be him right enough,' said a voice from behind the constable.

'He hasnae done onything, has he?' Jock asked apprehensively.

'Na, na,' said the invisible speaker, pushing forward to explain. 'He's a patient at Ballochmore and has some queer-like notions. He's aye trying to get oot bird-watching an such like.'

The boys helped as they could and carried on down to the road and their bikes and the long run home.

It was half way up the Duke's Pass when Davie stopped shoving his heavy cycle and turned to Jock.

'Hey, Jock, dae ye min whit yon doctor-chappie said?'

'When?'

'Aboot the aul man. "Queer-like notions," he said. "Like bird-watching." Whit a cheek!'

'Aye, it is that.'

'Whit dae they ken aboot birds onywey?'

And with a deal of standing on their pedals, they went on up the road for Aberfoyle and Paisley.

41   The Meikelour Beech Hedge near Blairgowrie—planted after the Forty-five and the
country's highest hedge (trimmed by the fire brigade).

Tait's Tomb

We were daft on horses in those days in Clackmannanshire—and lucky that we could indulge the passion. Both wee Hugh and I haunted the stables down at the Lower Mains, willing, unpaid slaves. Mrs Kirkton, who owned and ran the stables, was young and pretty. That she was a widow with a young family to bring up, that our help was a relief, however slight—these were things of which we were completely ignorant. Ours was a shortsighted, purely selfish indulgence: a love of the beast, of the free rhythm, of the sensual smell of life. The ultimate joy was to walk some tiny beginner home to the Back Road or the Old Town (nice and far away) and then come back riding.

Mrs Kirkton loved horses and loved kids, and never knew when to stop. Constantly we would still be going over the jumps in Trigger's Field at dusk, and we were forever clopping down Bridge Street with the echoes and moonlight playing tricks among the square-cut buildings. The time comes back now as a single, singing summer; if it rained, or some pony was intractable or some horse ill, if tiny tots cried and tempers ran tight, these are forgotten.

Often too, when tuition was over, we would go out on the Tilly Road, for Mrs Kirkton had rented fields there and was also helping to look after a herd of Shetland ponies which Lord Haverton had built up. One night Hugh and I had been to the cinema at Tilly. We came out too late for the last bus, which did not worry us, and too late for a chip supper, which did concern us, and set us grumbling on the three miles home. At the top of the brae we clambered over the wall to visit the sandpit to see if the sand-martins had returned, then wended on along the snaking road, lined on one side by the ruler of railway line and crowded on the other by tall trees which danced in a hot, dry storm.

It was repulsively hot, the heavy breath of the gasping west wheezing at our backs, with not a chance of rain. The scarp of the Ochils ran blackly back into the weirdly-lit west. Over Sheardale Brae the moon glowered, as though hot inside and swelling, ready to burst over the tepid night. We were reduced to a panting silence, ill at ease in this mysterious menace of nature unnatural.

The trees rubbed their limbs against each other, swayed their tops, and rippled their foliage so that the world was full of moaning and groaning, of sighing and whispering, of rustling and hustling—of some huge primeval imminence that never materialised. We stole furtively down the middle of the road, stamping on each cat's eye for its soft-solid reality.

About half-way home the road makes a big sweep left round the pony meadows while the railway goes straight on. The woods were thicker on the left and at the back of them somewhere lay Haverton Castle, a building of red sandstone towers and turrets. This half-circle of fields contained the Haverton ponies, but in the middle lay the walled circle of gravestones always called 'Tait's Tomb'.

This was the family burial place of the Havertons' predecessors; a jungle compound full of brambles and adolescent-looking trees, with here and there monstrous marble urns and slabs and angels and the like; gentry all, with an admiral, an archbishop, forgotten beneath the rash of nettles. It was a place all boys and girls shunned and into which few adults would bother to penetrate.

As wee Hughie and I came to the opening out of the pony meadow the circle of wall rose starkly from the white moonfields. We stopped together. In that moment the wind died; silence struck swift and deep.

And fear struck. In an instant it had us by the heart. We both shook! I recall Hugh's knuckles white as he gripped my bare arm. My chest hurt with a heaviness like lead, my stomach muscles seemed tied in hanks. Neither of us could even open our mouths, for we would have screamed and screamed for relief.

Wee Hugh swears that in that sudden silence he clearly saw the tops of the trees in Tait's Tomb in movement—though the great beeches beside us surged up in cathedral silence. I saw nothing; but Tait's tomb to me also was the centre of our terror. The moon-washed mausoleum seemed utterly satanic—rather I should imagine as Alloway Kirk appeared to Tam o' Shanter 'in a bleeze'. We did not people it with warlocks and witches. It was still; if Hughie's trees moved, it was motion without noise. Yet the fear rooted us to the road as firmly as the beeches were rooted in the bluebell banks beside us.

We stood I suppose mere seconds before I managed to gasp 'Run!' and we shot off. We ran in terror—for remember the road made a great sweep—convinced that something from the tomb was tearing across the fields to cut us off. We felt that if only we could pass that silent, unblinking wall of stone we would be safe, secure from its unknown horror.

The silence was the greatest terror of all.

We ran and ran; how we ran.

Eventually we turned the faraway bend and sped past a house: the spell broke.

Then how we gasped and wrenched our driven bodies. We lay on the ground, rolling in emotion and howling with the mad laughter of release. But we were silent and uncommunicative as we walked the last mile home.

The next night we were going over the jumps in Trigger's Field. Mrs Kirkton had been along at Lord Haverton's all evening, but her car drew up at last. 'Tim! Hugh!' she cried, without getting out.

We trotted over. Her face turned up to ours bore the marks of hard work and worry. 'Sorry to be late, lads. Can you just pack up now, please.'

Our faces fell, but orders were orders. I was about to nudge my horse when she added: 'You know the pony meadows. I've been there all day. The ponyman says that two of the mares dropped their foals last night and they were all wild and frightened this morning. Something awful must have happened last night to scare them.'

As we did not answer, she added, 'See you at the Mains,' and drove off. I ran my hand down the horse's neck, feeling the comforting strength there. Yet last night even the Shelties had gone mad out by Tait's tomb; the terror had not been ours alone.

To this day I cannot pass the spot at ease; more than a quarter of a century though it be since the night when boys—and ponies—ran unexplicably in terror from Tait's Tomb.

42 Leuchars Kirk in Fife—a Romanesque treasure.

The Cross

To enter for the Cross-Country at all one had to undertake six practice runs during the previous weeks. Then on the great Saturday, the first Saturday in May, the dedicated line up on the First Hockey Pitch, for triplicate departures: juniors, intermediates and seniors. The awkward and the athlete, en masse, in house-colour kaleidoscope, vanish through the Old Gates for the Burnside and Easter Mains. Parents and former pupils, staff—and the few infirm or ashamed—hang in clusters, chatting, remembering, barely hearing the Games Master's commentary as he gathered information from the various check points run by the Combined Cadet Force Signals Section. I, too, do my remembering.

Of races long ago. Of my first. Of the dramatic second. Of the endless practices. The public school disciplining of a twelve year old.

I was lucky not to be a Boarder of course. Their practices were so often dreadfully organised by big bullying House Captains or the Sports Captains. I could do mine at my own pleasure and pace, with friends or the dog Jock. Not infrequently bird-nesting or rabbit-hunting or the like played havoc with times and the training aspect, but nobody expected me to do more than gain the odd point; so long as I dutifully told my disinterested House Captain that another run had dutifully been followed, life went on its peaceful way.

It was an interesting enough route, even the short four-mile Junior version. From the Mains you went *down* almost to the River Dowan, then *up* by Hatton's Wood to Stevenson's and then Stoddart's Farms—quite a pech—before jarring down the Back Road and in again by the Prep School Gate. The winner did it in about twenty minutes; for his dedication he gained 10 points for his house, the second received 7, the third 5, than all those within five minutes of the winner 3 points, within 10 minutes 2 points, and if completing the course, 1 point; so everyone who could staggered round.

I had managed two dutiful points in my first year.

The dog Jock had often been a companion on the practice rounds. He was a typical boy's dog: a devoted fox terrier—a terror to all cats and postmen but loyal as could be. He was as kenspeckle a figure as myself for we seldom roamed apart. We knew every wood and burn, every den and hillside. We lived at the east end of the town too so he was well known to farmers Stoddart and Stevenson.

Both these gentlemen were elders in St Mungo's, our church, where grandfather was also an elder; both had families at school, though a bit younger than myself and all the mothers of course were Women's Guild members; so through many connections we all knew each other as folk do in a fairly small and closely-knit community.

I had completed a couple of rounds of Junior Cross practice in my second year when the Games Master drew me aside after PT.

'Oh, Beattie, it's been brought to my notice you do your Cross practices with a dog. It will have to stop. Understand?'

As I did not understand I returned, poor fool: 'Why sir?'

The reply was a slap and a 'You impertient brat. Because you're told.'

'But I want to know, sir . . .'

Five minutes later I went off to Latin with tingling hands, punished for insubordination—the art of not knowing when to keep one's mouth shut. Good training no doubt. It certainly helped me in later years to wiggle through National Service with my conduct described as 'exemplary'—and my contribution nil. The gods are always right.

Latin was mostly taken up in a baffled search for sanity somewhere in the recent incident. I had been called 'cheeky' and other incomprehensible words describing unknown attributes. I just was not. It was a completely unfair belting. Brought to his notice. Who? For crying out loud—no one objected the previous year. Or why? Everyone knew old Jock. It was just inconceivable that either Mr Stevenson or Mr Stoddart could have complained: dog and I roamed their land at will, even in the middle of lambing when we loved to 'help'. They could hardly have complained. Or could they? One's disillusionment at the conduct of adult examples came fast. Raeburn the PT bloke for instance had always been OK—yet loses the head at a simple 'Why?'—hits me—belts me. It was souring, illogical, so very unfair. Why could he not say why he was imposing a silly ban? Any time I could take the dog round that same course (for it's a natural walk) and no comment would follow, but because of this sacred season it was suddenly a crime, the mere questioning of which gained not helpful explanations but blows and accusations of being cheeky. It was hopeless and the day passed in misery. No more Crosses for me, thank you.

However, the gods were soon at it again. The House Captain this time. Cornwallis-Smith Senior (later to be thrown out of University and now running a garage, I believe).

'Beattie, you sod, this is the week before the Cross and you've only done two practices.'

'So? I'm not interested in your bloody Cross.'

'Oh, you're not are you? Well, you'll fit in the rest of your runs this week—and be running on Saturday—or I'll give you the beating of your life. The House needs even your miserable point. So crawl round or else . . .'

I was left to gaze after the retreating seventeen-year-old. My feelings welled up in tears as I walked home. I changed into shorts and plimsols. Jock watched, tail wagging in expectation.

'No, you mut, you're banned.'

Bark! Bark!

'No!'

The tail stopped wagging, slowly, unbelievingly.

'Oh, Jock, you don't understand either.'

I pulled him into my lap and roughed him up while hot tears dropped on my hands.
'I hate them all.'

Strange moral compunctions. Nobody ever dreamed of falsely claiming a practice
they had not in fact done. Yet what evils had been stirred up to set me off, dogless,
round that rainy course that evening. Beatings, threats, hates, fears panted through
head and heart as feet squelched the paths or crushed the overwhelming scent of
hyacinth into the air among the beech trees.

I ran blindly: in an emotional vacuum.

Mr Stevenson was standing with his two collies by the byre as I passed the yard.

'Hello, Alastair. Going to be Junior champion on Saturday?'

I forced a wan smile.

'Where's old Jock, your other half?'

'At home,' I gasped and was out of speaking range, glad not to have to explain fully.

So it certainly wasn't farmer Stevenson who had brought Jock to Raeburn's notice.
Thank goodness. He was a nice old chap. His dogs were great too. But why? Why?
Why? The whole affair had spoiled a week and now another had started; and it would
be full of it, a practice a day, a damned, damned jog, jog, silly, bloody, bloody practice
a day.

I toiled up to turn at Stoddart's Farm, Law Hill above, the sweeping view down to
the fertile valley below. Mr Stoddart was our elder and a great friend of grandfather's.
They both 'kept a bee' as they always put it. His was mainly a hilly sheep farm, high
above town and school and the lusher cow pastures. It was cleaner, brighter air up
there. I loved it and slowed to a walk, letting the balm of the evening's coolness flow
over my hot soul.

'Jock ill or something, Alastair?'

It was Mrs Stoddart.

'No, no.—He's—he's banned from doing Crosses with me.'

'Why?'

'I'm not told why. Just because I'm told.'

'Sounds damned silly. Are you in a hurry?'

'Not really. As long as I go round the daft course.'

'Good, can you take some daffs from the gate bit for your mother? She wants them
for church on Sunday. Save a trip later. They'll keep fine.'

'O.K.'

'Give her my love.'

'Cheerio.'

'Bye, Alastair.'

I picked an armful of daffodils and trundled down the Back Road, almost hoping to
meet the rat Raeburn. Perhaps he'd take exception to doing practices with bunches of
daffodils! It seemed it was just him who objected. I might be no damned good to him
but I knew more than he did about lots of things. I'd show him. The legal minimum.
His pound of flesh.

Each evening I dutifully did a run: moodily, with vengeful dedication rather than the old, carefree and careless dandering. I dodged a bit, careful to add to the route rather than cut it, in order to miss the farms. How could I explain to either Stevensons or Stoddarts? *They* asked *me* why the dog was banned! Perhaps as fellow irrational adults they might have been able to explain, but it was all hurtful enough without opening up further avenues of possibly painful misunderstanding. Best avoid the farms, for the week anyway.

Saturday came with its fuss. Cornwallis-Smith Senior had all our House lined up for a pep talk which took on the usual twittery Nelson touch of everyone expecting that every man will do his duty et cetera. I even gained a personal salvo.

'Good of you to come along, Beattie.'

It was wasted sarcasm. I was cold and miserably far away.

We toed the side lines of the first Hockey Pitch for the start. Raeburn raised his gun.

'Ready!'

The bang bounced us forward into our individual paths: ants in our mass yet each so entirely alone. What was *he* thinking? Did *he* hate this farce? What's *he* grinning at? Watch your elbows!

Through the Old Gates—the Burnside—the old road to the Easter Mains. Thank goodness it was the last run.

I could see my grandparents' house. Jock would be shut in the kitchen. Probably yapping his complaint.

I thumped on angrily, red vest stretching in the rhythm of deepening breath. Other reds were about, and greens, blues and yellows. 'The honour of the House' Raeburn was for ever preaching. 'House colours'—'School colours'—the glory of gods like Cornwallis-Smith, braids and badges, caps and cups, medals and medallions. (The bribes to justify the system. The knighthoods for forty years' drudgery and forty thousand cups of tea on the desk). Meaningless to Jock's master, running with emotional emptiness. Next year I'll have flu or something. They can have their race. Raeburn. Ra. Ra. Ra.

I grinned at Mr Stevenson who was standing outside his gate watching. Halfway alread.

'Go it, Alastair. You show 'em!'

Show 'em. I'd been wishing I could for days and days.

Then a brainwave. Perhaps I could drop out? Simply wander off up into the hills for the morning? Or go home? Tear that vital one point expected of me into tiny, tiny pieces.

The pull up to Stoddart's was no place for clear thinking. I passed a gaggle of various-coloured runners and realised there were only a handful ahead, including Inglis who had won last year. Possibly due to my private preoccupation, I was completely unpuffed and physically fresh. Suddenly I realised this. There was another way I could show them. I'd win the bloody race!

The thought certainly caused a rush of adrenalin. I immediately tripped over my own flipper feet and landed in the mud. I scrambled up again laughing at my madness; but as soon as the rhythm was restored my feet seemed to bang bang the message: 'Win! Win! Win! Win! . . .' Bang, bang, bang. Down the jarring brae of the Back Road. 'Win! Win! Win! Win!'

Without undue effort I passed the few stragglers who had slipped back from the leaders and tucked in at the rear of the leading knot of four. They looked tense with competitiveness, glancing at each other, planning, plotting like chess players as the End Game emerges from a cluttered board. It was almost funny.

They were runners though and I was not. I doubted if I could do any dramatic sprint across the playing fields. Inglis was 440 junior champ, too. He was edging into the lead already; half a mile from home. I'd have to go *now*. Being used to charging down the braes of the hills it was *my* ground. I bounded forward down the old Roman road which ran straight and steep into the town. I'd often done so before—usually in walking boots—so this was like skipping in comparison.

Halfway down and I'd passed all but Inglis. He was in my House too but being dedicated and a pet of the Cornwallis-Smiths of the school he was enemy as much as anyone. I drew level with him and a startled eye glanced to see who had come up. That glance could have cost him the race. Being about the last person he could expect he gave a perfect double take, staring and staring again, so his concentration broke and his stride faltered. I went through, pushing as hard as I could.

By the turn in at the Prep School Gate I had a clear fifty yards lead. But starting across that wide open expanse of hockey pitches was my undoing. The sheer enormity of my position horrified me. Ahead lay crowds and cheering: a scene and noise which was abhorrent to a shy youth whom the establishment had already consigned to the limbo of the inept. Prep kids were staring from their groups across the pitches. You could hear the incredulous, 'It's Beattie!' My resolution faltered. What had I done? Oh heavens!

And there was no way out. From the far out scattered Prep kids an ever-more solid funnel of spectators drained one towards the finishing tape. I was certain the cheers were for my House rather than me. I glanced back. Inglis was head back and sprinting—desperately trying to tear back the distance surprise and steepness had lost him. Och, it would be easy just to let him through. Let him face the palaver of prizes and praise.

Suddenly I spotted the House god. Cornwallis-Smith was inside the line with the other Captains to spur on their minions. But as I drew towards him I heard his bass trumpet call, 'Come on, Inglis!'

If he had hit me it could not have been more unkind. Inglis and I were both in the same House and both far enough ahead that nobody could pass us. It was a fatal disservice. Poor lad, he was coming on with all he could muster while I had slackened right off.

That call was a goad that jabbed me forward through every thought and feeling in a last blind burst. I passed the tape several strides ahead of Inglis.

'A gallant rally' the local rag was to call it.

We both sprawled on the grass, blown completely.

Cornwallis-Smith came up and shook my hand. 'Well run, Beattie. The House is proud of you.' I looked at him—and looked and looked. I could paint his portrait yet as he was that day. My loathing was complete, my reply all silence. He turned to pump Inglis up and down. Others were crossing the line steadily. The loudspeaker kept up its raucous commentary above the din of voices and sporadic cheers. The Seniors drifted off for their starting places. The Inters would be half way round their Cross already. The fuss had not been too bad. Raeburn and the Headmaster came over.

'Well, Beattie, your concentrated training seems to have worked wonders.'

The Head smiled and almost whispered (so I alone heard) 'There are races and race, boy, and reasons and reasons eh?'

His was the only firm handsake.

Ah well, it was all a long, long time ago. I stand here remembering it all so clearly. Somewhere up there my son will be passing Stoddart's Farm (the Stoddart who was a Prep kid in my day), ready for the jarring descent of the Back Road. It is his first race.

43   The summit of Scotland—Ben Nevis.

The Fisherman's Release

The water was clear and cool above the stones, flowing with a quiet laughter, lit by the quivering sunlight that filtered through the trees.

Old Andra leant over the parapet of the footbridge watching the flow, gazing through the crisp movement for the dark grey shapes; but there was only the dappled granite, worn smoth and round, there was only a rusty bicycle wheel to which clung a body of grass and twigs and heather. His eye sought under the peaty bank but no shadow moved there.

He startled at the cry of a hunting kestrel up in the wood and stared into the trees. No bird flew out. Nothing seemed to stir apart from the waters below his feet. The silence and beauty of it suddenly swept over him like a physical thing. He slowly ran his eye over the scene: the long glade, green and gay with soggy spaghnum moss and edged with the purple-brown of heather clumps; dead stumps and fallen trees lay skeleton white in contrast to the twisted red barks of the old Scots pines and their dark green canopies; the sky beyond stretched lightly blue above the rise of hills. He thought of the Moine Mor up there, the Great Moss, the savannahs of space where the turf was soft and the air breezy on the hottest day, where the plaintive cry of the golden plovers wept at the folly of men and the ptarmigan chicks ran at one's feet. There had been grand days fishing those high hill streams, tasty trout to lay on the scullery slab back in Fife on a Sunday night.

One of the tumbled trees moved though there was no wind— so he spotted the stag. His weakened eyes could not count its points. It lay quietly, watching the old man, unafraid but cautious, toning in against the heather, its antlers as mossy as the sterile debris of the old forest itself. It belonged to the forest, to the comfort of the trees, it was at home on the long slopes of the Bhreac, in the corries and snow-streaked tops. He envied the stag for the freedom of its ways.

He glanced back to the stream below—and tensed at once for a shadow glided out from the rough water where the stream fell to the gorge. It moved effortlessly, slowing bending and unbending its strong shape, nosing up against the invisible current with lithe ease. Andra stood silent, motionless, as the salmon slowly ascended.

He was right above its long, grey form, so he cold pick out the thrust of its jaw and the impersonal stare of its eyes and the coloured markings along its length.

His sciatica gave a twinge of pain so he jerked back. There was a flash below and the stream ran empty as before.

Andra sighed, cursing the weakness of his body. He picked up his rod to move down from the bridge to the great pools of the Linn.

He did not regard himself as really old. Seventy-nine next month. But he had taken it out of himself as a wild youth, he had worked hard, had survived two serious industrial accidents and had been unfortunate in married life.

In fact, anyone who knew his wife, Meg Ballantyne, immediately felt sorry for her husband.

The fire had long gone from his soul; the spirit had wilted, the flesh grown weak. His hands, fitting the rod together, shook noticeably.

He had not fished for long when a picnic party arrived, an English family, loud with health and jarring laughter. Andra peered unenthusiastically over his spectacles at their advance: cameras and handbags and fancy heels sinking into the peaty soil.

'Daft gowks,' he muttered.

They passed without greeting, members of the plastic age, a generation who simply puzzled old Andra. He wished he'd got the south bank instead of Archie McLeod—the road there ran further in among the trees.

'Erchie'll be doon by the Lang Pool,' he guessed.

The last member of the picnic party stopped and eyed him with the cool curiosity of eleven years.

'Are you fishing?'

'Naw! I'm jist gi'eing ma line a wash!'

The boy flushed, stood irresolute for a moment and then fled.

Andra stood cursing himself for an ill-tempered old fool.

The hurt was done however. Too late to call our, 'I'm sorry, sonny!'

The waters were loud here, bashing their creamy way down worn channels in the grey rock, or lying in golden pools carved out of the granite. One of the greatest salmon rivers in Scotland and he had its freedom, a privilege normally bought for £300 a week; his for the asking in return for a wartime service to the owner.

He remembered when he had been no older than the boy he had hurt. He and two friends had walked through the Lairig and come on this stretch of falls and pools towards evening. They had lain on the smooth, white, sun-warm rocks and watched the enormous salmon lying in the bottom of the pools. They had bent a safety pin and tied their boot-laces together and 'fished'. They had dangled their lines right before the great creatures but the fish were wiser than they knew and it was beans again in the frying pan that night before the long walk down to Braemore.

'An aw yon laddie kens is sittin on his hunkers in a caur aw day.'

He had forgotten his line and the fly lay at the end of the pool dashing from side to side in the rush of living waters.

'It's aw Meg's fault!' he suddenly cried, reeling in.

He had married latish and his choice had been bad. He should have seen the shallow depth behind the young laughter, but he had gone headlong and tied himself to the tigress, the tireless nature which had worn down his own. Thirty-two years under those claws would have marked the hardiest. Andra had slowly shrivelled, turned grey, and of nights haunted 'The Bucking Hind' and at weekends escaped to the fishing. Anything to be away from Meg. Even that freedom was dearly bought.

'Ye dinna care fir me ony mair. Ye like yir fushin better,' had been his farewell the night before.

It was true of course.

He pictured the return.

'An take yir dirty fish oot o ma kitchen! An look at yir claes! Hoo dae ye think I'll get them cleaned? I'll no be a skivvy fir the likes o you!'

Somehow these days he did not even seem to take many fish home. Not that that made things better.

'Ye gang awa aw weekend an ye dinna even bring a bliddy thing back wi ye. Can ye no even catch a supper noo?'

Perhaps Archie would give him one of his basket. He was a wily lad who always had a good catch, for all he was just forty and new to the game.

Archie had come to live next door and he had a car in which he gladly took old Andra to his haunts in return for being taught the grand game. Pupil, though, had long passed master.

Andra remembered his line again. His cast was a bad one, striking the polished rock on the far side. He tried again and felt the old thrill as it landed fair and floated down through the bubbles into the deep pool.

'Aw, it's graun jist tae be here.'

Archie and he had come up to the wee hamlet at ten the night before; to Mary Macdonald's, with Mary herself soon producing tea and scones, with the same bedroom under the slope of roof, the same view over fields to the river and the wide heather hills. It was the pattern of escape built over recent years. Mary understood. It was easy to stand in the kitchen door after supper while she bustled about—and unburden the cares of life. The menace of Meg seemed remote in that warm place.

Andra always lay in bed there with a great content—savouring the unusual peace, the absence of a nightly nagging, the blessed noises of the highland dusk: the call of the black-headed gulls or peewits or oyster-catchers, and, in the autumn, the distant challenge of the stags, and at all times, the muted flow of the great river, freed from its mountain swiftness and the wanderings in the big forest. He would watch the lace curtains billow and rattle on their rail, gossamer-like in the moonlight. The wrinkles would ease their grip from his face and the dreams were always of long ago.

The Leven had been his earliest playground and then he discovered the Ochils on the edge of Fife and their hill burns. When he had served his time a gang of them from the mill had bought the rights to Lochan Uaine in Glen Bhuidheanaich. Halcyon days, only given up for the pretty face of Margaret Lamont, willingly, given for Andra held little back. His rods went into the loft and his waders were more often used on the potato patch between the house and the line out to the pit bing.

But how quickly it had spoilt; Meg's impatience and temper, endless petty quarrels. And childless.

Andra reeled in again and changed flies. A Butcher would be better for the Long Pool. He would fish opposite Archie for a while, enjoying his portly, friendly presence, yet separated by the width of water and the roar of the Linn. He picked his way carefully along the path until he reached the Long Pool. Archie was there sure enough and they waved to each other and Archie shouted something that the older man could not catch, but he smiled in return. Archie held up two fingers.

'Ach, he's fir the Fife Cup this year,' sighed Andra—without envy. (A Ballantyne, be it said, was engraved on the cup opposite the dates, 1920, 1923, 1924, 1937, and 1946!)

He enjoyed the Long Pool with its shady trees. He felt the peace of the forest again seeping into him.

He had meant to see if the stag had moved when he had left the footbridge, but had forgotten.

It was so easy to forget these days.

'Aye, an ah shid jist forget tae gang hame as weel,' he said aloud and then felt aghast at the very idea, at its impudent possibility.

Why not?

'Jist think, Andra lad; nae mair frae the auld girner.' Then with a frightened glance round he added, 'Gawd, if she kent whit ah'm thinkin the noo!'

He cast violently, splashily, so Archie noticed, but the train of thought had entered the long tunnel of his stolid reasoning. Why did he put up with it? With her? But to do otherwise was the notion that shocked him.

'I've aye done the dacent thing.'

He watched the pool, pondering. Its quicksilver light flickered back off his wizened face. He looked round at the deep forest. He squinted up into the blue, cloudless sky. Here was content.

'Sax bob a nicht at Mary's . . . that's . . . twa pun a week maybe. I could dae it tae.'

He pulled out a handkerchief and dabbed at his brow. The hand was very shaky.

'Gawd, man, tak a grip o yirsel!'

But the idea would not go. It broke out with a roar in his ears and its sudden sunshine of madness struck like a blow.

HE WOULD NOT GO HOME!

After supper Andra and Archie always went 'fir a wee walk'. Archie normally had to contain himself for Andra's slow steps, but this night he was soon crying,

'Hey, Andra, haud yir horses, mun!'

Normally Andra was full of talk but this night he was silent and withdrawn, yet with his face alight as Archie had never know it.

Mary would have said he was 'fey'; Archie being a right Fifer was merely puzzled and as he later admitted, 'a wee bitty worried'.

'Whit's gat intae ye the day? Ye fished the Lang Pool like I've never seen onybody fish. (Five salmon, the heaviest 14 pounds, as against Archie's early two.) Ye scoffed aw the curranty-loaf at tea and ye're walkin me aff ma feet.'

Andra laughed.

'Tell ye the morn. I've got a graun notion.'

Inside he was simply stomping along, singing: 'I'll no gang hame! I'll no gang hame! . . .'

How could he tell Archie?

He would have to tomorrow, for they always left after an early high tea in the front room Mary used on Sundays. His thoughts ran on—

'Erchie will dae his nut! An Meg . . .' He laughed outright.

Archie frowned at the old man. He had never known him like this.

'Aye, old Meg! Well, she can just hae some o her ain medicine.'

He smiled at the marshalled trees behind the wobbly deer fence. He could have danced had he known how. Instead he strode along with his head thrown back and arms swinging. He had not felt so energetic or free since he came to the hills as a boy.

'I can bide jist as ah like an dae aw the things she's aye stapped. I'm free!'

And he really believed it.

They walked down to the old chief's castle and back. Mary commented on Andra's flushed appearance.

'You have been doing ower much the day, Andrew Ballantyne.'

'Ach, awa! I've never felt betta!'

'Wha caught aw the fush may I ask?' he poked at Archie.

Archie smiled wanly. 'he's got a secret, Mary, he'll no let on aboot. I dinnae ken, he's near walked me intae the grun. An he's been laughin away tae hi'sel aw day.'

'Weel, sup yir milk and off tae bed wi the both of you.'

They complied happily enough, like tired youngsters on a summer holiday evening, in their own thoughts, dreamily, untidily scattering their clothing and snuggling down in the cool linen.

Moonlight and the gentle flow of waters. Lace curtains swaying in the ghost of a breeze. Waking slid into sleeping before the first owl's call and dreams soon set smiles on their faces.

Archie woke once in the night to hear old Andra talking in his sleep:

'I'll no gang hame! I'LL NO GANG HAME!'

Archie thought, 'I widna blame ye; wi yon auld witch waitin,' and was soon thoughtlessly asleep again.

He woke later than usual. Andra normally woke him. He felt a bit annoyed.

'Hey, Andra! It's time we were up,' he called across the room.

But Andra did not answer—nor ever would—and his cry in the night had been very truth.

HE'D NO GANG HAME.

It was neighbourly Archie who arranged the funeral. And it was friend Archie who inserted the column in the local paper:

Andrew Ballantyne, the well-known angler from Calton, died peacefully in his sleep last Sunday morning, while staying at Inverspee in the Cairngorms. He was 78. As a young man he had an international reputation and was President of the Fife Association from 1938 to 1946, when he characteristically ended his extended presidency by winning the Fife Trophy for the fifth time. His many friends, young and old, will miss his cheery company, and to his wife, Margaret, we extend our sympathy in her bereavement.